GABLE

A PICTORIAL BIOGRAPHY

GABLE
A PICTORIAL BIOGRAPHY

JEAN GARCEAU
with
INEZ COCKE

Publishers • GROSSET & DUNLAP • New York
A FILMWAYS COMPANY

To Clark —
The King,
a gentleman,
my friend.

CREDITS

Copyright © 1961 by Jean Garceau and Inez Cocke
Additional photographs copyright © 1977 by Jean Garceau
All rights reserved
Published simultaneously in Canada
Library of Congress catalog card number 61-13898
ISBN 0-448-14358-5 (hardcover)
ISBN 0-448-14359-3 (paperback)

First printing 1977
Printed in the United States.

ON December 30, 1960, the Associated Press Editors' poll listed the death of Clark Gable as the top news story of the year in the entertainment world, for it marked the end of the golden, glamorous era in motion pictures which he dominated.

For over thirty years, in sixty-seven motion pictures, he was the idol of millions, the rugged sex symbol, the pace and style setter; a survivor where other stars either aged or lapsed into obscurity; the greatest money-maker of all time for his studio; the publicly acclaimed, uncontested "King" of Hollywood.

Gone With the Wind, a huge box-office success, has now won an even larger audience through television. All those who knew and loved Clark are seeing him again in his greatest role. And he is being rediscovered by a new and critical generation. That his appeal is still universal and timeless is best expressed in a question asked by a teenaged girl after seeing Clark as Rhett Butler:

"Mom, why don't they have actors like that now?"

Clark Gable was a man who became a legend in his own time. Wherever he went he made news, generated excitement, speculation, an atmosphere of mystery. To women, young and old, he was the romantic ideal with the little-boy quality that made every woman want to mother him. To men, he was the tough, two-fisted, rugged epitome of all the qualities they admired. To young people he represented the goal to be achieved. His advice to them was "hard work." But more than hard work put him on top and kept him there. Clark had an indestructible quality about him, plus an ability to change character with the changing times.

Reams have been written about him, but the true story of Clark Gable — the man behind the glamor and the legend — has never been told. In these pages I have tried to present the man as I knew him, based on my twenty-one years of close personal association. Ours was never an "employer and employee" relationship, but rather a working partnership with mutual respect for each other's special talents and abilities.

Twenty-one years is a long time; time in which to take the measure of a man, to know what he was really like in happiness and triumph, in tragedy and in defeat. My grateful thanks are extended to all whose generous assistance helped me recreate this portrait of Clark Gable.

JEAN GARCEAU

Sherman Oaks, California

To Corney Mr Ghu Guy Like me No Matter How badly I play tennis
Clark

CLARK GABLE and Carole Lombard were rehearsing a time step in Carole's living room when I arrived at her house in Bel Air that October day in 1938.

The phonograph was going and Carole was having a difficult time because her partner seemed rather awkward.

"No, no!" she was saying as I came in. "Remember, it's one, two, three . . . *kick!* One, two, three . . . *kick!*" Then the music ground to a stop and both collapsed on a sofa, breathless with laughter.

"Jean," Carole said when she saw me, "I want you to meet a big moose with two left feet!"

"In other words, just a clumsy country boy," Clark said, grinning. He held out his hand. It was a wonderful, firm handshake. I shall like this man, I thought.

He was wearing slacks and a turtleneck sweater and his hair was mussed, but he radiated such charm and vitality that I began to see what people meant when they said a sort of magic happened when he was present. When he smiled his crooked smile he seemed much handsomer than he was on the screen.

Carole had asked me to bring some business papers from the Myron Selznick Agency. She rang for tea, then went away to look at them, leaving me with Clark.

We talked about *Idiot's Delight*, which he was making with Norma Shearer. The part called for him to dance with a chorus line and the studio had hired longtime burlesque comedian and soft-shoe artist Jo Yule, Mickey Rooney's father, to coach him. Carole, who'd been a hoofer in her Mack Sennett days, was also helping him with the routines.

"Alfred Lunt originated the role on the stage," Clark said. "I've got some big shoes to fill."

This modesty is refreshing, I thought, for Clark was tremendously popular and I knew Metro-Goldwyn-Mayer considered him their most valuable male star. Following his Academy Award in 1935 for *It Happened One Night,* he'd made a string of successes, such as *San Francisco* and *Mutiny on the Bounty,* receiving the award nomination for the latter film.

Men admired and respected, women idolized him. Everything he said or did or wore was news. A newspaper editors' poll conducted by Ed Sullivan, the columnist, had named him "King" of the movies, and no one had ever challenged his right to the title. As a final criterion of success, his foot- and hand-prints had been duly recorded in the forecourt of Grauman's Chinese Theater in Hollywood before hordes of shrieking fans.

And now he was going to play Rhett Butler in *Gone With the Wind.* Errol Flynn, Gary Cooper and others had been touted for the part, but the fans—millions of them—had written David Selznick, the producer, demanding Clark. We knew "in the trade" that Metro-Goldwyn-Mayer

Gable and friend. Clark autographed this photograph to Corney Jackson: "To Corney This guy likes me no matter how I play tennis."
(1940) COURTESY OF CLARENCE S. BULL. PRIVATE COLLECTION OF CORNWELL JACKSON

had driven a hard bargain for his services. Selznick had to agree to release the film through them in order to get Clark.

"Are you excited about playing Rhett?" I asked.

"Frankly, I'm scared to death," he said seriously. "He's a tremendous challenge. I've read the book over and over, trying to feel my way into the character. I hope I can do justice to him."

"But the fans all want you in the part," I said.

"That's just the point," he replied. "It's like starting with five million critics. I can't let them down."

Carole came back with the papers in time to hear his last remark.

"Jean," she said, "this man's a worrier."

The next day Carole asked me to work for her exclusively as personal secretary and business manager. I realized then that the meeting with Clark had not been sheer coincidence, that she'd deliberately staged it so that he might "look me over."

It was a flattering offer but I hesitated, for it meant leaving the Selznick staff. Myron Selznick, brother of David O., the producer, was one of the most powerful and influential Hollywood agents and the only one at that time who furnished a business management service for his clients, some of whom were among the biggest names in the motion picture industry. I was the personal contact on several accounts, which included Carole, Fredric March, Ida Lupino and William Powell. The hours there were from nine to six, which meant a great deal to me, for I was (and still am) interested in being Mrs. Russel Garceau and providing the proper after-office-hours home life for the husband to whom I had

then been married for eight years. I knew that "Fieldsie" (Madalynne Fields), Carole's secretary, had recently retired to marry Walter Lang, the director, and I wasn't sure that I could fill her shoes and still have a home life of my own, for Fieldsie had lived with Carole; she had been companion, friend, secretary, *alter ego*, for many years.

We talked it over and Carole promised that we'd keep things on a strictly business, nine-to-six basis. "If you're game to try it, I am," she said, so I handed in my resignation, moved into an office in Carole's home, and from that day on I was one of the family. This was one of the most important decisions of my life—one I have never regretted.

Carole's house was an English Tudor type on St. Cloud Road. Her mother, Mrs. Elizabeth Peters, whom we all called Bessie, lived in nearby Brentwood. There were two brothers, Frederick (Freddie), a Bullock's department store executive, and Stuart, a stockbroker. A warm relationship existed between Carole and her family, and she and Bessie were especially close.

When I took over her business affairs, Carole was making *Made For Each Other* with Jimmy Stewart for David Selznick and was one of the highest-paid free-lance stars in the business. Despite the fact that she was a delightful madcap, she had a reputation for being a shrewd businesswoman, a fact I was able to confirm when we went over her investment portfolio.

Her agent was Myron Selznick, but he never fought any battles with the "front office" for her. Carole fought her own battles with the "brass," her own and those of the people who worked around her, for she knew her Hollywood, inside and out.

Everyone on the set adored her—cameramen, electricians, crew, make-up men, hairdressers, studio police. She was gay, she was witty, she was kind and generous. She was "one of them," sympathizing with their troubles and problems, always ready to lend a helping hand. To them she was "regular" and they respected her, for Carole had made it the hard way.

Her real name was Jane Peters. Born October 6, 1909, in Fort Wayne, Indiana, she and her family moved to California when she was seven. At eleven Carole got her first taste of motion pictures when a neighbor recommended her for the part of Monte Blue's little sister in *The Perfect Crime*. Her first film pay was fifty dollars.

After that Carole was ready for a film career. "School comes first," Bessie had insisted, so it wasn't till Carole was fifteen, had finished junior high and won a lot of Charleston dance contests, that she got another bit part in *Marriage in Transit*. (Incidentally, her biggest competitor in the Charleston contest was a girl named Lucille LeSueur, who was known in her films as Joan Crawford.)

Now there was no holding her. She literally fought her way up through the bit parts to a series of hard-riding cowgirl roles in Buck Jones Westerns on the Fox lot, at a salary of seventy-five dollars a week.

In 1925 an automobile accident sidelined her for a year with a deep cut in her face, which ran from her upper lip to the middle of her cheek. But the resulting tiny scar served only to accentuate her beauty, and she went on to two hectic years in Mack Sennett comedies, where custard pie throwing and bathing beauties were the stock in trade.

"The theory was that if you could 'take it' there, you could do anything," Carole said. "I was on the receiving end of many a pie."

She made the grade, and when Pathe came along with an offer of one hundred and fifty dollars a week, Carole jumped at it. "I thought I was in the big money," she laughed.

Joseph P. Kennedy, the President's father, was head of Pathe at the time. He told Carole she was too fat (one hundred and twenty-one pounds). Carole readily agreed to a daily course of reducing treatments from Madame Sylvia, the studio's noted figure expert, but not before she got in a parting shot at Kennedy.

"You're not so skinny yourself," she called out, slamming the door behind her.

So both of them ended up taking turns in Madame Sylvia's torture chamber—Kennedy for the sake of his pride, Carole for the sake of her career. Madame's touch was sure but hardly tender. Carole lost ten pounds and thereafter kept her weight at one hundred and twelve. There is no record of the poundage Mr. Kennedy lost.

The Pathe contract led to one at Paramount, where she met and co-starred with William Powell in *Man of the World*. It was released in 1931 and in June of that year she and Powell were married. They soon discovered they were incompatible. It was a case of two peole striving for careers, each with a different outlook on life. An amicable separation followed, then divorce in 1933, with both still good friends.

Carole attained stardom with such hit pictures as *Twentieth Century, My*

4   *Man Godfrey* and *The Princess Comes Across.* She received an Academy Award nomination for her work in *Godfrey.* John Barrymore, who co-starred with her in *Twentieth Century,* said, "She is perhaps the greatest actress I ever worked with."

Carole had two big hit pictures in 1937, the hilarious *True Confession* for Paramount and her first Technicolor film, *Nothing Sacred,* for David Selznick. She paid income taxes that year on four hundred and sixty-five thousand dollars.

Thus when I went to work for her, in the fall of 1938, she had "arrived."

"Clark and I are going to be married as soon as he's free," she told me that morning.

Clark had been separated from his wife Ria, who was a good many years his senior, for several years, but there'd been no final divorce action. Carole told me that Ria, who'd been a chic, thrice-married divorcee before becoming Mrs. Gable, was holding out for a huge financial settlement, pending a final decree. Until then, wedding plans were to be very hush-hush, although all Hollywood knew of their romance, for they were seen together constantly.

Carole had met Clark in 1932 when they'd co-starred in *No Man of Her Own* at Paramount. They'd clowned and gagged their way all through that production, but didn't see each other after that until Jock Whitney gave his famous gag party on February 7, 1936. If there was one thing Carole loved, it was a gag. She outdid herself for the occasion. Attired in a hospital gown, she had herself carried into the party on a stretcher borne by two white-coated attendants. Clark thought she was great. It was fun to be with her again and this time he was free to ask for a date.

The following Valentine's Day Carole sent Clark an ancient, battered, wheezy old Model A she'd found in a junkyard. It was plastered all over with tiny red hearts. Clark loved it and, going right along with the gag, called for Carole that evening in the noisy old rattletrap. In full evening dress, they drove off to a party. From then on, they'd been kindred spirits.

A business manager's job has many facets. She not only handles income and investments, she keeps financial accounts, prepares tax statements, pays bills, finds houses, hires servants, does trouble shooting of all kinds.

When *Made for Each Other* was finished, Carole and I started house hunting for a place to live after she and Clark were married. We spent days roaming through all the available properties on the "B Circuit," which in movie parlance stands for Beverly Hills, Brentwood and Bel Air. We found nothing she liked.

Then a brochure came in the mail describing the Raoul Walsh ranch in Encino, out in the San Fernando Valley. It was up for sale. Usually I threw this type of literature away but on a hunch I showed it to Carole. She took one look, let out a yell and called Clark, who came rushing over.

They were both excited, for they had visited Raoul, a prominent director, many times, and knew and loved

Clark's favorite picture of Carole Lombard. She inscribed it to him on the back with these words: "Pa Dear, I love you, Ma" He kept the photo at the studio on his dressing table and beside it, a single red rose that Carole sent him each day. (1936) COURTESY OF GEORGE HURRELL

his place. They got in touch with him at once and bought the property then and there. We all drove out to look at it.

The Walsh ranch was eight miles from Bel Air, reached via one of the canyon passes through the hills to the north of Hollywood.

At that time the San Fernando Valley was not as built-up as it is today. The ranches were widely scattered and there were vast citrus groves reaching to the distant mountains beyond.

Raoul's place, which consisted of twenty acres, lay in open country in a beautiful little valley at the foot of a gently rolling hill.

"Let's buy the hill, too," Clark said. "It will give us more privacy." (This added five acres to the ranch.)

There was a main house, stables for nine horses, a hay barn, workshop and garage. Raoul used the ranch as a week-end place and kept his horses and sulky there. He also maintained a short track where the horses were worked out.

Paddocks and stables were enclosed with split-rail fences, but the property fronting on the road and the great curving driveway leading to the house were not fenced in and Clark decided that he'd like to keep it that way to preserve the rural effect.

The trees were beautiful. Giant pepper and eucalyptus were everywhere, providing wonderful shade. There was a citrus orchard of oranges, lemons and grapefruit as well as many avocado trees, peaches, plums, figs and apricots. The paddocks and fields were planted to alfalfa and red oats.

The house was a two-story Connecticut farmhouse, with tall chimneys of clinker brick. Thirteen years old, it had been designed by Malcolm Brown of Metro-Goldwyn-Mayer. Clark and Carole were like excited children, dashing up and down stairs, in and out of the rooms, calling to each other, planning changes while I trailed them with a notebook.

Raoul had never really lived there, so despite the fireplaces, furnaces would have to be installed, kitchen and service porch enlarged, additional servants' quarters added on to the garage, and a caretaker's cottage built, for Clark wanted to plant additional citrus trees and put the farm on a paying basis. I was to get bids so the remodeling could begin as soon as they were married.

One of Clark's pet names for Carole was "Ma," while she always called him "Pa."

"I've always wanted a place like this," he said, looking around, his eyes shining. "It will be the first home I've had since I was a boy that I can really call my own." He put his arm around Carole. "Ma, I think we're going to be very happy here."

The financial negotiations for the divorce settlement with Ria hit a snag. Russell Birdwell, Carole's publicity agent, recommended W. I. Gilbert, Sr., a prominent lawyer, and Clark asked him to take over the case. It was due to his efforts that an amicable settlement was finally made, and the divorce was granted March 6, 1939. Clark and Carole were now free to marry.

But by that time, Clark was deeply involved in *Gone With the Wind*. The shooting schedule made it virtually impossible for him to get away for the quiet wedding without fanfare or publicity which he and Carole wanted.

Otto Winkler, a publicity man at Metro-Goldwyn-Mayer, handled all of Clark's personal publicity and contacts. They were good friends, so Clark asked Otto to make arrangements for the wedding.

"Get it all set up," he said, "so we can go the minute I get some free time."

Otto scouted around for a week, looking for a place where the marriage could be performed without ballyhoo. He finally decided on Kingman, Arizona. It was not too far (350 miles) from Hollywood and he found a minister that he liked, the Reverend Kenneth Engle, of the First Methodist-Episcopal Church. He told the Reverend Engle that he planned to bring some friends over to be married, but did not reveal their identity.

The days dragged on. Then, unexpectedly, Clark found that he had two days off from shooting—March 29 and 30. "This is just the break we've been waiting for," he said.

The next problem was to elude the reporters, for it was very difficult for stars as prominent as Clark and Carole to make a move without publicity.

A second break came. A full-scale, white-tie, splash preview of *The Story of Alexander Graham Bell,* starring Don Ameche and Loretta Young, was scheduled in San Francisco on the night of the twenty-eighth, with civic and motion picture leaders in attendance. The elite of the movie world, together with all the top columnists and reporters, departed for the Bay City!

"It's like a cloak-and-dagger mystery," Carole said, when she told me of their plans.

Clark was living in North Hollywood, in a house he rented from Alice Terry Ingram. At 4:30 on the morning of the twenty-ninth he drove over to Carole's house. Together they went to pick up Otto. The trio then drove to Kingman in Otto's car. All wore shabby old clothes to escape recognition.

Upon arriving in Kingman they went directly to the courthouse for the license. Clark told me later that Viola Olson, the clerk at the marriage license bureau, practically collapsed when she recognized them and could hardly fill out the necessary forms in her excitement.

As they came down the steps of the courthouse, a reporter from the local paper drove up in a press car and parked in front of them. "That stopped us for a moment," Clark said. "We were sure the game was up. But he didn't give us a second glance." What a scoop he missed!

The minister had been alerted by Otto, and he and his wife were waiting at their home just outside the city. The Engles were hospitable, friendly people. Carole and Clark changed clothes before the wedding. The ceremony was quiet and dignified, with Mrs. Engle and a neighbor serving as witnesses.

I had arrived at Carole's house that morning as usual, and Bessie and I spent the day together, waiting for the news. One paper had assigned a reporter to keep a daytime watch on Carole's house, just in case, but of course he saw nothing.

Carole's brother Stuart came out during the afternoon and, without telling him what was going on, we managed to detain him for fear that somehow the news would leak prematurely.

Then the call came through from Clark and Carole. It was official. They were married. There was much excitement and laughter as they talked first to Bessie and Stuart and then to me. Bessie was delighted when Clark said, "You've got a son-in-law, Mom!" The servants were overjoyed when we told them, although I think they had suspected what was happening.

In Hollywood the rivalry among movie columnists and newsmen is so great, each vying for scoops, that it's always desirable to break a story to them simultaneously, if possible. Otto now called all the wire services and papers, briefing them on the news, and invited all of the reporters to a reception at Carole's the next morning. The newlyweds returned home late that night.

Carole had a cook named Jessie who was a regular Mrs. Five by Five. Carole called her "Miss Majess."

Early the next morning Jessie ran out in her nightgown to pick up the morning paper and inadvertently locked herself out of the house. Frantic, not wishing to disturb the bride and groom, she managed to open one of the downstairs front windows and tried to crawl back inside. Halfway through, she got hopelessly stuck.

This was the sight that greeted me when I arrived a little later. There was Jessie, groaning helplessly, her legs paddling up and down furiously. Somehow I got the door unlocked, pried Jessie loose—and she scooted back into the house just as a group of early-bird reporters and photographers descended upon us!

We set up a buffet in the living room and served sandwiches, coffee and cake to the newsmen. Soon Clark and Carole appeared, were interviewed, posed for pictures. Carole wore her wedding suit, a gray flannel with a gray and white polka-dot vest, gray shoes and hose. Clark wore a navy blue suit and a dark tie. Both were radiant with happiness.

Clark moved into Carole's house and the next day he went back to being Rhett Butler. Soon after that Carole began shooting *In Name Only* with Cary Grant for RKO. Business as usual. The honeymoon would have to wait.

Work on the ranch now began. The place was like a lodestone. Every spare moment Clark or Carole had, we raced out to check the progress of the remodeling and the construction of the caretaker's cottage. The three of us spent many hours sitting on the floor before a huge fire in the dining room, deep in plans and specifications of all kinds, while workmen swarmed around us.

Besides the construction work, outside irrigation lines were being repaired, power lines changed, cesspools installed, fences mended, trees pruned. Some of the bids were fantastic. One in particular, for work on the pepper trees, was way out of line.

"To heck with it," Clark decided. "Let's leave 'em as they are—they'll outlive us all."

Carole and I spent our days haunting antique shops, buying things for the ranch house.

At last the construction work was finished, the house and all the other buildings painted white, with dark green, almost black shutters, in true New England style. Then Carole began decorating and furnishing.

Her first and only thought was to make it a *man's* home—livable, comfortable, warm, beautiful. Tom Douglas, a prominent decorator, handled the interiors for her; but Carole had exquisite taste, knew exactly what she wanted and the effects she wished to achieve. She loved color and knew how to use it. The results were charming.

Clark finished shooting *Gone With the Wind* in June and the move to the ranch was made soon after. This was a major undertaking. We all worked like mad and were in a state of collapse at the end of the day. The servants were too tired even to prepare a meal.

Carole was all for phoning the Brown Derby to send out some food when Bessie appeared, laden with great bowls of salad and casseroles of hot food, ready to serve. So the first meal at the ranch was an impromptu picnic on the patio.

Just as we finished, Clark turned to Carole and said, "Hey, Ma, I want Jeanie to look after my business, too. How about it?"

"Oh, no you don't!" Carole squawked. "I found her first!"

"Oh, come on, Ma, let's make her community property," Clark teased.

Carole's eyes took on a wicked gleam. "It's going to cost you money," she said. (Clark was always conservative when it came to expense, and she liked to kid him about it.)

Clark laughed. "I knew that. How much?"

"Halvers," Carole said, her eyes narrowing.

"Sold!" Clark said. "Jeanie, you're half mine!"

"If she's going to work for you, she's got to have more money," Carole decided. "Jeanie, your salary is raised!"

I was too tired to do anything but sit there in a happy daze.

Clark was very proud of his "old lady" and the job she'd done. When I left that night they were wandering around, hand in hand, looking things over. Carole constantly ribbed Clark about his title of "King."

"Well, old King," she said, "you've finally got a castle."

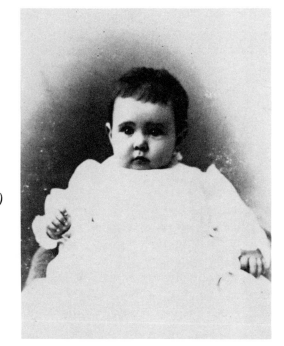

107

Record of Births, Probate Court,

DATE	Number	NAME IN FULL	DATE OF BIRTH			PLACE OF BIRTH			SEX	
			Year	Month	Day	State	County	City Town or Township	Male	Female

Clark Gable's birth certificate. Note entry made as "Female," much to Father Gable's chagrin.

Clark in his first year. (1901)
COURTESY OF GEORGE ANNA BURKE

CLARK'S father, William H. Gable, lived in a small home in Hollywood with his wife, Edna, and an aunt whom Clark called "Pinkie." Before her marriage Edna, a quiet, gentle woman, had been the widow of William's brother.

Father Gable, as we all called him, was in his late sixties, and very like Clark in general appearance, mannerisms and disposition. That is, they were both big Dutchmen, had deep convictions, unwavering integrity, were given to moods of impenetrable silence, and were stubborn as mules.

They were not demonstrative with each other, but father and son were on affectionate terms and the elder Gables were frequent visitors at the ranch. Carole was fond of both and liked having them for Sunday brunch. Clark was their sole support.

Carole loved scrapbooks and picture albums. She had a little Brownie box camera and was always snapping pictures to chronicle their activities. Besides her own career scrapbooks, she asked me if I'd start a series for Clark.

In sorting out his papers, I found his birth certificate, old theater programs and handbills, newspaper clippings, pictures and other souvenirs he'd collected along the way. I was fascinated.

Reporters were constantly besieging Clark for interviews, or asking me for information about him. I was forever making up long lists of their questions, against which he could check "Yes" or "No" or go into detail if he wished. Soon I was asking questions of my own.

Gradually, from these interviews and his personal papers and from Father Gable and Clark himself, I learned something of his early life and career. His experiences gave me an insight into what had gone into the making of his rather complex personality. The road to the "castle" in the San Fernando Valley had been a long, hard one.

His father, William H. "Bill" Gable, was of Pennsylvania Dutch ancestry whose original name, "Goebel" had been Anglicized to "Gable." His wife's maiden name was Adeline Hershelman and her parents were Holland-born farmers living in Meadville, Pennsylvania.

Bill Gable owned his own drilling rig and was a speculative oil driller or "wildcatter." In 1900, an oil boom developed in Harrison County, Ohio, and the Gables moved from Meadville to Cadiz, Ohio, where Bill went to work in the nearby Bricker oil fields.

At the time of Clark's birth— February 1, 1901—the Gables were living on the top floor of a two-story white clapboard house at 138 Charleston Street. (Cadiz advertises itself as "the proudest small town in America" and postcard pictures of the Gable birthplace are on sale in the local drugstore.)

Clark made his entry into the world at 5:30 on that February morning under the aegis of Dr. John S. Campbell.

Adeline Gable registered her son's

birth at Harrison County courthouse on February 1, 1901, giving his name as "Clark Gable." Through a clerical error, the record of births listed him as "Female." This was a cause of much concern to Gable Senior until it was corrected.

"They'd have known he was a boy if they'd seen him," he said. "He weighed nearly eleven pounds when he was born and was all feet and ears."

Probably the closest friends to the couple when Clark was born were their downstairs neighbors, the Reeses. Adeline, a pretty, delicate woman, was ill a great deal and Mrs. Reese helped care for her and the baby until Bill was forced to take her back to Meadville, where she died at her parents' home when Clark was seven months old.

Clark was left in his grandparents' care while his father continued his roving oil operations. Within a year or two, Bill Gable settled in Hopedale, a small town six miles from Cadiz, and went to board with the Dunlap family.

The Dunlaps were fairly well-to-do. There were two sons, Edison and John, and two daughters, Ella and Jennie. All were well educated, well-bred. Jennie, a slender, gracious woman, was considered the old maid of the family.

In 1906, Bill married Jennie and they established their own home in Hopedale and Bill went to Meadville to get his son.

"The best day of my boyhood was the day I came to live with my step-mother," Clark once said. "She was a gentle, loving woman, one of the kindest human beings I have ever known."

In the following years, Bill Gable's fortunes prospered and he provided a large, comfortable home for his family.

The house was a two-story, three-bedroom structure and was nicely furnished. "They weren't rich, but they had all they needed," a neighbor says.

As he grew up, Clark was almost entirely under Jennie's devoted guidance, for his father was away most of the time except on weekends, when he drove home in his Model T Ford coupe. Jennie was the first of many women who were to influence Clark's life.

She saw to it that he had a normal, happy boyhood. Jennie herself was a happy person, gay and talkative. She was known as a "fussy" dresser and loved to have people around her. From her Clark learned kindness, courtesy, a simple dignity and a deep respect for the rights of others.

Clark had a birthday party every year and all the local children were invited to share his cake and refreshments.

"She spoiled me and I loved it," Clark said. "I had the first bicycle of any kid in town."

The Gable house was directly across the street from the Methodist Church and Clark went to Sunday School there every Sunday. Sometime later, William Gable became Sunday School superintendent. He was greatly loved by all the children, who called him "Bill."

Hopedale had a population of five hundred people at that time. The school was a small one, but the teachers were excellent. Clark's first teacher was Fanny Thompson. Later, in high school, he came under the jurisdiction of George Dunlap (no relation to Jennie), Mary Frost, Ann Webster, Stuart Nease and "Miss" Purvis.

Among his close friends were Andy Means and Tommy Lewis, Mar-

Clark and father, William Gable. (1920)
COURTESY OF GEORGE ANNA BURKE

CLARK GABLE SHOWN WITH RELATIVES

The serious-faced boy you see in the above picture is none other than Clark Gable, now one of the most famous movie actors in America. And can you wonder that he is serious with his four aunts, mother and uncle around him?

Those pictured in the front row are: from left to right— Clark Gable, Mrs. Nancy Thompson, his aunt and mother of Mrs. John Nation, of Ravenna; Mrs. Mirar Dunlap and Mrs. Blothia Caves, both aunts of Clark. Second row: Mrs. William Gable, his stepmother, Robert Caves, his uncle, and Ella Dunlop his aunt.

Insert is another picture of Clark taken when he was a small boy.

• • •

From Ravenna Daily Record, *January 23, 1932.* COURTESY OF RAVENNA RECORD-COURIER
AND GEORGE ANNA BURKE

Thelma Lewis and Clark just after appearing together in their high school play, "The Arrival of Kitty." (1916)

jorie Miller, Marie Winland, John Sagrilla and the Hoobler boys. Tommy Lewis had a sister, Thelma, who was red-haired and known as the "prettiest girl in Hopedale."

Soon Clark was escorting Thelma to and from the Epworth League meetings at the Methodist Church and to the various other young people's social gatherings, including Sunday School picnics.

"Clark was my first date," Thelma recalls. "He was not particularly good-looking. His ears were too large.

"He was very lazy about school work," she continues. "He'd never do his homework and I practically put him through his freshman year in high school by letting him copy my Latin and Algebra assignments. We had a spelling match every Friday, however, and he was quite good in that."

The high school students put on plays at the old Patton Opera House in Hopedale, constructing their own scenery. Clark's first dramatic role was a roustabout in *The Arrival of Kitty*, in which Thelma took the part of Kitty and Andy Means had the lead opposite her.

Clark also played an alto horn in the school band, and Jennie tried to teach him to play the piano but finally had to give it up.

"Clark had a very good voice," Thelma says. "Jennie played the piano for us while we sang duets. 'Beautiful Isle of Somewhere' was his favorite song then."

The local Means Hotel boasted a player piano and the young people of the town learned to dance to its music. Thelma reports that Clark was all feet and never became a good dancer. Although quite shy, he was popular and was invited to all the parties.

"We all loved to go to Clark's home," Thelma says. "Jennie was a wonderful cook and we always had such good times there."

In the summers, Clark visited his father's parents, Charles and Nancy Gable, who owned a farm near Meadville. There he learned to do farm chores and care for horses.

When Clark was fifteen and in his sophomore year in high school, Jennie's health began to fail and she prevailed on his father to abandon the oil business and settle down on a farm in Portage County in northeastern Ohio, near the town of Ravenna.

Clark became a farm boy and started his junior year in high school. Their home was outside the town and it was difficult for him to adjust from the familiar, closely knit school and social life of Hopedale to the new and larger school environment, and to his classmates at Ravenna, a town of nine thousand inhabitants.

Now six feet tall, weighing one hundred and fifty-five pounds, he was shy and awkward, not too popular with the girls.

"He had his eye on the pretty girls all right, but was too timid to do anything about it," a friend commented. A good athlete, Clark played on the school baseball team and also played the French horn in the school band. His grades were in the "passing" bracket except in spelling, in which he made excellent marks.

Farms in Ohio were not run on the highly mechanized scale of today. It was hard, grubby work and Clark hated it. An accident in a farm wagon gave him an ambition and an objective. He liked the gruff old country doctor who attended him and after several talks with the physician decided he'd like to have a career in medicine.

In April 1917, the United States entered World War I. That fall, just before he was to enter his senior year in high school, Clark had a visit from Andy Means, his old Hopedale friend. Andy suggested that they go to Akron, sixty miles away, and look for jobs. Clark leaped at the opportunity to escape the farm. In Akron he could finish high school in night classes and go on to pre-med work at Akron University.

The decision precipitated his first clash with his father. It was a case of two implacable Dutchmen pitted against each other. Father Gable believed that a strong, able-bodied man should work with his hands. If Clark wasn't going to be a farmer, then an oil man was his next choice. There was a terrible quarrel, with Gable Senior issuing ultimatums.

Jennie took Clark's side and stood up for him. Somehow she persuaded her husband to let Clark go.

"If it hadn't been for her, I'd probably still be farming in Ohio," Clark said years later.

To the eyes of a country boy, Akron was a bewildering big city of bright lights and strange people. Clark had very little money and said later that he was more than a little scared, but he set out to find a job.

A wartime work boom was on and a harassed employment man took it for granted that the big raw-boned fellow was eighteen. Clark wound up as a timekeeper in one of the big rubber plants. Then he enrolled in night school.

One evening Clark sat down in a short-order restaurant next to two actors from the Clark-Lilly Players, a stock company at the local music hall, and got into conversation with them. Flattered by his wide-eyed interest, they invited him backstage to see the current play, *Bird of Paradise*.

Clark had never witnessed a professional theatrical performance, and by the time the final curtain was rung down he had the smell of greasepaint in his nostrils and was completely and forever in love with show business.

He started cutting classes, haunted the theater every night, and promptly quit his job at the rubber plant when his friends offered him a job as callboy. He received no salary, but besides calling actors to go on the stage a callboy made tips running errands for the cast, doing odd jobs, and being generally useful.

"I never failed to get my people out in front of the curtain in time, even if it meant sewing buttons on their costumes, which I often did," Clark said.

He slept in the theater, took showers at the "Y", used his tips for eating money, and was nearly always hungry but happy.

Then they gave him a walk-on part calling for three words of dialogue: "Good evening, sir." According to Clark, that first appearance on stage was one of the greatest thrills of his life.

Occasional bit parts followed, but there were many weeks when Clark made no money at all, except for tips. Worried, Jennie secretly sent him parcels of food and homemade bread. Father Gable demanded that he come home at once. Work without pay was beyond his ken. To Clark, quitting this bright new world was inconceivable.

Jennie died the following year. In response to a wire from his father, Clark rushed home in time to be with her in her last moments. Her death was a deep personal loss to him. "I felt I'd lost my greatest friend," he said.

After her funeral there was another bitter quarrel with his father.

This time there was no gentle Jennie to intercede for Clark.

An oil boom had developed in Oklahoma and Father Gable decided to sell the farm and return to his first love—oil drilling. He wanted Clark to go with him, but Clark refused.

"I won't give up the theater," he said. "I want to try my luck in New York."

To his father this was sheer madness.

"I told him when he got hungry enough and was ready to quit his shenanigans and come to Oklahoma I'd make an oil man out of him."

The postwar depression was setting in when Clark arrived in New York. Talented young actors were a dime a dozen. Clark found his Akron stock company experience no open sesame to Broadway. After weeks of various odd jobs, he was hired as callboy for a new play at the Plymouth Theater. Clark was in heaven. At least he could be *in* the theater if not *of* it.

The play, *The Jest*, was produced by Arthur Hopkins and starred John and Lionel Barrymore. It opened September 19, 1919. Night after night an eager callboy rapped reverently on the doors of the Barrymore dressing rooms. "Half an hour, please sir." The brothers took an interest in Clark and a friendship developed between Lionel and the callboy that was of great importance later in Clark's career.

The play ran for one hundred and seventy-nine performances, and then Clark was jobless again. He lived in a tiny walk-up hall bedroom, ate sketchy meals at lunch stands. His savings melted away as he made the rounds of casting offices and theater managers. There were no jobs of any kind for tall, dark-haired amateur actors, or even callboys, no matter how earnest and willing.

Clark was forced to capitulate. He decided to play it Father Gable's way, be an oil man for a while. But he told himself he wasn't quitting the theatrical world. He was just going to be "at liberty" for a time.

Father Gable was at work in a new field near Bigheart, Oklahoma. It was a matter of deep satisfaction to him to have Clark join him. Clark was hired as an apprentice at twelve dollars a day.

Accommodations were primitive. The oil crews slept in tents, food was coarse and expensive, and the winter winds sweeping in off the Oklahoma prairies were bitter.

Drilling for oil was an around-the-clock business with the wildcatters. Equipment was old and frequently in need of repair; the derricks were shaky wooden structures at best.

An apprentice is a general handy man and Jack-of-all-jobs. He is at the bidding of the blacksmith, the tool dresser, the driller. Clark chopped wood to keep the fires going in the boilers, swung a heavy sledgehammer to pound a sharp edge on the red-hot drill bits held by the blacksmith, took his turn on the platform at the top of the derrick to oil the bearings on the rig, pulled the heavy pipe sections into place for coupling as the drill bored deeper, re-stacked the sections when the drill was brought up again.

He took his turn working every shift around the clock. His shoulders broadened with the heavy labor, he grew lean and tough—and he saved his money, not for one minute forgetting his dreams of the theater.

A year later, Clark read a newspaper account of a repertory company being organized in Kansas City. He announced his intention of quitting the oil fields and joining them.

This was a terrible shock to his father. Once again the two Dutch temperaments clashed and the quarrel that followed was an explosive and bitter one.

"I told the stubborn mule that if he left me this time, he needn't ever come back," Father Gable said later. "I was through with him."

Clark left. It was to be five years before his father heard from him again.

The newly organized Jewell Players were a tent-show repertory company, with ambitious plans for touring the Middle West after a stand in Kansas City.

On the basis of his husky physique, Clark was engaged as a prop and general utility man at ten dollars a week, with a promise of a chance at character parts as the occasion demanded.

For nearly two years, the company toured the small towns of the Middle West, staging their shows in a tent in summer, hiring local town halls and opera houses in the winter.

The routine was much like that of a traveling circus. Immediately upon arrival the tent went up; then the company staged an impromptu parade down the main street, ballyhooing the evening's performance. Clark doubled in brass at many jobs; drove tent stakes, played a French horn in the band during the parade, was in the orchestra during the overture before the curtain went up, and then ran backstage, changed clothes, donned makeup and waited for his cue to go on stage.

"Actually they'd hired me for my muscles, but I thought I was an actor," he said.

The company was always in financial straits. The winter of 1922 was a bitter one. Heavy snowstorms kept audiences at home. Receipts dwindled and the company was finally stranded in Butte, Montana.

Clark had only a couple of dollars in his pocket. Other members of the troupe were sending out SOS messages to families and friends. Clark debated writing to his father but the memory of their last quarrel was still with him. Too proud, too stubborn, to ask for help, he climbed into an empty boxcar on a westbound freight train.

"It was that or go to work in the copper mines," he said. "Besides, I thought it'd be warmer on the coast."

Tired, hungry, dirty, Clark jumped off the boxcar when the train made a stop at Bend, a small town in central Oregon. "I was afraid I'd be picked up as a vagrant if they found me on board," he said. "The car was almost in front of a lumber company's office. I went inside to get warm and found that they were hiring men, no questions asked. In ten minutes I was on the payroll."

Clark spent the next three months in a lumber camp on one end of a huge cross-saw. The man on the opposite end was a powerful Swede named Thorsen. It was hard work keeping up with Thorsen, who seemed indefatigable but Clark stuck it out.

He was sitting in my office when he told me of the experience. Looking down at his hands he said, "I can remember when they were chapped and torn and raw. The other men in the camp wore heavy work gloves. I didn't have the money to buy any so I had to do without. At night I'd get the camp cook to give me vinegar to help heal them and lard to soften the sting of the vinegar. It toughened them up. By the time I had the money for the gloves, my hands were so hard and callused I didn't need 'em."

When he had enough money saved, Clark went north to Portland. "It was the nearest big city, and I thought I might find a theater there," he explained.

In Portland, Clark got a job in a department store as a salesman for men's neckwear. A fellow employee, Earle Larimore, was directing an amateur acting group, the Red Lantern Players. When he learned of Clark's experience, he gave him a bit part in the current production, *Nothing but the Truth*. Later, Earle organized a stock company in Astoria, about a hundred miles northwest of Portland. He invited Clark to join the group, and Clark gladly quit his job to do so.

Billed as "The Astoria Players," the company opened in Astoria on July 23, 1922, in *When Women Rule*. Clark played the role of Eliza, a Negro cook who becomes chief of police. (This was the only time he ever appeared in blackface.)

Other plays presented included *Blundering Billy*, with Clark as a seaman. In *The Villun Still Pursued Her*, Clark was dressed as a baby, and seen on stage in a huge crib.

The venture was a cooperative one and the box office receipts were prorated. Clark never drew more than a few dollars a week, with one exception. A local fair pulled in big crowds from the surrounding countryside and the show profited thereby. The take that week netted him ten dollars.

The company played a string of little towns up and down the Columbia River, then finally folded in Astoria. Among the group was a pretty girl named Franz Doerfler, whose father owned a prosperous farm at Silverton in the Willamette Valley. Clark was broke, so Franz took him home with her and her father gave him a job picking hops.

Martin Doerfler and his wife,

Franz's sister Margaret, and her brother Fritz treated Clark as one of the family. When the hop season was over, Clark went to work for the Silverton Lumber Company at three dollars and twenty cents a day.

For five weeks he carried chains for a surveying party in the Oregon woods. Next he was on a construction gang as a "brush hooker," cutting low brush ahead of the construction crew.

Ingrained Dutch thrift made Clark save every penny he could. Meantime, he continued to see Franz at every opportunity, for they were both interested in the theater and had a lot in common. When Clark had one hundred dollars saved, he asked Franz to marry him. Together they would go to Portland.

Franz loved Clark but she had quite a bit of Dutch practicality herself. She thought he was having too hard a time supporting himself without taking on the responsibility of a wife. As for the theater, she didn't think Clark had much future as an actor. She told the shy, awkward, twenty-one-year-old lumberjack that marriage for them, in view of the circumstances, would be disastrous.

Clark took his damaged ego to Portland, where he worked for a while for an automobile accessory firm. Then he got a job as a classified advertising solicitor for the *Portland Oregonian*, at fifteen dollars a week. This was a key spot for keeping an eye on available jobs, and when the local telephone company advertised for a lineman, Clark took time off to answer the ad himself and got the job.

One day he got a call to repair a phone line at Portland's newly organized Little Theater, which was under the direction of Josephine Dillon. After he had fixed the wire, Clark stood in

Josephine Dillon, 1923. When they met, Clark was 24; she was 36, talented, mature and brilliant.

the back of the theater watching Miss Dillon direct her players. When the class was over, he spoke to her, told her of his interest in the theater, and said he'd done some acting with the Jewell Players in Montana.

Josephine was impressed with him and suggested that he join her group. Once again Clark had met a woman who was to shape and influence his life.

Josephine Dillon was a newcomer to Portland, having arrived in the fall of 1922 to play in stock opposite Edward Everett Horton. At the end of the season, she decided to remain in the city and start a little theater group. She rented a large old-fashioned house, converted the first floor into the theater and used the upper floor for her

personal living quarters. (Portland's largest movie theater, the Broadway, now stands on the site of this house.)

Soon her advertisement for classes in a "school of the theater" was appearing in the local paper and on hotel menus. The Little Theater "caught on." It became fashionable for the wealthy and cultured to patronize it.

Josephine had a splendid background as an educator in the dramatic arts when she embarked on this venture. Born in Denver in 1888, she was graduated from Stanford University in 1908 and completed her education in New York and Paris.

Besides being a talented actress, she had been a lecturer on speech and acting techniques and a prominent figure in the Liberty Theater of the United States Army School during World War I. For a time she was secretary to Rupert Hughes.

When Clark met Josephine she was thirty-six—mature, brilliant, and what is most important, painstaking. She saw the latent possibilities in the broad-shouldered young man, and decided to channel his dogged Dutch persistence into constructive effort.

Josephine felt that Clark's voice needed intensive training, as he had acquired a mixture of accents from different sections of the country and his conversation was full of Pennsylvania Dutch idiom. His voice was hard in quality and rather high-pitched, which is often characteristic of big men.

Soon she had Clark at the piano for long periods, trying for pitch and accuracy of tone. Patiently they worked together to bring his voice down to a lower register and establish quality and resonance.

Josephine's method was to have her students do their breathing exercises while in motion, in order to avoid stilted attitudes and at the same time relax muscles.

Clark walked to and from his room to his job twice a day—he went home for lunch—and now he learned to do his breathing exercises while walking.

"He had the straight-lipped, set mouth of the do-it-or-die character, the man who has had to fight things through alone, and who tells nothing," Josephine says in her book.[1]

She thought he looked over-worked and undernourished, and because his general physical condition was so poor ("he looked like a gorgeous skeleton"), Josephine encouraged him to give up his telephone job that summer. She arranged for him to work on a farm near Salem. That fall, he returned to Portland in much better health, deeply tanned from outdoor activity.

Josephine now got him a job singing in the dining room of the Portland Hotel. This was *the* fashionable social center.

"Clark wasn't much of a singer," a friend writes, "but the wealthy old ladies who made up the hotel's clientele were happy just to look at the handsome young man. Miss Dillon had him finish his program every evening with 'Mother Machree,' which always went over big."

Meanwhile, Josephine continued to coach Clark. They read plays together; he acted in the plays the theater produced. An old play program for March 21, 1924, lists him in the part of Menian Deacon in *Miss Lulu Bett,* with Freida Pubols. The Portland group also took their plays to other towns in the vicinity.

Under Josephine's patient and skillful guidance, Clark began to learn the rudiments of acting. "She taught me timing, co-ordination, how to make an entrance," he wrote years later.

In the summer of 1924, Josephine decided to give up her theater group and return to Los Angeles. A good many stage shows were being produced there and she felt that opportunities for her services would be greater.

That fall she wrote to Clark outlining the possibilities for theatrical work. She suggested that it might be good training for him if he were to get some professional experience in California, with the New York stage as his eventual goal.

Clark left at once for California. His dream of becoming a good actor was about to take on reality. To him, Josephine represented theatrical "class." Too, her father had been District Attorney in Los Angeles prior to his death. Josephine's sister, Fannie, was an accomplished composer and teacher of classical music. Another sister, Enrica, was singing in opera in Italy. Josephine herself was brilliant, vital. Clark was fascinated by her. They were married December 13, 1924, by the Reverend H.W. Meadows, in a quiet ceremony in the church office.

They moved into a twenty-dollar-a-month bungalow court apartment in Hollywood, and Josephine got a job reading scripts for the Palmer Photoplay Corporation and advertised for dramatic students. Clark bought a secondhand car for fifty-six dollars and began making the rounds of the theatrical producers.

The venture was discouraging. He failed to find anything on the legitimate stage, and decided that movie work would be the next best thing, although at the time he had no thought of a movie career. Almost immediately he got a bit part in *White Man,* with

[1] *Modern Acting:* A Guide for Stage, Screen and Radio. Prentice-Hall, Inc. 1940.

Alice Joyce and Kenneth Harland. The job lasted ten days and paid fifteen dollars a day.

This bonanza fired him with enthusiasm over his prospects. Mary Pickford, Charles Chaplin, Douglas Fairbanks, Harold Lloyd were the big names and the big money-makers of the day. If they could roll up a fortune, so could he.

But the part in *White Man* was the last one of any consequence. All he could get thereafter was extra work at five dollars a day, though one day's work, in *The Merry Widow* with Mae Murray and John Gilbert, paid seven-fifty. Meanwhile, Josephine continued to coach and encourage him.

In the summer of 1925, Louis O. Macloon and his wife, Lillian Albertson, brought their production of *Romeo and Juliet* to the coast. The stars were Jane Cowl and Rollo Peters. It was customary to select a group of extras in each locality to serve in crowd scenes, and Clark got a job as a spear carrier at thirty-five dollars a week.

"I remember him as a sturdy, raw and unschooled young man, brimful of ambition," Rollo Peters says. "We were impressed with his determination and sincerity, however, and our management engaged him to travel with the troupe till the season ended. He served—and well—as leader of the extras. One thing I recall about him was his great modesty."

After *Romeo and Juliet* closed, Lillian offered Clark a small part in *What Price Glory?* Fortunately for Clark, the actor playing the part of Sergeant Quirk left the show soon after the opening, and Clark got the role. The play ran for two months at the Playhouse. Lillian cast him in subsequent productions of *Madame X* and *Lady Frederick.*

Clark in What Price Glory. *(1925)*

In the summer of 1926, Lionel Barrymore directed and starred in a revival of *The Copperhead* on the stage in Los Angeles. He remembered Clark from his callboy days during the New York run of *The Jest,* and gave him the part of the juvenile lead in. his new production.

Lionel was Clark's idol, and the opportunity was a tremendous one for him. In later years he loved to tell the story of his dreadful stage *faux pas* on the show's opening night. He accidentally dropped his hat into what was supposed to be a deep well on the stage. Instinctively, he reached down and retrieved it. The audience roared.

Backstage, Lionel went into a truly spectacular Barrymore rage, gave Clark a tongue-lashing that terrified him. Clark thought he was fired, but Lionel finally cooled down and kept him in the cast, because he really liked Clark and thought he had talent.

After *Copperhead* closed, Ernest Lubitsch gave Clark a chance at a big part in a picture with Pola Negri and Rod LaRocque. Somehow, Clark failed to perform a bit of "business" to Lubitsch's liking on the first take, and another extra got the part. "I was crushed by my failure," Clark said.

Motion pictures had not begun to talk. The screen's leading men were suave and passionate lovers such as Valentino, John Gilbert, Ricardo Cortez. Clark felt that he was a "roughneck" and that there was no future in films for him.

After weeks of discouragement, he got the role of the reporter in a stock company production of *Chicago,* with Nancy Carroll, which played for several weeks at the Music Box on Hollywood Boulevard.

There Clark was seen by a scout from a Houston stock company who was in Hollywood to recruit players, including a second lead. He offered Clark a job and Clark, on Josephine's advice, accepted it. It meant separation, but it would give him valuable stage experience and a steady income. Having made less than a thousand dollars in the last two years, Clark needed no further urging.

The Gene Lewis Players put on two plays a week. It was rigorous training for Clark, meaning endless cramming to learn his lines, but with his usual persistence he forced himself to perform prodigious feats of memorizing.

"I was never a quick study," Clark said. "I really had to grind." Soon he was playing leads and his salary was raised to seventy-five dollars a week.

When the stock company season ended, many of the players planned to go to New York. They urged Clark to go with them. He was faced with a decision: Should he return to Hollywood where his stage and film work had been so scarce and unprofitable? Or go to New York, where there was every possibility that he might get another stock company engagement from the booking offices there?

"I couldn't get New York out of my mind," Clark told me. "When I went there this time I'd have letters of recommendation from the Houston company. It was too good a chance to miss. I settled for New York."

CHAPTER THREE

CLARK'S earlier experience in New York had been as a callboy for an Arthur Hopkins production, *The Jest.* Clark felt it was an auspicious omen when Lillian Albertson sent him to see Hopkins, who was casting *Machinal,* a new play by Sophie Treadwell.

Hopkins looked him over, was impressed by his background and experience, and assigned him a role opposite Zita Johann, the lead. Clark was elated but, as he confessed later, "loaded with stage fright."

Now the whole tempo of his theatrical experience changed completely. He was amazed at the ease with which Hopkins conducted rehearsals. The cast sat in a circle on the stage under a single work-light while Hopkins discussed the play and its purpose and what he saw in each individual character. "His manner, tone of voice, and attitude were quiet and easy and inspired our confidence," Clark said.

After four weeks' rehearsal, Hopkins took *Machinal* to New Haven for a three-day tryout. Clark had a bad case of opening night jitters and lost all semblance of the characterization he had carefully rehearsed.

"I was the typical stock company actor from the provinces, panicking at the thought of Broadway," Clark said later. "I tried too hard."

That night after the show, and again the next morning at the brush-up rehearsal, he expected Hopkins to give him his notice; but the producer said nothing.

Clark's performances for the next two nights were even more ragged. At last, he could stand it no longer. He went to Hopkins and suggested that another actor be hired to replace him. Hopkins remained perfectly calm, refusing to admit that Clark's performance was bad. Instead he told him to relax, that he'd be all right after they got to New York.

Machinal opened at the Plymouth Theater in New York September 7, 1928. Hopkins came backstage before the curtain and assured the cast that he would be in his customary seat in the back row, where he'd sat during rehearsals. "He suggested that we forget the house was full of people and play it the way we'd rehearsed it for him," Clark said.

Hopkins's little pep talk worked. Clark lost his fears, made his entrance on cue, and played with strength and assurance.

In the audience that night were aristocratic, well-to-do divorcee Maria ("Ria") Langham, her daughter George Anna, and her half-brother Booth Franklin, all of Houston.

"We noticed that there were several players from Houston in the cast," Ria says. "My brother, who was also an actor, knew them and suggested that we go backstage after the play to visit. I had seen Clark in stock in Houston but had never met him. After the show, we were introduced and he went on to supper with us."

The group waited up to read the reviews in the early morning papers. The notices were all good.

Clark and Ria Langham Gable, his second wife, married in Santa Ana, California, on June 19, 1931. COURTESY OF
GEORGE ANNA BURKE

The *New York Times* reported that Clark was "an engaging adventurer" and "played the casual, good-humored lover without a hackneyed gesture." The *Telegraph* described him as "young, vigorous, brutally masculine."

Clark was relieved and happy. Years later he wrote a tribute to Arthur Hopkins, saying that had he been in the hands of a director with less understanding and knowledge of the theater and its players, he might never have opened on Broadway.

Some of the critics claimed that *Machinal* was a dramatization of the recent sensational Ruth Snyder-Judd Gray murder trial. Sophie Treadwell, the author, denied this, insisting that the struggle of an individual against callous inhumanity in the mechanical age was her theme. The initial interest in the play that had flared so high gradually died. It closed after ten weeks.

Clark was "at liberty," and could not find another job. Josephine visited him that winter and urged him to return to California, but Clark felt there was no future for him in films, and that if he was to have a career in acting it would be on the stage in New York or playing in stock around the country.

"We were drifting apart, and we both knew it," Clark said.

Josephine went back to California. In March 1929 she quietly filed for divorce.

Ria Langham's daughter George Anna was a teen-ager in school at Tarrytown, and Ria and her younger son were established in an apartment in New York. She extended a warm and friendly welcome to the lonely and discouraged Clark.

Ria was eleven years Clark's senior. A small woman with auburn hair, she was "regal" in her bearing and was considered a "fascinating hostess."

Born Maria Franklin, she had been married three times and had two sons and a daughter. Clark was entertained in her home, met her friends, and found her attractive and companionable.

"He was unknown, very discouraged and had little money," Ria says. "However, I thought he had great charm and potential. No agent would take him and he couldn't seem to get another part after *Machinal*. But I encouraged him to stay in show business as I believed he had a great deal to offer. I persuaded him to take voice lessons from Frances Robinson-Duff, the noted dramatic coach, and to keep trying a little longer."

Early in the fall, Clark was cast in *Hawk Island*, a play by Howard Irving Young, which opened at the Longacre Theater September 16, 1929, under the production banner of Thomas Kilpatrick.

Clark's role was that of Gregory Sloane, host to a house party on a remote island. Bored, he and a visiting mystery writer plot a fake murder to stir up a little excitement. The whole thing backfires when the writer is killed by an irate husband and Sloane is charged with the murder.

The critics thought Mr. Young had an interesting premise but had failed to follow through. The *Times* noted that "the principal player is Clark Gable, who came to light in Mr. Hopkins's *Machinal* a season ago. He is fully equal to the demands that Mr. Young puts upon him."

The play closed after twenty-four performances. Another flop, Elmer Boross's *Blind Windows*, which opened in Philadelphia with Clark in

the cast, was a discouraging follow-up to *Hawk Island*.

"I couldn't get a job, but at least I could see other actors at work and study their techniques," Clark said. "I bought cheap balcony seats for *Journey's End* and Francine Larrimore's *Let Us Be Gay*. Katharine Cornell was playing in *Dishonorerd Lady*, Constance Collier in *The Matriarch*. All that winter I was on the outside looking in."

In the spring of 1930, A. H. Woods cast Clark opposite Alice Brady in his production of *Love, Honor and Betray*, which opened at the Eltinge on March 13. Alice played a *femme fatale* who visits a cemetery and has a reunion with the ghosts of three men prominent in her love life: one the youth she jilted, one the fat millionaire she married, and the third her lover—played by Clark. At the final curtain, Alice has her eye on her daughter's lover, a handsome chauffeur. (George Brent played the chauffeur; the daughter was Glenda Farrell.)

The *Times* reviewer wrote "Clark Gable is personable as the lover," but decided that the "stage designer gave the best performance."

"This one lasted all of four weeks," Clark said. "I thought my luck was picking up."

Josephine's final divorce decree was granted on March 30, 1930. Their parting was a friendly one. Clark always praised the important part she had played in his career.

"I shall always be grateful for her patient and skillful teaching," he told interviewers in later years.

While still playing in *Love, Honor and Betray*, Clark had a letter from Macloon and Albertson, who were interested in presenting a West Coast production of *The Last Mile*, then playing to packed houses in New York.

They suggested that Clark see it. "You're just right for Killer Mears," they said.

Clark went to see *The Last Mile*, and at once became a devoted fan of Spencer Tracy, who had originated the role of Mears, the condemned killer in Cell Five who stages a jail break. Tracy's characterization was described as "ruthless...dominant."

Clark liked what he saw and, encouraged by Ria, took the next train for California.

He found the atmosphere in Hollywood had changed. Sound had arrived. Public interest in silent movies was dying. Studio heads were in a state of panic over their tremendous investments and silent star contracts.

Highly technical sound mixing had not been perfected. Audiences jeered at the high, falsetto tones of erstwhile idols such as John Gilbert and William Haines, who were falling from favor.

The movie makers were seeking actors with good voices for sound films. Drama and voice schools were flourishing. Josephine Dillon's coaching services were in great demand.

Los Angeles was having a lush theatrical season. Thirteen theaters were playing to capacity houses, with some of the best players in New York in their casts. Movie scouts attended every opening.

His appearance in *The Last Mile* at the Majestic Theater in Los Angeles was something of a triumphant return for Clark. The discouraged stage and film bit player who had left in 1927 was now making three hundred dollars a week and was out to show what he could do. He brought ruthless drive and authority to his role as the convict fighting against death in the chair.

At the end of the first performance, Lionel Barrymore, who was at Metro-Goldwyn-Mayer in the dual capacity of director-actor, came backstage to see Clark. He was enthusiastic over his performance. "I think you're a good bet for pictures," he said. "I want to arrange a screen test for you at my studio."

On the day set for the test Lionel was away on location. For some reason, possibly because of Clark's rangy physique and dark hair, he was made up as a "native" and asked to do a scene from *Bird of Paradise*.

"I was sure this was good luck for me, because it was the first play I'd ever seen, years ago in Akron," Clark said. But he always shuddered when he went on to describe this experience. "They covered my entire body with some sort of dark goop," he said, "wrapped me in a loincloth and stuck a red flower behind my ear. I was all elbows and knees and felt like a fool. Naturally I acted like one."

When the test was screened in a projection room for the studio executives, they outdid each other in screaming "No." They told Lionel his protege had nothing and they weren't interested.

Ruth Collier, an agent, and her associate Minna Wallis also saw the test. Ruth got in touch with Clark to ask if she might represent him. Clark gratefully agreed, but was dubious about his prospects. Ruth assigned Minna to handle his affairs.

Enterprising Minna, the sister of producer-director Hal Wallis, took Clark out to Pathe where E. B. Derr was casting *The Painted Desert*, a medium-budget western starring William Boyd and Helen Twelvetrees.

"They asked me if I could ride," Clark said. "I'd never been on a horse in my life but I lied in my teeth and said 'Yes.'"

Later that day Minna called him to congratulate him on being cast as the "heavy," at a salary of seven hundred and fifty dollars a week.

"How much time do I have?" Clark asked. "I've got to learn to ride."

Minna groaned and rushed him out to a riding stable in the San Fernando Valley for a daily two-hour session with a horse.

"I was so stiff and sore the first few days I could hardly walk, but I stuck it out," Clark said. "Five weeks later when the film went on location in Arizona, I could ride well enough to get by."

In the film he had one big scene where he blows up a mine. Technicians made careful arrangements but something went wrong. In the ensuing explosion, one man was killed, several others injured. Clark was knocked flat by falling rocks and sand but fortunately was unhurt. The experience was a deeply depressing one and he returned to Hollywood in a very discouraged frame of mind.

Minna knew he was very unsure of himself and that the only remedy for this was to get him another job, keep him working.

She took her client over to Warner Brothers and got him a bit part in *Night Nurse,* starring Barbara Stanwyck and Ben Lyon. Clark played another "heavy," a brutal chauffeur who starves two children to death. For some reason *Night Nurse* was not released until a year or so later, so Clark had no immediate "exposure."

While he was at Warners, Minna touted him for a part in *Little Caesar.* Darryl Zanuck, then a Warner executive, made a test of him in a scene from *The Last Mile.* He showed it to Jack Warner. To this day Mr. Warner tells how he turned Clark down. "What can you do with a guy with ears like that?" he is reported to have said.

This was another bitter disappointment for Clark. He'd had such high hopes after his successful "comeback" in *The Last Mile.* He felt he had failed again.

Ria Langham now appeared on the scene to spend the winter in California. Clark was delighted to see her. Once again a mature and gracious woman was on hand to give him encouragement, counsel, understanding. Clark had enjoyed her companionship in New York. In his loneliness and insecurity he turned to her. They became inseparable.

Undaunted by the failure of the Warner test, Minna went to Pandro S. Berman at RKO and sold him on the idea of putting Clark under contract. While these negotiations were in progress, Lionel Barrymore arranged another test for Clark at Metro-Goldwyn-Mayer.

This time Lionel took complete charge, rehearsed the scene with Clark, and personally supervised the test. He saw to it that Clark was properly groomed in a well-fitting suit from Wardrobe and directed the make-up man to tape back the offending ears. He asked the cameraman to experiment with the lighting in order to photograph Clark to greatest advantage.

Clark's teeth were unevenly spaced and not very attractive.

"Keep your mouth closed, son, until you get those front teeth capped," Lionel advised.

The test showed Clark in three-quarter profile. When it was screened, Irving Thalberg, the rising young production genius at the studio, saw it and told Minna he wanted Clark under contract.

Minna called Clark and found he was en route home from New York where he'd been negotiating to return to Broadway in *A Farewell to Arms,* with Elissa Landi.

Unaware of the contract awaiting him, Clark stopped off in Hopedale to see Thelma and his other old friends. He found that Thelma had married Harold Hoobler and was living in nearby Bloomfield, so he went over to see them.

"Harold was in his shirt sleeves, washing up before dinner," Thelma says. "We heard a knock and when I opened the door, there stood Clark. I shall never forget it. He had on a derby, was carrying a cane, and wore gloves. He tried to be so sophisticated," she continues, "and kept calling me 'my dear' until we were convinced he'd 'gone Hollywood' completely. Harold invited him to stay for dinner but Clark declined. I was secretly relieved, for it was a New England boiled dinner and I was sure it wouldn't be fancy enough for him."

When Clark got back to Hollywood, Minna told him of the offers from RKO and MGM. Clark's experience in films had not been too happy and he felt he should continue in the theater. He took his problem to Ria.

"I begged him to stay in pictures, Ria says. "He had a contract with Louis Macloon but I told him he could get out of it."

Clark took her advice and decided in favor of signing with MGM. He was put under short-term contract by the studio on December 4, 1930, at a salary of three hundred and fifty dollars a week.

Minna went to work on her client.

Clark's teeth were capped; and she got him out of the very *gauche* black suit with white stripes and the high collar and gaudy tie he was wearing, seeing to it that his wardrobe became more appropriate for a young contract player. Ria picked up where Minna left off; gradually the rough edges began to be smoothed away.

MGM put Clark to work at once in *The Easiest Way,* starring Constance Bennett, Adolphe Menjou and Robert Montgomery, who was then the studio's romantic young leading man. Clark's role was minor. He was the laundryman husband of Anita Page, while Constance Bennett was involved in a triangular affair with Menjou and Montgomery.

Clark "registered" in this role. People began to make inquiries. Joan Crawford saw him and asked to have him play opposite her in *Dance, Fools, Dance.* In this Clark was cast as a gang leader, wore a black homburg and looked properly menacing. The *New York Times* review said, "His characterization of the gang chieftain is a vivid and authentic piece of acting."

Alert Minna realized that Clark was on his way and wangled a dressing room at the studio for him. Clark had his first studio portrait sitting. He took the proofs to Minna's house that night, spread them all out on the floor and asked Minna to help him select the best ones.

The studio rushed him into *The Secret Six,* with Wally Beery and newcomer Jean Harlow, starring Johnny Mack Brown. Clark played a reporter, a sympathetic character.

A loan-out to First National followed *The Secret Six.* Clark played another gangster in *The Finger Points,* with Richard Barthelmess and Fay

Wray, a story of the death of the Chicago reporter Jack Lingle at the hands of the Capone mob.

When the MGM brass saw *The Finger Points,* they decided that Clark had "great potentialities." Joan Crawford had just finished *Laughing Sinners* with Johnny Mack Brown, a tale of a shady lady who is redeemed by the love of a good man, a Salvation Army worker. All her scenes with Brown were re-shot with Clark, as the Salvation Army worker. This was not a success. He didn't register as a romantic lead. The studio decided his appeal was more aggressive. He projected masculine sex with a knowing, crooked smile.

Clarence Brown, the director, saw Clark in the studio commissary one day and decided he'd be right for the role of the gangster in *A Free Soul* with Norma Shearer, who was playing the daring and uninhibited daughter of a criminal lawyer addicted to alcohol.

Larry Barbier, of MGM's Publicity Department, was on the set during the shooting of Clark's first scene. "When Brown saw him, he said, 'We've got to do something with those ears,'" Larry recalls. "He told the make-up man to tape Clark's ears close to his head."

A Free Soul, 1931, with Norma Shearer made Clark an overnight sensation. He brought a new element to the screen—masculine sex appeal. COURTESY OF MGM

"Clark shot a few minutes this way and then tore the tape off," Larry continues. "He said, 'I'm not going to use this stuff. Either you take me as I am or I will go back to New York.' That ended the business about his ears. Thereafter, the makeup man simply darkened them so they didn't pick up too much light."

Brown had selected Clark because the gangster had to be attractive enough to appeal to the high-born girl, yet show he was no gentleman by slapping her down when she needed it.

"Clark was in agony over playing the scene," Lionel Barrymore said. "He wanted to give it everything and really slap Norma, as Brown directed, but he was plagued by the thought that she was Irving Thalberg's wife and Metro's biggest star. He was afraid that if he really belted her, it might ruin his chances in films. Norma solved his problem for him. When it came to the big slap scene, she told him to follow Brown's orders, slap her and mean it."

Clark slapped and slapped hard. The scene was so brutal that Louis B. Mayer, studio head, wanted it cut out of the finished print, but was persuaded to leave it in.

When the picture was released, in June 1931, Clark was an overnight sensation. Thousands of letters poured in about his performance. Exhibitors wired, "Who is this new he-man?"

Lionel Barrymore won an Oscar for his portrayal of the drunken father, but the film made Clark a star in his own right. The public, it seems, was fed up with suave, romantic lovers. Clark brought a new element to the screen—virile masculine sex appeal.

"The secretaries and the girls in the studio stenographic pool are always a good barometer," Larry Barbier says. "Something like an elec-tric shock now ran along the studio grapevine. When he walked into the commissary for lunch all eyes were upon him. Suddenly everyone was aware of Clark Gable."

Clark's contract was rewritten, on a one-year basis. His salary was raised to eleven hundred and fifty dollars a week, with the studio setting five hundred of this aside in a trust fund each week.

The word went forth that the "Valentino style" of make-up for him was out. Hereafter Clark's rugged he-man qualities were to be emphasized. Howard Strickling, publicity chief of MGM, was told to give him what is known as "the build-up."

Howard and Clark got together for a long talk. It was the beginning of what was to be a lifelong and enduring friendship. Portrait and publicity stills were ordered, background stories started flowing to the columns, interviews with feature writers were set up.

He made *Sporting Blood,* a racing story, with Ernest Torrence and Madge Evans; and then Greta Garbo asked to have him as her leading man in *Susan Lenox.*

"Clark was grateful for all the attention," a friend says. "He'd been beaten down in both films and the theater so many times that he found it hard to believe it was all happening to him."

Clark celebrated by buying his first sports car, a secondhand Duesenberg. He was so proud of it that friends accused him of sleeping in it.

"He said he remembered when he'd slept in worse places," one reports. "He couldn't forget his early struggles."

Flushed with success, Clark went to see Ria Langham. She had been a good companion and staunch supporter during the hard times. It was Ria who had encouraged him, taught him to believe in himself. Now he felt that he had something to offer her.

They were married before Justice of the Peace Kenneth E. Morrison in Santa Ana, California on June 19, 1931. Joe Sherman of the MGM Publicity staff was one of the witnesses.

At the time of her marriage to Clark, Ria and her children were living in a house on San Ysidro, a small street behind Mary Pickford's home. Fredric March was their neighbor.

"When Clark's father came to live with us, we moved to Brentwood, renting a house at 220 North Bristol Street," Ria says. "Barbara Stanwyck was living just across the street and Joan Crawford's house was several doors down. Father Gable stayed with us several months until he married Edna."

The whole pattern of Clark's life now changed; he was head of a family. "George Anna was fourteen, my son eight. He fell in love with them and they with him," Ria says. "The boy was crazy about him and Clark took him hunting on many occasions."

At first the Gables lived very simply, for Clark was working hard to establish himself, and Ria, who was very social, entertained only on weekends. She took charge of the financial accounts, telling Clark that there were to be no presents or extravagances until he'd paid all his debts.

Hunting, fishing and camping-out were Clark's favorite diversions and he wanted Ria to share them with him. He took her on various weekend trips to his favorite haunts.

One of these was "Rainbow" Gibson's fishing lodge on the Rogue River in Oregon, just east of Grant's Pass.

Gable and Peggy Gibson, 1933. The Gibsons owned the We Ask U Inn on the Rogue River in Oregon, where Clark loved to go fishing.

Rainbow was famous as a guide and fisherman, and Clark liked to fish the well-known Pierce Riffle for salmon in the spring and steelhead in the fall.

The lodge was called the We Ask U Inn, and was a sprawling structure with a huge living room, great stone fireplace and deep comfortable chairs and sofas. Guest cabins were scattered among the beautiful madrona, fir, pine and cedar trees.

The Gibsons had three little girls: Sybil, who was fourteen, Carol, twelve, and Vee, ten. Clark was very fond of the whole family and felt at home there.

"Ria was typically society but very friendly," Sybil recalls. "She didn't fish, just sat around and waited for Clark."

Other sports-loving friends were Harry and Nan Fleischmann of the Fleischmann's Yeast family. Harry's father and his Uncle Max, the company founders, had brought the yeast from Europe to introduce it on the American market.

Harry owned a skeet club and Clark took Ria there frequently, although she didn't shoot. In fact, it soon became apparent that Ria was a "patient spectator" on these trips.

"Clark's career was just getting started then," Nan Fleischmann says. "He was earning his first important money, and he was cautious with it. He told me that it was his greatest ambition to have twenty thousand dollars in cash."

When Clark reported for *Susan Lenox* with Greta Garbo he had a bad case of the jitters, and was actually scared of the star; but Robert Leonard, the director, told him to relax, he'd find she was wonderful.

Everyone on the set seemed to adore her, and Clark soon found her very friendly and cooperative. He admired her businesslike approach and deep concentration on the scene at hand. Promptly at five o'clock each afternoon, Miss Garbo quit work, no matter what was going on. This made a deep impression on Clark. He resolved that one day there would be a clause in *his* contract to this effect.

Playing with Greta was a big boost for his career and Clark was rushed into the role of a politician in *Possessed*, with Joan Crawford. He was then cast as a naval aviator in *Hell Divers* with Wallace Beery and as a minister in *Polly of the Circus*.

Marion Davies was his leading lady in *Polly*, and William Randolph Hearst was a frequent visitor on the set, for he was supervising Marion's wardrobe. Hearst, impressed with Clark and his growing popularity, suggested that he demand a raise in salary, and promised to put in a good word for him.

"I encouraged him in this also," Ria says. "Night after night he'd come home exhausted, fuming because the other stars in his films were making more money. He felt he was the drawing card and that tremendous pride of his was hurt because his salary was less."

Hell Divers was released and was a huge success. Clark was emboldened to follow Hearst's and Ria's advice to demand a raise. The studio wrote a new two-year contract for him at two thousand dollars a week, five hundred dollars of this still reserved in a trust fund each week.

Ria now began to surround Clark with the luxury and social life she felt befitted his status as a popular young film star. She had always moved in the upper echelons socially and her formal dinner guest lists included the David Selznicks, Mary Pickford, Sam and

Frances Goldwyn, Norma Shearer, Irving Thalberg and other ranking Hollywood stars and personalities.

There were parties, yachting trips, and weekends at San Simeon, the Hearst Ranch. "Clark enjoyed it all for a while, but he was rather temperamental and for many weekends he'd do nothing but hunt," Ria says. "He always felt more comfortable in sports clothes. Clark had a deep inferiority complex and was highly sensitive," she continues. "I remember when he bought his first expensive sports car. It was quite flashy and he was bursting with pride when he drove it to the studio. Then a slighting remark about it, made in jest, infuriated him. He sold the car immediately at a tremendous loss.

"It was the same way with his clothes," she observed. "If anything critical was said about them, he never wore them again. I used to urge him to stand up and fight back, to say, 'I like this, whether you do or not,' but he never would."

Although Clark had learned to ride for his role in *The Painted Desert*, he continued to take riding lessons, this time at the Valdez Riding Stables in Coldwater Canyon. The Valdez couple were known as "Val and Mrs. Val." Val was an expert horseman, as was his wife, who was a movie stunt woman.

"Clark became an excellent rider," Mrs. Val says. "He also took roping lessons and became quite proficient at it. Robert Taylor and Zeppo Marx were out here at the same time."

The Valdezes liked Clark, but found him hard to get acquainted with at first, he seemed so reticent. "He acted as if he had been 'taken' and he had a reserve that was hard to penetrate," Mrs. Val says. "Often Val and I

thought we'd broken through, only to find him very aloof the next time we saw him."

Norma Shearer, the wife of Irving Thalberg and now "Queen" of the Metro lot, selected Clark to play opposite her in *Strange Interlude*. Clark had the role of the long-suffering and "understanding" lover—the picture did nothing for him; but the subsequent *Red Dust*, with Jean Harlow, was a sexy drama that had Clark playing the "he-man" again. It was a big box-office success.

Red Dust was Clark's first film under Victor Fleming's direction and he and Fleming became close friends. The script was written by John Lee Mahim, with whom Clark was to be closely associated later on.

Just before going into *Strange Interlude*, Clark and Ria had their first separation. Ria took the children and went to New York for a while. When the film was finished, Clark telephoned her and asked her to come back. They were reconciled and their life together went on as before.

"Actually Clark was very insecure," a friend says. "His sudden popularity puzzled and confused him and he didn't quite know how to handle it. He was beginning to find his marriage to Ria restrictive, but he clung to her for he'd grown to depend on her strength and reassurance."

In 1932 Paramount Pictures was in a slump, but the studio executives had high hopes for a promising story called *No Man of Her Own*, a comedy about a fascinating gambler and a small-town librarian. Miriam Hopkins was slated for the librarian role and Wesley Ruggles was to direct.

Then Miss Hopkins withdrew from the part, which was assigned to Carole Lombard. "I suggested Clark for the

Gable with Jean Harlow in Red Dust, *1932.* COURTESY OF MGM

me he was going to 'make hay' while he could."

Ruggles found Clark very prompt, businesslike and absorbed in doing a good job. Clark frequently called him in to discuss various lines, sometimes suggested changes, but always deferred to Ruggles's decisions. "You're the boss," was his attitude.

The picture took six weeks to shoot and Clark and Carole devised innumerable gags on each other. At the party on the final day of shooting, Carole presented Clark with a huge ham with his picture imprinted on the label. He, in turn, gave her a pair of dilapidated outsize ballet shoes "for dancing."

Clark's next three pictures were not very successful despite the fact that he was cast with Helen Hayes in a remake of *The White Sister* and *Night Flight* and was teamed again with Jean Harlow in *Hold Your Man.*

Helen Hayes and Ria became great friends. Gloria Swanson, Marlene Dietrich, Joan Crawford, Countess di Frasso, Joe Schenck and the Richard Barthelmesses were among the group entertained by the Gables.

"Irving Thalberg said I provided the 'frame' for showing Clark off," Ria says. "He congratulated me on having seen his potentialities and said I could surely 'pick 'em.' I was always arranging a screen test for some young hopeful."

Clark continued to shun the formal social life, however, and spent his spare time hunting with his cronies, among whom was Eddie Mannix, one of the MGM executives, who later became vice president and general manager. "Clark trusted Eddie and always took his advice about his film roles," a friend said.

He became interested in Masonry

gambler," Ruggles says. "I remembered him from the one-reelers when I'd used him and Janet Gaynor as extras at five dollars a day."

The Paramount executives were dubious about Clark's ability to play comedy; they had him typed as a "killer." But they ended up by making a deal with MGM for his services.

"Clark and Carole 'clicked' right from the start, and made a good comedy team," Ruggles says. "I was impressed with the progress Clark had made. One day I stopped by his dressing room to ask how things were going for him. It was Clark's opinion that he wasn't going to 'last long' and he told

and was initiated an Entered Apprentice Mason in Beverly Hills Lodge No. 528, Free and Accepted Masons of the State of California on September 19, 1933, becoming a Master Mason on October 31st.

The next year he petitioned for and received the degrees of the Royal Arch, in Santa Monica Bay Chapter No. 97, and the Commandery in Santa Monica Bay Commandery No. 61, Knights Templar. Later he was made a member of Al Malaikah Temple of the Ancient and Arabic Order of the Nobles of the Mystic Shrine in Los Angeles.

In June 1933, while on a bear hunt in Nevada with his friend Dr. Franklin Thorpe, he had an attack of appendicitis. He was put on a diet which failed to relieve the condition and in August he had his tonsils and appendix removed by Dr. Thorpe at the Cedars of Lebanon Hospital in Los Angeles.

After his recovery from his illness, Clark returned to the studio and was cast as the second lead opposite Joan Crawford and Franchot Tone in *Dancing Lady.*

"Clark felt this was a step down for him, that he hadn't done anything really worthwhile since *Susan Lenox* and that he'd fallen into the category of 'just a good leading man,' " a friend says. "He went to the front office and complained. To discipline him, they loaned him out to Columbia for a picture Frank Capra was going to make."

The picture in question was a comedy based on a story by Samuel Hopkins Adams called *Night Bus* and involved a runaway heiress and a newspaperman on a Miami-to-New York bus.

MGM had originally owned the story but had sold it to Columbia, which was then a secondary company.

Harry Cohn, head of Columbia, wanted Myrna Loy and Robert Montgomery for the leads. Myrna had read the script and rejected it, and when Cohn went to Louis B. Mayer to borrow Montgomery, Mayer persuaded him to take Gable instead.

When Clark heard of his loan-out to Columbia, and to a minor producer at that, he felt that his career was really in jeopardy.

"He came storming home, threatening to quit Metro, walk out on his contract," Ria relates. "I told him that if that would make him happy to go ahead and do it, but I thought it would be smarter to make the picture, do the best he could and see what happened."

Claudette Colbert had been

Joan Crawford was one of Clark's most popular leading ladies. Here they are in their first film together, Dancing Lady, *1933.* COURTESY OF MGM

signed to play opposite him and she and Clark got together and compared notes.

"Clark wasn't actually dissatisfied with the story," Claudette says. "He was just irritated that MGM had farmed him out. As for me, I went into it deliberately—and with pleasure; because I had never met Clark and, like every other woman in the country, thought he was divine and, secondly, because I admired Frank Capra and had made my very first picture for him.

"Comedies were not 'the thing' in that glamorous era, but I loved comedy, having played it on Broadway. And as Paramount was putting me in rather dull 'nice women' roles, I jumped at this gay prospect of looking at Gable every day and getting paid besides!"

"Capra was terribly disappointed when he had to settle for Gable," Joe Walker, Capra's long-time cameraman, says. "When Gable came over to see him about it, Capra told me to stick around. They had an hour-and-a-half session together, and when it was over, they both came out smiling. Capra put his arm around Gable's shoulder and said, 'Joe, everything is fine. This boy is going to be just great in the part.' "

Joe recalls that when they walked out into the studio's patio courtyard, Capra nudged him to look up at the windows around the court. "Every female in the place was hanging out, trying to get a look at Gable," Joe says.

"The 'image' of Clark, the strength in his face that we came to know later, had not yet come through on camera," Joe recalls. "He was still very young-looking and we had to light him carefully. After several days' shooting, Clark asked Capra how he was doing. 'Oh, you'll get by,' Capra said. Actually he was delighted with the rushes."

"We all had a good time shooting the picture," Claudette says, "but neither Clark nor I had the remotest idea that it would be a sensation. We thought it was very funny, however, and Clark broke up—take after take—in some of the scenes."

The film was shot on a "tight" budget of three hundred and fifty thousand dollars. The hours were long and hard. "Many nights we worked all night," Joe says. "The bus scenes were very difficult, because we didn't have 'breakaways' in those days. We had to shoot in the actual cramped quarters inside a bus. We shot the night-in-a-haystack scene under a circus tent on the RKO ranch. Capra devised the dubbing-in of the sound of frogs and crickets, which was an innovation at that time."

When the picture was finished, Clark went back to Metro, to find his status unchanged. He was just another good leading man. He went into *Men in White* in the role of an idealistic doctor, opposite Myrna Loy, and was teamed with her again in *Manhattan Melodrama*, as a gangster.

His career was in the doldrums; and, as if to prove it, Ruth Collier, his agent, sold his contract. In Hollywood this is known as "unloading" a client whose future seems uncertain.

"Clark was terribly discouraged," a friend says. "He felt *It Happened One Night* was going to be a flop; his marriage was not going well, and when his agent sold him out he really touched bottom."

Clark's new agent Phil Berg and his associate Bob Coryell had great faith in Clark, however. "We paid twenty-five thousand dollars for his contract," Bob says, "and we soon had reason to congratulate ourselves on a profitable buy."

It Happened One Night (1934) was Gable's breakthrough film. Both Clark and Claudette Colbert won Academy Awards for their performances. Gable's stardom was finally established. COURTESY OF COLUMBIA STUDIOS

It Happened One Night was released in February 1934, and was an overnight box-office sensation. Audiences loved Clark and Claudette in their light comedy roles. Everywhere people sang "The Man on the Flying Trapeze."

Clark in his role of the newspaperman, set several masculine styles. Mustaches, the symbol of the dilettante, now became fashionable for rugged males. The fact that he wore no undershirt in the film caused an immediate decline in sales, to the great discomfort of the manufacturers. Bus-line operators, on the other hand, loved the free publicity for bus travel, and reported a healthy increase in the number of female passengers, who were doubtless seeking an experience similar to Claudette's.

When it was announced that he'd been nominated for best actor of the year in *It Happened One Night,* Clark considered it just a "streak of luck." "There are so many good actors in the business," he said. "I just happened to hit it by chance."

"Clark was almost afraid to believe that he might win," Bob says. "He was constantly pointing to other once popular actors who were now on the skids. 'This could happen to me,' he always said."

The 1934 Academy Awards presentations were to be made at a dinner in the Biltmore Bowl (a dining room) at the Biltmore Hotel, February 27, 1935.

Voting procedures were different then. The polls closed at five o'clock on the day of the awards, and the dinner was held at eight—which always meant a frantic last-minute counting of votes.

Over a thousand people were seated in the Bowl; six thousand standees crammed the lobby and foyer.

"Clark had not wanted to attend, but Ria and George Anna persuaded him," a friend says. "He looked uncomfortable in a stiff collar and a dinner jacket."

Claudette Colbert had also received a nomination, but she was so certain that Bette Davis was going to win (for *Of Human Bondage*) that she didn't show up. She was about to board the "Chief" for New York when friends reached her and persuaded her to accompany them to the Bowl.

Major Nathan Levinson, acting president of the Motion Picture Academy, introduced Lionel Barrymore—who'd won an award for his role in *A Free Soul*. Lionel, in turn, introduced Irvin S. Cobb, the master of ceremonies. Cobb's wit lent humor and charm to his presentation of the Oscars. *It Happened One Night* swept the boards with five surprise awards. It was rated the best picture of the year; Robert Riskin won for his screen play, Frank Capra for direction, and the co-stars, Clark and Claudette, for best actor and actress of the year.

Clark accepted his Oscar, grinned broadly, and said "Thank you." Claudette, dressed for travel in a suit and hat, was overcome with emotion, cried as she took possession of hers.

"They held up the 'Chief' a half hour for me," Claudette says. "I clutched my Oscar, hugged everybody,

Three Hollywood Greats: Irving Thalberg, Gable, and Frank Capra at the 1934 Academy presentations. Gable is leaning against a table to seem the same height as his two shorter companions. PRIVATE COLLECTION OF HOWARD STRICKLING

felt like a fool in my traveling suit and hat, and remained in a state of shock until well past Albuquerque."

Clark now became the fair-haired boy of the MGM lot. A new seven-year contract was negotiated at a salary of four thousand dollars a week for three years, with escalator clauses raising the total to forty-five hundred dollars for the next two years and five thousand weekly for the two years thereafter.

His popularity soared. When Columbia staged the premiere of Grace Moore's *One Night of Love* in San Francisco at the opening of the Orpheum Theater, Miss Moore was unable to attend. Marco Wolff, of the firm of Fanchon and Marco, owners of the Orpheum Theater, asked Harry Cohn of Columbia to send him a big star in her stead. Cohn promised him Clark Gable.

"I really didn't think he could do it," Marco says, "but Gable's career had been greatly benefited by *It Happened One Night* and he was grateful to Cohn. He agreed to appear with a group of other top stars.

"The only one who made the headlines was Gable," Marco relates. "They featured his name in four-inch type—you would have thought war was being declared.

"I have given and attended many theater openings and premieres," he continues, "but never have I seen anything like the reception given Gable. The master of ceremonies tried to introduce the other stars, but the audience was on its feet yelling 'Gable, Gable!' "

When Clark left the theater after the premiere to return to the St. Francis Hotel, the people waiting to see him had blocked the traffic at Post and Geary and Powell, and the cable cars had stopped running. Women left their cars in the middle of the street and rushed forward to try to get a glimpse of him. "It was the most electrifying sight I have ever witnessed," Marco says.

Trouble with Ria continued. "Clark was restless and unhappy," Ria comments. "He was like a child who has been surfeited with candy. His success was too sudden, too overwhelming. He couldn't adjust to it. We would separate, and then he couldn't rest until we were together again."

Clark found social life irksome. He began spending much time away from home. He was a frequent visitor at Phil Berg's, where he met and played tennis with Cornwell ("Corney") Jackson, who was then secretary to Rupert Hughes.

"Clark was an indifferent player," Corney says. "I used to ride him about it. 'With your brawn and muscle you could beat everyone on the courts,' I used to tell him. But Clark never took the game seriously."

It was Clark's admiration and liking for Corney that influenced Phil Berg to ask Corney to join his agency staff. "I owe a lot of my success to Clark," Corney says.

One evening when Clark and Corney were at Phil's house for dinner, Clark announced that he thought it only fair for him to take a tenth of Phil's beautiful silver dinner service. "You take 10 per cent of all my money," he said.

"Clark actually picked up about a tenth of the silver and took it out of the dining room," Corney says. "But he left it somewhere in the house before he went home."

Sometimes Ria accompanied Clark to the tennis matches at the Los Angeles

Tennis Club. "She had quite a motherly quality," Corney recalls. "Clark was always rather suppressed when he was with her, like a small boy on his good behavior."

Clark's next two pictures, *Chained* and *Forsaking All Others*, were glossy melodramas based on trite stories, as was *After Office Hours* with Constance Bennett. Then Darryl Zanuck borrowed him for *The Call of the Wild* with Loretta Young. Clark played a gambler-miner and the reviewers noted that "Clark is out of dinner clothes and into a more natural role."

When the picture was finished, Clark left on a trip to South America, to "think things over." "He flew down the West Coast and it was thrilling to hear him tell of his flight over the Andes," Corney recalls. "The flying was rough, and at one point the plane suddenly lost altitude and they barely skirted mountain peaks. Clark said he wouldn't have missed it for anything, but wouldn't do it again. He was not too keen about flying after that."

Clark was mobbed by fans everywhere he went. In Buenos Aires the Argentine girls swarmed the airport to bid him farewell. He later described the trip as "miserable" and said he was glad to get back. When he did return, he had arrived at a decision. He and Ria separated.

"I understood what was happening," Ria says. "He was under tremendous pressure. It was a combination of too much work, too sudden success and the fact that women fairly threw themselves at him all the time.

"Basically he had good sound Dutch principles, and no one could be sweeter at times, but he could also be stubborn and perverse," she continues. "I tried to make him see that his happiness would have to come from within himself."

Clark moved out of the house and into the Beverly Wilshire Hotel in December 1935. When newsmen phoned him, Clark suggested that they talk to Ria.

Clark's stock reply to interviewers who questioned him about either Josephine or Ria was always, "Let the Lady tell it." He was never known to say anything derogatory about either one.

Early in 1936, Clark met Carole again at a party, and they began to date; but he was also seen about town with other glamorous stars, including Merle Oberon, with whom he shared a table at the Academy Awards banquet at the Biltmore Hotel.

George Anna, Ria's daughter, had married Dr. Thomas W. Burke, a young Houston physician, the year before. Clark was very fond of her and had flown to Houston to give her away and had presented her with a lovely diamond and ruby bracelet. In February 1936, George Anna had a son and Clark's critics said that he had separated from Ria just in time to escape being a "step-grandfather."

After *China Seas* with Jean Harlow, Clark was proposed for the role of Fletcher Christian in *Mutiny on the Bounty*, owned by Frank Lloyd. Lloyd had arranged a production deal with MGM, with himself as director.

Clark didn't want the role. It would mean shaving his mustache and he thought he'd look silly in the knee breeches and sailor's pigtail he'd have to wear. Besides, he thought Charles Laughton, who was slated for Captain Bligh, and Franchot Tone, who was to play Midshipman Byam, had more important parts.

Bob Cobb (then owner of the Brown Derby restaurants), Gail Patrick Cobb, Clark, and Carole at a Western costume party. (1936) COURTESY OF FRED PETERS

Eddie Mannix talked him into it, and told him he'd have key scenes with Movita, a lovely Polynesian who was signed to play the native girl. This meant that Clark would have the "love interest"—which Clark knew was important at the box office.

Most of the outdoor scenes were shot off Catalina Island, and the cast was at sea all day on a replica of the *Bounty.* They swam and fished and shot at sharks. Clark loved the outdoor atmosphere. He later said that *Mutiny* was one of the films he enjoyed most. When it was released, he was nominated for an Academy Award.

Clark's next film, *Wife vs. Secre-* tary, with Myrna Loy and Jean Harlow, was a routine triangle story; then Jeanette MacDonald asked to have him play opposite her in *San Francisco,* in the role of the owner of a Barbary Coast cabaret. Jeanette was to be a "good" girl from the Middle West who sings in his place, going on to star at the local opera house. The 1906 earthquake would resolve the story; Clark was to rescue the girl. Spencer Tracy was cast as a rugged mission priest.

Clark objected to his role. He thought the emphasis would be placed on Jeanette and her songs. Jeanette was so eager to have him in the film that she was willing to go off salary while waiting until he was available. Once again, Clark's good friend and hunting companion Eddie Mannix talked him into it.

The special effects depicting the earthquake and the ensuing fire were spectacular. In one scene, Clark fights his way through crowds and wreckage and is buried beneath a falling brick wall. Although the bricks were made of *papier-mâché,* Clark's shoulder was injured and he suffered discomfort from it for several years afterwards.

During the filming of *San Francisco* a change in make-up men was made and Stan Campbell was assigned to Clark. They became good friends, and Stan worked for Clark thereafter, at Clark's request.

San Francisco was a box-office success; it advanced Clark's career and made a star out of Spencer Tracy. It received the 1936 Photoplay Award for the best picture of the year.

"Clark's next two pictures, *Cain and Mabel* and *Love On the Run,* weren't up to standard and it worried him," Corney says. "Although he was on top in all the popularity polls, he always insisted that it wasn't going to last, that he'd just been lucky. We were driving down Sunset Boulevard one day and passed a cheap little hotel. 'I used to live there,' Clark said. 'I'd hate to have to do it again.' "

CHAPTER FOUR

NINETEEN-THIRTY-SEVEN was an eventful year for Clark, publicity-wise. On January 20 his foot- and hand-prints were placed in the forecourt of Grauman's Chinese Theater, that familiar landmark and tourist attraction in Hollywood. Next to an Oscar, this was the film capital's highest mark of distinction. It meant your position was now assured, unassailable; you had made it.

The footprint ceremony originated in 1927, when Sid Grauman, a noted theater-chain owner and Hollywood personality, was about to open his new Chinese theater on Hollywood Boulevard. He went over to the United Artists lot to see Mary Pickford. The cement in front of her dressing room (bungalow) had just been laid. Not realizing it was still wet, Sid stepped into it. The sight of his footprints gave him an idea.

When he saw Mary, he said, "Why not have the footprints of the top stars in front of my Chinese theater? It will honor the star, be good for the theater and for the film industry. I want yours to be the first ones there."

Mary liked the suggestion, and at the star-studded opening ceremonies and premiere of Cecil B. DeMille's *King of Kings* on May 27, 1927, her footprints were made in a square of wet cement in the theater forecourt. The event was covered by the newsreels and wire services, and the footprint ceremony got wide publicity. A precedent was set, a custom born.

Clark inscribed his prints, "To Sid, Who Is a Great Guy." The crown of fans that day was estimated as the largest ever on hand for the ceremony. (This record stood for twenty-four years and was never equaled until January 1961, when Doris Day's footprints were recorded.)

In April, Clark made the headlines again. This time he was in a Federal Court in Los Angeles as a witness for the prosecution in the United States Government's case against one Violet Norton, an Englishwoman, and Jack L. Smith, a Los Angeles private detective, who were indicted for illegal use of the mails to "Obtain money and property from Clark Gable under fraudulent pretenses and promises."

The background story on the case, as brought out in court, was incredible. It seems that Violet Norton, a British housewife, went to see *It Happened One Night* at her home theater in Essex. When Clark appeared on the screen, Violet decided that he was none other than Frank Billings, a light o' love who'd fathered her daughter Gwendoline in September 1922, then disappeared from her life. Subsequently, and because of her dalliance with Frank, Violet's husband had abandoned her. Gwendoline was born in June 1923.

After seeing the film, Violet promptly wrote to Clark, reminding him of their "flyming affair" and advising him of Gwendoline's claim upon him. "The letter was so fantastic, I threw it away," Clark said.

Nothing daunted over Clark's silence, Violet and Gwendoline, now a pretty girl of thirteen, packed their belongings and set out for Canada, arriving in Winnipeg late in 1935. Violet now began a campaign to prove that Clark was the father of her child.

At first she attempted to insert an advertisement in an American motion picture magazine, seeking an actor interested in "helping to support the child of Clark Gable." She offered to make such an actor the child's godfather.

She also wrote Mae West, suggesting that Mae "give Clark Gable's daughter a start in life," and reported that her husband had abandoned her because of Gable. Violet also generously offered to make Mae little Gwendoline's godmother. She claimed that Gwendoline looked a great deal like Mae.

When these letters failed to elicit replies, Violet continued her mail campaign. She wrote to the British Consul at Los Angeles, soliciting his aid, and even sent a similar letter to the United States District Attorney. Both letters were mailed from Winnipeg.

During 1936, Violet continued to press her case, offering the "story of Clark Gable's child" to various newspaper columnists. Somehow, she enlisted the sympathies of a retired Canadian businessman, who financed a trip to California for her and Gwendoline in December of that year.

Arriving in Hollywood, Violet engaged the services of Jack L. Smith, a private detective, who was to act as her liaison agent in putting the pressure on Clark to acknowledge her claim and provide for Gwendoline.

Smith approached the secretary treasurer of the Motion Picture Producers Association, suggested establishing a trust fund for $150,000 for Gwendoline "to avoid unfavorable publicity for both Clark Gable and MGM Studios." He also demanded blood tests be made of Clark to establish paternity of the Norton child.

Smith also told his story to Ralph Wheelwright of the MGM publicity staff. The studio took prompt action. The United States Attorney's office was more than interested. Mrs. Norton's use of the mails had not gone unreported nor unnoted.

The case came to trial in Federal Judge George Cosgrave's court on April 22, 1937, before an all-male jury of builders, brokers, jobbers, salesmen and retired businessmen.

Daily long lines of waiting women fought to get into the courtroom. Clark had to be brought into court via a back entrance in order to escape the milling crowds of curious spectators outside. Vendors hawked peanuts and cheap photographs of Clark on the street in front of the building, lending a carnival atmosphere to the proceedings. Photographers and newsmen had a field day.

Full details of his early life and rise to fame were recounted by Clark and a series of witnesses, as Assistant United States Attorney Jack Powell established that Clark was an American, had been in Oregon in 1922, and had never been issued a passport to leave the country.

Violet, a florid, gray-haired woman of forty-seven, introduced as evidence a photograph of Frank Billings in British Army uniform, insisted that Clark and Frank were one and the same man she had known in Essex in 1922. While Clark was on the stand, her lawyer asked the court's permission to have Mrs. Norton inspect Clark at close range to satisfy herself that he *was* Clark Gable. The judge overruled this on the grounds that "anyone in the court can see that the witness is Clark Gable."

Father Gable, making one of his rare public appearances, took the stand to testify that Clark was American born and bred and that "there have been Gables in this country for over four hundred years."

The president of a Silverton, Oregon, lumber company produced payroll vouchers to show that Clark had been a $3.20-a-day employee in his lumber camps during 1922. ("Best damn woodchopper I ever had.") The payroll clerk for the *Portland Oregonian* vouched for the fact that Clark had been an advertising solicitor for that newspaper for six weeks at fifteen dollars a week.

The star witness was Franz Doerfler, Clark's former sweetheart, who told of their romance and his proposal of marriage. She pinpointed the month of September 1922 as the time when Clark was a guest at her father's ranch in Oregon, thus completely refuting Mrs. Norton's claim that Clark was in England at that time. Franz concluded her testimony by stating that she was Clark's "Number One Fan." Clark was the cynosure of all eyes as he gallantly escorted Franz to and from the witness stand.

Clark himself was smiling and completely at ease during the three-day trial, and calmly took camera shots of his accuser and her extremely pretty daughter, Gwendoline, throughout the proceedings.

All of Clark's old Astoria Theater friends wrote or wired, offering their testimony in his behalf, if necessary. One stated that he'd furnish snapshots to prove that he and Clark "rode the rods to Portland" when they were broke and stranded.

The case had some interesting side aspects. While it was being tried, little Gwendoline was in the care of a woman friend of her mother's. This enterprising person took the child and the story to Ria. Ria was more amused than annoyed. "Utterly impossible," she said, and sent the woman packing. When Josephine Dillon received a similar visit, she sent Clark word that she would be glad to help him in any way, if necessary.

A surprise witness for the prosecution was Harry Billings, brother of the Frank Billings in question, who testified that Clark was not his brother. Despite his testimony and that of the other witnesses, Violet refused to concede she had made a mistake. Dramatically pointing to Clark, she screamed, "He is the father of my child," as the case went to the jury.

The jury's verdict exonerated Detective Smith and Violet's Canadian benefactor, but convicted her of use of the mails to defraud. She was judged not guilty of conspiracy to mulct money and property. The judge set a later date for hearing an application for probation, and Violet Norton was eventually deported.

During the trial, Clark was impressed with the straightforward news coverage given the case by Otto Winkler, a reporter he knew on the *Los Angeles Examiner.* He went to Howard Strickling and said, "Let's get Otto—I'd like to have him working for me."

After the trial, Howard offered Otto a job on the MGM publicity staff and Otto became Clark's personal publicity and public relations man thereafter.

When it was all over, Clark was praised for his courage in taking a public stand to refute the charges and clear his name.

One incident occurring during the trial is indicative of Clark's nature. He took the opportunity while in the Federal Building to ask the United

States District Attorney if he might inspect his income-tax returns, to check his earnings report against that submitted by the studio. It was arranged for him to see the papers after hours. Clark wanted to use an electric adding machine which had been disconnected. Overlooking a plug on the baseboard, he attempted to connect it to an overhead light fixture and gave himself quite an electric shock.

"That's Gable for you," Carole said when she heard the story. "Always an eye on those payroll figures."

Mickey Rooney and Judy Garland were youngsters on the MGM contract list. As Clark's popularity increased, his voice and his walk began to be widely imitated. Mickey was noted for his skit on Clark. Judy, who was thirteen then, had a schoolgirl crush on him. One day she and Roger Edens, a promising young musician, wrote some lyrics to the tune of "You Made Me Love You." They were called "Dear Mr. Gable," and Judy had a chance to sing them to Clark at a birthday party being given him on one of the sound stages.

Clark was delighted with the song and the studio executives were so pleased with it that they decided to have Judy sing it in *Broadway Melody of 1938.* "Dear Mr. Gable" became a great hit.

Clark's name became such a byword that the expression "Who do you think you are—Clark Gable?" came into being as the perfect retort, guaranteed to put one in one's place, reduce egos. In other words, the ultimate putdown.

With his motion picture career in high gear, Clark was now in great demand for radio shows, and appeared with Marlene Dietrich in *The Legion-naire and the Lady,* the first Lux Theater program to originate from Hollywood. Clark's radio assignments were handled by Corney Jackson of Phil Berg's office.

In the spring of 1937, Lux signed Clark to do *Farewell to Arms* with Josephine Hutchinson.

At that time five thousand dollars was the top figure for any star appearing on the show. Clark wanted seven thousand, five hundred and Corney felt he was worth it, but the Lux people had a five-thousand-dollar limit.

While waiting to start the show one day, Clark turned to a fellow player and announced that he was getting seven thousand, five hundred dollars for his services. Corney told Clark he hadn't been able to get that figure for him.

"But I told you I wouldn't work for five thousand dollars," Clark replied.

After much discussion, Corney agreed to give Clark his personal check for two thousand, five hundred to make up the difference.

That afternoon when the two men drove to the tennis club together, Clark said, "I guess that check made quite a hole in your bankroll, didn't it?"

Corney agreed that it did. Whereupon Clark put his arm around Corney's shoulders and gave him back the check. "I was just letting you sweat it out for a while," he said.

"When it came to the billing on the radio shows," Corney recalls, "all the stars and their agents jockeyed for top billing, but not Clark. He was always willing to let the leading lady and the others come first. He'd settle every time for the last name announced—which just so happened to be the best spot, for it was the one that people remembered."

Clark's last radio appearance, in March 1939, was in *It Happened One Night*, when he and Claudette Colbert were reunited in their award-winning roles.

Love on the Run had received such poor notices that MGM decided on a complete change of characterization for Clark. He was cast as Charles Parnell, the Irish patriot who fought for Home Rule. Myrna Loy played Katie O'Shea, whose affair with Parnell brings about his ruin.

Clark prepared for the part carefully, let his sideburns and mustache grow and practiced an accent with Irish overtones, for Parnell's mother had been an American and it was not necessary for him to develop an authentic Irish brogue.

When it was time to make up for the picture, Stan, the makeup man, brought in a special stove and curling iron for the low-flowing mustache.

"I curled the long ends up into beautiful curves," Stan says, "but my iron was too hot and when Clark touched the tips, they fell into ashes. I was worried but Clark just laughed and said, "To heck with it, we'll just have to use what mustache I've got left!"

The picture was released early in June, preceded by a huge advertising campaign. By this time Clark and Carole were having a serious romance. She showered the MGM lot with special little *Parnell* stickers.

Parnell was the biggest flop of Clark's career. Thousands of indignant fans wrote to the studio protesting the miscasting. They did not want Gable to abandon his he-man roles to portray political or historical figures who let women bring about their downfall. They wanted him in the familiar mas-

Gable with Carole and good friend Corney Jackson after making a radio broadcast. (1938) COURTESY OF CORNWELL JACKSON

Clark, Carole, and Louis B. Mayer at the 1938 MGM annual picnic. PRIVATE COLLECTION OF HOWARD STRICKLING

Ed Sullivan, Spencer Tracy, Louis B. Mayer, Myrna Loy, and Clark at the formal coronation ceremony at MGM. Twenty million votes were cast establishing Loy as the Queen of movies and Gable, as he would always thereafter be known, the King. (1938) PRIVATE COLLECTION OF HOWARD STRICKLING

culine, "tough-with-the-women" characterizations.

Clark's friends all ribbed him unmercifully over the *Parnell* fiasco. Clark took it all good-naturedly but said in private: "No one is ever going to sell me a bill of goods again. I know my limitations and I really am at my best in an open shirt, blue jeans and boots."

(Carole had had thousands of *Parnell* stickers printed, and after their marriage she stuck them in everything imaginable around the house. They were always turning up in Clark's books, his clothes, the food and other unexpected places.)

MGM returned to typecasting in Clark's next picture and teamed him up with Jean Harlow again, in *Saratoga*. Lionel Barrymore, Frank Morgan and Walter Pidgeon were in the cast. Jean died during the filming of the picture and the front office was faced with a decision: Should they begin all over again, using another actress, or use Mary Dees, Jean's stand-in, for the scenes still to be shot?

Three girls were tested with a complete remake in mind. One of these was twenty-year-old Virginia Grey, a charming blonde MGM had under contract at seventy-five dollars a week. Clark made the test scene with Virginia.

"I was terribly nervous when they called me about the test," Virginia says. "I'd been told Clark was a real lady-killer and I was on my guard. 'He's not going to get anywhere with me,' I said to myself.

"To my astonishment," she continues, "he was very businesslike and such a gentleman. He was so kind and helped me so much that I felt I had a real friend."

MGM finally decided to finish the picture with Miss Dees (whose face never appeared on the screen), and Virginia went back to the contract list, waiting for a "break."

Thereafter, Clark used his influence to see that she got parts in all of his pictures, if possible.

That fall Clark made front-page news. Ed Sullivan was covering Hollywood for the *Chicago Tribune-New York Daily News* syndicate. Harry Brand, publicity director at 20th Century-Fox, suggested that Ed run a "King and Queen of the Movies" contest in all of his syndicate papers.

The papers handled the balloting in each city and, according to Ed's records, twenty million votes were cast by readers of the fifty-five key city newspapers in the syndicate. The results established Clark as "King" and Myrna Loy as "Queen."

A formal coronation ceremony was held at MGM with Ed Sullivan as master of ceremonies. Each crown was decorated with the mastheads of the newspapers handling the competition.

"The story got world-wide coverage via the news services, because of the importance of the papers involved in the balloting," said Ed. "Additionally, each paper in the competition played it up as a front-page story, so the coverage was enormous."

The title of "King" stuck with Clark thereafter and became his nickname throughout the industry. When one said "The King," there was no mistaking the fact that you were referring to Clark Gable. Carole and his friends often kidded him about it and Clark always took it with good grace, although he frequently looked a little sheepish.

Test Pilot was a role after Clark's heart, for his old friend Victor Fleming was directing and he was playing with two of the men he admired most, Lionel Barrymore and Spencer Tracy. Myrna Loy was his leading lady and Grey had a bit part in the production.

The company went on four different Air Force locations in order to get authentic shots. Clark's sequences were shot at March Air Force Base at Riverside, then under the command of Colonel R. E. Olds.

Clark met two men on location who were to become good friends and companions. They were Paul Mantz, the famous flier, who was directing the aerial sequences, and Al Menasco, the founder of Menasco Motors, who was instrumental in borrowing the special Sikorsky test plane used by Clark in the picture. Al had designed and built the first inverted inline engine, had been a test pilot in World War I, and was a close friend of Jimmy Doolittle's. Ray Moore, who did Clark's stunt flying, lived with Al at his San Gabriel home during the filming of the picture and Clark spent many happy hours there with these three men.

The B-17 bombers were the newest development in military aircraft at that time and the Air Force permitted their use in the film in order to exploit them. Clark was keenly interested in the handling of the bombers, and persuaded the pilot to let him fly one, with the pilot giving directions from the dual control.

All during the filming of *Test Pilot* Spencer Tracy, who was playing the part of Clark's hard-boiled mechanic, made frequent derogatory references to *Parnell*, which kept the crew in a state of hilarity. One day Spencer left early because he was not involved in any part of the sequences to be shot that afternoon. Clark tried to retaliate for all the ribbing by calling after him,

"Good-by, you Wisconsin ham, and don't bother to come back tomorrow either."

Spencer turned to Myrna. "Just remember, dear Myrna," he said, "when I walk out this door, all you have left is Parnell." Clark threw his script at him, Spencer ducked and they both burst into laughter.

Clark thought "Spence" was the greatest actor in the world. In one sequence in *Pilot* Clark and Myrna are in the front seat of a car and Spencer is riding in the rear. He dominates the whole scene.

"Any other star but Clark would have had them cut that shot," Stan Campbell says, "but Clark was never jealous of his fellow players. When the film was screened, he said, 'Look at that guy Tracy, sitting there doing nothing and stealing our scene.' He thought it was wonderful that Spence showed up so well."

When the film was previewed, MGM sent the invitations via air mail from Culver City to Los Angeles, a distance of seven air miles. Clark and Myrna launched the plane for this shortest air-mail flight in history. Flying time, four and a half minutes.

Clark was teamed again with Myrna Loy in *Too Hot to Handle,* which was a mediocre story about a daredevil newsreel photographer who rescues Myrna from a burning plane crash. Such shots are made with what is known as "controlled fire." But in this case, the fire got out of hand. Director Jack Conway ordered the scene halted and directed firemen to drag Myrna out of danger.

"Keep 'em turning, Jack," Clark yelled. "I'll get her." And he did. There was nothing "phony" about it. The story made front pages all over the country, with photographs of the rescue taken from the actual film.

Idiot's Delight, *1938. Clark with a troupe of dancers from the film. Virginia Grey, who later became a close friend, is on the extreme right.* COURTESY OF MGM

In mid-August of 1938, David Selznick announced that Clark has been signed to play Rhett Butler in *Gone With the Wind.*

"Clark's publicity was simply fantastic," Corney Jackson recalls. "The studio was giving him the 'A' treatment, of course, but he made a lot on his own by just *being* Clark Gable. Everywhere he and Carole went, they were mobbed. They almost stole the show from Norma Shearer at the world premiere of *Marie Antoinette.*"

Clark's popularity led Miss Shearer to choose him as her leading man for *Idiot's Delight,* which began shooting in the fall of 1938. Carole was helping him with the dance routines when I went to work for her.

"Clark isn't the happy-go-lucky, carefree man the public sees," she told me one day. "He's not had a very happy life and is inclined to be de-

Carole Lombard, 1938. This shot was taken at Harry Fleischmann's duck club.

pressed and worried. I want to make it up to him if I can and you've got to help me. Let's keep the gags going, get him to relax and be happy."

Carole really worked at it. She sent Clark a full ballet outfit including some outsize dancing slippers while he was rehearsing the *Idiot's Delight* dances. (Virginia Grey was one of the chorus girls.) Corney Jackson was on the set when the dance sequences were shot.

Carole had a huge bouquet delivered to him when the 'take' was over," Corney says. "Just as if he were a prima donna. Clark thought everything she did was terrific."

Clark was good at gags himself. When he called Carole I found I could never recognize his voice. It embarrassed me for I had thought I was rather experienced at handling telephone calls. One day I turned to her and said, "Why can't I recognize Clark's voice?"

"He changes it deliberately," Carole replied. "He gets a kick out of fooling you, so even if you do recognize it, just go along with the gag and pretend you don't."

Early in November Carole said, "Jeanie, we'd better get started on the Christmas shopping."

Thereafter we went to Beverly Hills or Los Angeles for all-day shopping sprees and I watched in amazement as Carole played Lady Bountiful. She never stopped at one gift; there were always several for each member of her family and her personal friends.

Carole never had any of the stores do her gift wrapping. The presents were all sent to the house in Bel Air and stacked in a spare bedroom. Before she was through you could hardly make your way around the room without falling over stacks of boxes.

I shall never forget the first time she said, "Now we'll begin to wrap." I had never wrapped a package in my life.

"I'm really no good at this sort of thing. I wouldn't know where to start," I said.

"Come on," she replied, "let's sit here on the floor and I'll show you."

She had laid in a supply of beautiful papers and ribbons and was far better than any professional at wrapping exquisite packages. Each gift was ticketed, checked against her list and arrangements made for its delivery.

I must confess that I was an awkward amateur and that Carole wrapped most of the gifts, but it was the beginning of many Christmas, birthday and other gift wrap sessions we had and I soon learned to love it. Gradually I improved, and finally was able to do a fair job.

Carole had a brownish beige Pekingese called Pushface who had been used in *My Man Godfrey*. Pushface, who was getting along in years, died just before Christmas. Ellie, one of the maids, adored the dog and told Carole she would dispose of her.

Carole planned a family party at her home for Christmas and of course Clark was to spend it with them. The house was gaily decorated, a huge tree set up in the living room.

Although I was aware of her generosity, I was not prepared for the lovely Persian coat Carole gave me on Christmas Eve, nor for the bonus check I later found in the pocket.

Clark was at the house when I came in after Christmas. "We had quite a do here," he said. "Ellie took Pushface to a taxidermist and had her stuffed. She was sitting in Carole's chair when we went in to dinner, and when Ma saw her, she screamed the house down."

"Look what I found on my door-step Christmas morning," Carole said, pointing to a huge plaster statue of himself that Clark had sent her. It weighed several hundred pounds and was a remarkable likeness. Carole loved it and kept it around for a conversation piece for a while—often hung her hat on it.

Clark's "real" gift to her that Christmas was a beautiful yellow Cadillac convertible.

Although Clark had been announced for *Gone With the Wind* in August, it was December before David Selznick found the Scarlett he wanted, Vivien Leigh. The actual shooting started in late January 1939. Carole sent Clark a string of stuffed white doves on the first day of shooting. These he kept draped over his mirror thereafter.

At first there were many delays because Clark's wardrobe was ill-fitting.

"That's the only time I ever saw Clark angry," Stan Campbell says. "There he was knocking himself out to make the character perfect and the clothes were terrible."

Selznick finally called in MacIntosh, a Hollywood tailor, to remake everything.

Almost from the first, the production was plagued by director trouble. Things were not going well and Clark thought there should be a replacement. He went to bat for Victor Fleming, urging Mr. Selznick to hire him, for he had worked with Victor many times and had great respect for him.

"Victor has the gutty style this script needs," he said. Selznick finally made the change and Clark was much happier under Victor's guidance.

Clark loved working with Vivien Leigh, Olivia de Havilland and others in the cast, especially little Cammie King, who played the part of Rhett's

Gable in his most famous role, as Rhett Butler. (1939)
COURTESY OF MGM

Scene from Gone With the Wind. *Rhett took Scarlett to New Orleans on their honeymoon. Scarlett, who loved the food above all, gorged herself with pastries, remembering the endless goobers, dried peas, and sweet potatoes at Tara.*
COURTESY OF MGM

This shot of Clark, Olivia de Havilland and Vivien Leigh relaxing on the set of Gone With the Wind *was taken by Lee Garmes. Garmes was director of photography during the first part of work on the film.* PRIVATE COLLECTION OF LEE GARMES

Painting done of Gable as Rhett in a Yankee jail. COURTESY OF CHARLES DIERKOP

Carole and Clark at a Hollywood premier. (1937)

child, Bonnie. The pony scene where Bonnie is thrown from her horse was shot in Pasadena and Carole and I went out to watch the takes.

Clark brought Cammie over to see us. "This is my real sweetheart," he told Carole, and she pretended to be very jealous. Clark was always crazy about children and he never forgot Cammie. (Years later he had a chance meeting with her in London. She was eighteen then and on her way to a finishing school in Switzerland. Clark was delighted with her beauty and the fact that she still called him "Father Rhett.")

The schedule was a grueling one, and as usual the cast and crew relieved the tension with gags. During the filming of the scene where Rhett carries Scarlett upstairs, Victor and the crew decided to play a joke on Clark. They had him carry Vivien up the long winding staircase for a dozen retakes. Vivien was in on the secret and always managed to do something to make Clark think she had spoiled the shot. Clark was literally exhausted and ready to explode at his co-star, but he never complained.

"The first take was perfect, Clark," Fleming finally said. "The others were just for laughs."

In March 1939 Clark won his freedom from Ria. He and Carole were married on the twenty-ninth, and we made the move to the ranch in Encino that summer.

Carole Lombard and Clark Gable meet the photographers on the morning after their marriage. (1939) COURTESY OF MGM

Otto Winkler, Carole, Clark and Howard Strickling posing together the day after the Gable-Lombard marriage. PRIVATE COLLECTION OF HOWARD STRICKLING

That first summer at the ranch was a busy, happy one. Clark had no immediate film commitments and he and Carole were free to settle down and enjoy their new life together.

There were any number of projects going on at once. Clark wanted the ranch to be self-sustaining, at least to pay the taxes if nothing more. We were soon deep in nursery catalogues, agricultural bulletins and tracts on soil improvement.

Clark was fascinated by the thought of scientific farming with modern equipment and began buying machines, tools and gadgets of all kinds. A small yellow Caterpillar tractor became his prize possession. He even had a road scraper.

"I've done so much farm work the hard way, this is going to be fun," he said.

There were two hundred and fifty citrus trees on the place and Clark added an additional hundred and twenty-five. He helped Fred, the new caretaker, dig the holes to plant them and invest in a wonderful spray machine for spraying whitewash on tree trunks and fences. When Carole came out to inspect progress, he even sprayed *her*.

The house was Carole's domain. "I want this to be a real home," she said, "not just a house." She was determined to create an atmosphere where Clark could find the quiet and relaxation that he craved.

Until their marriage, she had been a silken siren, a glamorous party girl. Her career now rated second with her. She told Myron Selznick that she wouldn't sign for a film unless Clark was working. When he was free, she wanted to be free also. "Clark comes first," she said. Meantime she set about making herself over for him.

Clark liked hunting, fishing, riding and camping, and the people who enjoyed these. He ordered a specially built Dodge truck with four-wheel drive and had the body outfitted for camping and sleeping, so that he and Carole would be ready to go when the hunting season opened.

Carole took shooting lessons, learning to handle a .22 caliber rifle. She became a crack shot. She had superbly cut play and sports clothes made.

"I want to be ready to go anywhere, do anything Clark wants to do," she said.

For Clark she was fulfillment, a pal and partner in everything. She roamed the ranch with him in casual clothes during the day and her hair was frequently in pigtails, but in the evenings she was always sleek and lovely in a glamorous housecoat.

It was a household of gaiety, laughter, corny jokes and gag gifts. Everything centered around Clark, his likes and dislikes. Carole enjoyed and had fun at everything she did. If Clark was moody or silent, she clowned until he smiled again. He adored her, thought she was the most exciting,

Entrance to the Gable home.

amusing, desirable woman in the world.

They rode horseback frequently. Carole had given Clark a saddle-bred sorrel show horse named Sonny, which he loved. He gave her a palomino gelding, but it turned out to be a bit rough to ride, so they finally sold it and acquired Melody, a bay polo pony. Although Carole was an expert horsewoman, having got her training in the Buck Jones westerns, she gradually gave it up. She longed for a baby and had the notion that horseback riding might lessen her chances for becoming a mother.

They both had beautiful handmade saddles which they'd secured through Clark's old friends, Val and Mrs. Val of the Valdez Riding Stables in Coldwater Canyon. The Valdezes were frequent visitors at the ranch, and the ranch horses were groomed and received other professional care at the Valdez stables.

One evening Clark invited Val and Mrs. Val in for dinner and Val objected: he was afraid his stable boots might soil the carpet or chairs. Clark and Carole both protested, "If we can't enjoy our home with our friends, we don't want it."

Mr. and Mrs. Valdez interested Clark and Carole in leather tooling, and Clark built a little workshop in one of the barns where they could pursue this hobby. Both took lessons from a Captain Hardy in Beverly Hills and became very proficient at it.

Dogs were an important part of the ménage. Bobby, a shorthaired German pointer, was Clark's prized hunting dog, and later went with them on all their trips. Commissioner, a dachshund, was named after Clark's great friend Kenny Watters, who was fire commissioner in Santa Barbara. Tuffy, a boxer, was the watchdog.

We inherited a cat with the place—a black and white male who was called Tommy. Tommy was quite wild; he was unfriendly except with Juanita, the maid, and gradually came to be known as "Juanita's cat."

The staff consisted of Fred, the ranch caretaker, and his wife; a cook; a maid; and a butler-valet. Fred and his wife occupied the caretaker's cottage; the other servants occupied quarters in the house and alongside the garage.

At first the house servants had been a problem. When we'd moved, Carole had counted on having Jessie, her long-time cook, and Juanita, her personal and studio maid, with her. But Jessie, a superb cook with a highly emotional love life, had a new boy friend in Bel Air and decided she couldn't live "in the country." Juanita was Jessie's niece, and she, too, acted as if Encino were out in the boondocks. Both left our service.

Clark hated formal dinners, big parties, and the necessity to dress for them. He enjoyed being at home, having a group of close friends in for dinner, with quiet talk afterwards.

The Howard Stricklings, who had a ranch nearby, were frequent guests. I had met "Howdie" at the studio, of course, but did not know until they visited the ranch that his wife was Gail Greenstreet, an old schoolmate of mine in Seattle. It was great fun to renew our friendship.

Fieldsie and her husband, Walter Lang, who'd directed Carole in two of her films, were at the ranch a great deal. Fieldsie and Carole had been Mack Sennett girls together and the bond between them was very close. Fieldsie, Carole and impish Daphne Pollard had been a popular Sennett trio, romping their way through some hiliarious sequences.

Carole with her two kittens and Bobby. (1941) COURTESY OF RKO

Carole and Clark relaxing after lunch on their patio, with their two Siamese cats. (1941)

Carole walking her Palomino. Photo is autographed to me: To Jean Dear, You're a "Honey." Devotedly, Carole. (1940)

"Fieldsie and I shared a room, our clothes, an old car and even our dates through all those hectic days," Carole told me. "I love her dearly."

The Goffs (he was Abner of *Lum and Abner*), the Andy Devines, the Buster Colliers, and the Al Menascos were in this group of close friends, as were Nan and Harry Fleischmann, Clark's boon hunting companions. Al Menasco had a Ford agency in Culver City and he and Clark had much in common, for both were crazy about cars.

Of course everyone raved about the house and Clark loved to show guests around on the "fifty-cent tour," as he called it. It gave him a chance to sing Carole's praises as a decorator.

"Ma sure knows her stuff," he'd say with pride.

"Watch him or he'll collect the fifty cents," Carole teased.

The living room was huge, with white-paneled woodwork, a white brick and paneled fireplace, and a wonderful staircase leading to the second floor, the bannister and railing of authentic Colonial design.

The wall-to-wall carpeting was canary yellow, specially woven and tufted. The windows, of many-paned authentic Early American glass, were draped with gay English prints in a red and green hollyhock pattern on white backgrounds.

Two large yellow sofas were flanked by wing-back chairs upholstered in red quilted linen, and two huge green club chairs. One of these became Clark's favorite and I used to leave his mail there for him at night. Beautiful pine coffee tables and an antique glass cabinet housing exquisite antique pitchers of all kinds completed the decor of the room.

Men in particular used to pause in the doorway to comment, "This is a real home."

Opening off the living room, separated from it by sliding doors, was the dining room, one of the most beautiful I've ever seen. It was fun to hear the exclamations of delight when guests first saw it.

The walls were of natural pine, the beamed ceiling painted grayish white, and the huge fireplace of clinker brick had an offset of brick at one side where a beautiful Sheffield lazy susan and an especially fine collection of old pink Staffordshire were kept.

An open bar counter was backgrounded by an interesting collection of antique and modern glassware. A game table, with a round leaf that could be added, was near the bar.

The dining table was a long, stretcher, tavern type, a reproduction that had been in Clark's home before they were married. Captains' chairs picked up here and there at antique shops, braided rugs in red and beige tones, and rare old horse prints on the walls completed the Early American tavern effect Carole wanted.

When the dining table was first moved to the ranch it was not antiqued to suit Carole, so she sent it to a refinisher who set it outside to weather. Every so often Carole and Clark would say, "Let's go visit our table!" They'd pour water on it, snub out burning cigarettes on the surface and even take turns pounding it with a heavy chain! This hastened the weathering process, and when the table was finally polished and in use, it was a thing of beauty.

Despite the servant problem, Carole ran the house beautifully. Breakfast and lunch were informal meals, lunch usually served on trays in the white-bricked patio. Here she'd used old Vermont courthouse furniture, painted yellow, with matching cushions.

At dinner Carole insisted on formal service, whether guests were present or not. No linen except napkins was used on the gleaming tavern table, which was set with exquisite Waterford crystal and Spode. Antique kerosene lamps furnished the light. The flatware was antique silver, the knives pistol-handled and very rare. The blades were polished daily and sharpened with emery and a razor strop.

Carole's menus featured "he-man" food. Clark was a steak and potato guy, and loved baked beans and spareribs, corn bread, stewed chicken and dumplings, hamburgers with onions, chocolate cake and home-made ice cream. The men always raved about the food. Women sighed over their figures, forgot their diets and enjoyed it too!

The room that Clark loved to show was his gun room, the most talked-about, publicized room in the whole house. A specially constructed gun case occupied one wall. Here Clark kept his prized hunting guns, old pistols and other firearms. The leather gun cases were hand-tooled and beautiful. Comfortable built-in sofas and lounge chairs and old English prints made this a real man's refuge.

A downstairs bedroom was turned into a charming office for me. Yellow toile wallpaper, yellow linen draperies, a blue-green sofa and a large business desk and chair were installed, along with the usual files, an intercom and telephone system and other office paraphernalia. A bath and storage closet were included in my suite.

A lovely little powder room, done in white marble with green and white wallpaper; a glittering, efficient kitchen, service porch and an attractive maid's room completed the lower floor.

Upstairs there were two master bedroom suites and an attic storage closet where Clark eventually kept his hunting clothes.

Clark's bedroom was done in beige and brown, with quilted beige wallpaper, a large green couch and attractive green chintz curtains. The room had clipped dormer ceilings. The finish of the woodwork did not suit Carole so she had it removed and antiqued until it had just the right patina.

The bed was of brown tufted leather. Clark was proud of a rare old pine desk which David Selznick gave him at the conclusion of *Gone With the Wind*. He had bookcases built around the desk and a dictionary stand installed. Clark never tried to hide his lack of formal education. "I'm just a guy trying to learn," he'd say.

His bathroom was done in beige marble with glass shelves containing rare old bottles. His dressing room was mirrored and housed the enormous wardrobe necessary in his work, for men often furnished their own clothes in the picture business. It's the women who had wardrobes specially designed and created for them!

The tufted wallpaper was repeated in Carole's suite. Carpeted in white with white goatskin throw rugs, ankle deep, her bedroom contained an old mahogany four-poster bed with organdy tester and flounce, beautiful old mahogany bedside tables, antique lamps, a white sofa and chairs. The windows were draped in chintz and organdy.

Her dressing room and bath were completely mirrored and very glamorous, with a white fur rug on the floor, and silver and crystal fixtures in the white marble tub and lavatory.

Our accountant and tax consultant, Russell Bock, from the firm of Ernst and Ernst, audited our accounts periodically. Once, during new cook Louella's tenure, Carole was away when Bock was due. I told Louella the accountant was expected and suggested that she have some special dish for lunch, for I knew he enjoyed being at the ranch. To our surprise, Louella served lunch in the dining room and it soon became apparent that she had outdone herself. Course followed delicious course.

Afterwards, Clark complimented her on the meal. "But why were we so formal?" he asked.

"We had to have things nice for a *count*, Mr. Gable," she said reproachfully. Clark roared with laughter over her misinterpretation of Mr. Bock's profession.

After Louella, there were others. One day, Carole said, "This is ridiculous. We must get Jessie and Juanita back." To her delight, she found them both longing to return to their beloved mistress. They moved in, and we acquired a butler named Martin, and peace descended.

Martin was tall and handsome and could wear Clark's things. He came to be known as the best-dressed butler in the San Fernando Valley. He was an intelligent, loyal, efficient butler-valet for Clark. This staff remained at the ranch for many years.

Jessie had Sundays off and Clark and Carole loved to get their own dinners on Sunday nights. They'd eat in the kitchen on these occasions and the menu was often ham and eggs or baked beans and spareribs.

When a new picture for Clark was under consideration, the studio executives frequently lunched at the ranch, to discuss script, casting and other matters. They always demanded one of Jessie's "southern lunches": ham and eggs, hominy grits, enormous biscuits and honey.

"No one can do eggs like Jess," Clark always said—and threatened to widen the doors, for Jessie partook heavily of her own cuisine and was enormous.

Clark literally lived outdoors. When I couldn't locate him anywhere else on the ranch, I could always find him near the garage tinkering with one of the cars. He was an excellent mechanic and loved high-powered motors. Carole drove a yellow Cadillac that Clark had given her the Christmas before they were married. Clark changed cars every year or so. He had Lincolns, Chryslers, Fords, and later on Jaguars and a Mercedes Benz. He was the first man in town to drive a model SS Jaguar.

When there were no guests, the Gables spent the evenings quietly at home, reading, talking, listening to music. Clark liked to read in bed, fast-moving mystery and adventure stories.

An air of peace and contentment pervaded the place. There was a sense of love, security and happy activity. Both Carole and Clark made it a rule never to discuss business except in my office.

Whenever they returned to the house, they made a beeline for my suite, which became the "nerve center" of life at the ranch. It was the clearinghouse for their personal, business, ranch and studio affairs. Mail, telephone calls, publicity appointments, accounts and household management all centered in that pleasant yellow and blue office. Carole and Clark both called me "Jeanie." I called Carole by her first name too, but when

I addressed Clark, he was never anything but "Mr. G—." I was one of the family, treated with love, consideration and respect.

There was a family dinner party on Carole's birthday, October 6, complete with cake and candles and personal gifts. Clark gave her some beautiful diamond and ruby earrings, which she treasured, for these were her favorite stones.

Soon after that, Clark reported to the studio for *Strange Cargo,* opposite Joan Crawford, and Carole signed to play the role of a nurse in *Vigil in the Night,* with Brian Aherne, at RKO.

A few days before her picture was to start, Clark phoned me late one evening.

"Ma is in Cedars of Lebanon," he said. "They say it's her appendix. I've got a room next door and I'm staying right with her."

Carole's appendectomy was without complications, her recovery routine and rapid. By the second day she was clowning for the benefit of doctors and nurses, playing all sorts of practical jokes on them.

Clark slept at the hospital every night while she was there. So many friends came to call and her room was in such an uproar most of the time that her doctor had to lay down the law, curtail her visitors and insist she get more rest. Masses of flowers arrived every day, which she kept sending to the wards and to the children's wing.

The nurses were in a swoon over Clark. Carole's special nurses were besieged by offers of help from others so that they might catch a glimpse of their hero. Carole teased him unmercifully, because he was always shy and uncomfortable in the presence of adoring women.

"Jean, I really think Ma got sick so she could get some atmosphere for her picture," Clark said one day when I was there. He failed to duck in time to dodge the pillow Carole threw at him.

Within a few days she was back at the ranch; and at the end of the third week she was ready to go to work. "I'm as healthy as a horse," she assured Clark when he questioned her need for a longer recovery period.

With Clark working at MGM and Carole at RKO, I alternated between their studio dressing rooms and the ranch office, as business demanded.

As one of Metro's top contract stars, Clark had a luxurious permanent dressing room which consisted of a sitting room, dressing room, bath. The sitting room was done in red leather throughout, the walls hung with photographs and personal souvenirs of all kinds, including a particularly devastating caricature of Clark by Walt Disney, of which he was very proud.

Carole always sent him a single red rose everyday that he was working on the lot. Clark kept it in a bud vase on his dressing table in front of her photograph. Over his dressing room mirror he kept the string of stuffed white doves she had sent him at the beginning of *Gone With the Wind.* It was her symbol of love and peace between them.

In addition to his regular dressing room, Clark had the usual portable dressing room right on the sound stage where he was shooting. Actually these dressing rooms are small trailers and the interior of Clark's was done in knotty pine and red leather.

Both of Clark's dressing room doors were usually open and he loved visiting with the crew and cast, always interested in their problems, or delighted when the conversation turned to guns, hunting and fishing.

His stand-in, Lew Smith, was a big fellow, not quite as tall as Clark but with the same general build and coloring. He was devoted to Clark and they were close friends.

Stan Campbell, Clark's make-up man, who had been with him since *San Francisco*, was another friend and fan.

"Clark never had a star complex, never pulled rank," Stan says. "He knew his lines, never kept others waiting and was very businesslike."

Strange Cargo was Clark's eighth film with Joan Crawford. Others in the cast were Ian Hunter, Peter Lorre and Albert Dekker. Clark sent Joan red roses at the start of the picture, which was his custom with all his leading ladies. He admired Joan immensely and everyone agreed that they made a great team.

Clark's role in the picture was that of an escaped convict who fights his way through jungle and swamp. Frank Borzage, the director, had planned to shoot the exteriors on location at Pismo Beach, some miles north along the California coast, but they ran into a lot of early morning fog.

Each day, while waiting for the weather to clear, Clark, Joan and the entire cast and crew played ball on the beach. The heavy fogs continued, however, and Borzage finally had to bring his company back to the studio and shoot most of the film on stage sets.

Up until this time Clark had seldom used much make-up. Joan thought it would be an improvement and urged Stan to recommend it. Clark merely laughed at the suggestion.

Clark usually kept the radio going in his dressing room. "He was a great guy for band music," Stan says. "Change that station, Stan," he'd say, "get us a good band."

It is a custom in Hollywood to have a party on stage the last day of shooting, and the stars of the film usually give presents to the director, crew members and sometimes others in the cast. Clark never conformed to this practice.

"A man does a day's work and gets paid for it," he said. "He shouldn't expect anything more. I never got anything I didn't work for."

Clark was always quick to defend a co-worker, however, or to put in a good word for him at the front office.

Carole, as a free-lance star, was usually assigned one of the choice dressing rooms on the lot where she was working. Her quarters were always the scene of great activity. There were flowers, music, noise, ringing phones, excitement. Restless and high strung, she loved visitors, people around her. She traveled from dressing room to stage on a motor scooter, her hair flying in the breeze, and she had a smile, a cheery wave of the hand, an exchange of pleasantries for everyone.

Whether she was having a massage, being fitted for a gown or merely waiting for a scene, people vied to be of service to her.

Carole's contract gave her one hundred and fifty thousand dollars a picture and contained clauses giving her various rights, including that of choosing her own hairdresser, manicurist and crew members if she so desired.

One of her special people was Loretta Francel, a free-lance hairdresser everyone called "Bucket." Carole felt no one could dress her long blonde hair like Bucket, and where she went Bucket went too. When she was working, Carole was on the set at seven o'clock every morning so Bucket could give her a daily shampoo.

Her favorite manicurist, Peggy Mercer, a girl from the Ann Meredith Beauty Shop in Beverly Hills, was always in attendance, as was Betty, her stand-in. Carole also always saw to it that Pat Drew, a gaffer (electrician) who had lost a leg in a plane accident, worked on all her pictures.

She was the delight of Irene, the designer, who made all of Carole's clothes on and off the screen after Carole left Paramount.

"Whenever I'm asked to name the most exciting woman I've ever dressed, I say Carole," Irene said.

The fitters adored her, particularly Jennie, Irene's head fitter. In fact, all the girls used to fight for the privilege of working with Carole.

"She was a real 'clothes horse,'" Irene recalled. "Everything looked good on that beautiful figure. She knew clothes and she knew how to wear them."

Irene had little scope for her talents, however, in *Vigil in the Night,* for Carole wore a nurse's uniform most of the time. She played the part of a dedicated nurse who saves her younger sister, a probationer, from pending disgrace as the result of the girl's carelessness. Ann Shirley played the part of the sister and Brian Aherne was an idealistic physician.

Carole was never late, always knew her lines and was remarkable in her ability to concentrate. When she worked, she gave everything to what she was doing.

There was one highly emotional scene in *Vigil* where Carole was required to cry. She was so gay and fun-loving that it seemed as if this would be an impossibility. George Stevens, the director asked if there was anything, any device they might use that would put her in the mood, bring tears.

"Just leave me alone for a little," Carole said. "I'll cry."

When the scene was shot, Carole cried so convincingly and gave such a poignant performance that the crew applauded, and the scene helped make *Vigil in the Night* one of the best pictures about nurses ever made.

Having got herself into a melancholy mood, however, it was a little difficult for her to make an immediate transition to her own gay self. Director Stevens had to shoot around her for a while.

Much has been said and written about Carole's predilection for certain profane and four-letter words. I must admit that her conversation was spiced with what can only be described as "salty" expressions; but somehow, coming from Carole, they seemed to lose their offensiveness.

Carole never swore when she was angry, and I am convinced that she used this device deliberately many times to relieve tension on the set and put everyone at ease. It always seemed so spontaneous, and so *funny,* that one automatically forgave her. She did it at home, too, but never in anger, and I never heard her tell an off-color story.

When the picture was over, Carole staged a big party for cast and crew, gave gag gifts such as crutches and back braces and bedpans, which were quickly followed up by genuine gifts, carefully selected to show that she knew what the recipients liked.

Carole's kindness to struggling young players was well known in Hollywood. One afternoon while she was at Paramount, she met Margaret Tallichet, a pretty young typist from Dallas, Texas. Margaret told Carole of her ambition to crash motion pictures and Carole arranged an interview with David O. Selznick for her. After a bit in

Atlanta welcomed Clark and Carole with great affection. Here they are enroute from the airport to their hotel before the premier of GWTW. Mayor William E. Hartsfield is riding with them. COURTESY OF MGM

Clark, his Uncle Charlie, and Carole at the special luncheon in Atlanta for GWTW. COURTESY OF MGM

the 1937 *A Star Is Born* and subsequent, more important parts, Margaret married William Wyler, the director.

Carole also made a test with Cheryl Walker, a Rose Queen, who was trying for a movie career. Alice Marble, the tennis champion, was another of her protégées. Alice wanted to get into the movies and had worked toward it by singing in New York night clubs. In appreciation for Carole's help, she sent her two beautiful silver serving trays, engraved trophies she had won at tennis.

Lucille Ball is another star who got a helping hand from Carole. "Yes, Carole did help me many many times in my early days at RKO and Paramount," Lucille says, "mostly by being ready with good sound advice about people. Her intuitive grasp of people and situations was something I like to believe she taught me. She always encouraged me by saying that she saw in me a girl who would probably have the same problems she'd had, and that I should learn from her mistakes. I tried, but I could never see them. I really learned more from her successes. Her *joie de vivre* was the thing I liked most about her. I learned about people, love and laughter from her. She was really my guardian angel."

David Selznick scheduled the premiere of *Gone With the Wind* in Atlanta on December 15, 1939, and made arrangements for the film's stars to be in attendance. It was to be a regular, full-scale, Hollywood-style affair, and the governor of Georgia promptly declared the day a state-wide holiday. The city fathers planned a three-day gala celebration in honor of the occasion. Besides the premiere, there were to be balls, receptions and festivities of all kinds.

Clark and Carole's arrangements for the trip were all master-minded by Howard Strickling. Irene created special gowns for Carole and all of us worked hard to get everything in readiness.

There was much excitement on the eve of their take-off. Bucket, Carole's hairdresser, had been sent on ahead to await her in Atlanta, so I called Ann Meredith's shop and she sent a girl named Brownie out to the ranch to do Carole's hair and Peggy came along to do her nails.

While Carole was under the dryer, the top of it flew off and hit Brownie in the face, knocking her unconscious. We were all horrified. I called a doctor and he came out at once. It was necessary for him to take several stitches in Brownie's scalp but he assured Clark and Carole that there'd be no permanent damage to her pretty face. We were all relieved and grateful, and Brownie was a good sport about it all. She insisted on finishing the job, and combed and set Carole's hair. Somehow, despite the near-tragedy and the delay, they finally got off.

Clark, Carole and Howard Strickling flew to Atlanta in a chartered American Airlines plane, which had *Gone With the Wind* painted on its fuselage.

Tremendous crowds gave them a huge ovation at the airport as they deplaned and were greeted by a civic committee, headed by Mayor William B. Hartsfield. Carole was presented with a bouquet of yellow roses. She was radiant in black suit, black hat and sables. Clark wore gray tweeds and had a red carnation in his buttonhole. Police had to fight to hold back the wildly cheering fans.

Within a few minutes, a second plane arrived from New York with

David Selznick, Vivien Leigh, Laurence Olivier and Olivia de Havilland aboard.

The stars and their parties made the seven-mile ride to the city in open cars, Clark, Carole and Howard riding together. The entire route was lined with solid masses of almost hysterical fans, and Clark and Carole sat up on the back of their car to acknowledge their greetings.

Beginning with an outdoor reception that night, they were surrounded wherever they went by enthusiastic but respectful fans. All of the stars received their share of attention but, according to Howard, it was Clark the fans really wanted to see.

When Carole was introduced, she modestly announced that she was "going to let Mr. Gable do all the talking. I love you all."

Clark won them with his opening lines.

"You know," he said, "as I started down here this evening your good Mayor told me there were three hundred thousand people in Atlanta. I'm positive I saw at least *three million* happy faces, and I want you to know that your treatment of us has far exceeded our expectations."

The Grand Theater where the premiere was held seated two thousand people. Sale of the tickets was handled by the Community Chest at ten dollars apiece. The Mayor told Clark that there had been forty thousand requests for tickets.

The front of the theater was decorated to resemble the portico of Twelve Oaks, one of the antebellum mansions in the book. The blazing searchlights, the batteries of microphones and movie cameras, the newsmen and photographers, the surging crowds who cheered as the stars ar-

rived, were all history-making for Atlanta.

Carole was glamorous in slinky champagne satin and rubies, Clark impressively handsome in his white tie and tails.

"When the crowd saw them they let out the old rebel yell and would have torn them to pieces if the police hadn't held them back," a friend wrote me later. "They just couldn't get enough of the Gables."

Clark spoke very briefly in front of the microphones. "This is Margaret Mitchell's night and your night," he said. "Just let me be a spectator, going in to see *Gone With the Wind*."

Eight thousand tickets at ten dollars apiece were sold for a brilliant Junior League Ball the next night, where all the stars made an appearance. Carole, in black velvet and silver fox muff, received as much attention as Clark.

During the day there were smaller receptions and teas. Clark and Carole met Margaret Mitchell and he had an opportunity to thank her personally for the autographed copy of *Gone With the Wind* which she'd sent him when he'd been signed for the part. Miss Mitchell thought his portrayal of Rhett was superb, exactly as she'd envisioned her character.

The Daughters of the American Revolution presented Clark and Carole with a lovely woven Colonial bedspread and a set of rare old china demitasse cups and saucers.

Bucket is my authority for an incident in the Gables' departure from their hotel in Atlanta. That morning, just after Clark and Carole had checked out of their suite and left for the airport, Bucket was at the hotel desk and overheard a little old lady ask the desk clerk if she might engage the room occupied by Clark.

The clerk suggested that she register, but said there'd be a slight delay until the room was made up, the linens changed.

"Are you sure, now, it's the same room *he* had?" the little lady inquired anxiously.

"Yes, of course," the clerk replied.

Whereupon the old lady announced that she wanted immediate occupancy, and "Don't change the sheets," she said.

Clark and Carole returned to the ranch in midafternoon. After greeting me, Carole went right upstairs, but Clark lingered in my office for an hour, describing their trip, telling me what a great job Howard Strickling had done and voicing his pride over Carole, her beauty and glamour, her graciousness to the fans. "They were all at her feet," he said.

"I tried to keep out of the limelight as much as possible," Carole told me later. "This was Pa's triumph."

The day after Carole got back from Atlanta, we started the Christmas shopping.

Christmas week Carole decorated the lower floor with evergreens and holly and set up a huge white Christmas tree, covered with red lights and exquisite silver ornaments and frosted grapes. She thoughtfully provided the same lovely silver ornaments and grapes for the Garceau tree.

Bessie and Carole's brothers, Father Gable, Edna and Pinkie were invited to a family dinner.

"We're going to be very cozy and very gay," Carole said.

When I left, early Christmas Eve, Carole draped some lovely Baum marten furs over my shoulders and

Clark with Margaret Mitchell.

tucked a generous bonus check from the Gables into my handbag. She'd also remembered my husband Russ with a wonderful automobile robe and even had a nice gift for the college girl who helped me at home.

That year, Clark's "big" gift to Carole was an exquisite ruby heart, plus the usual collection of "woman stuff," such as hostess gowns, handbags, sweaters, scarves and perfume, especially Chanel No. 5, which was her favorite.

Carole loved to give Clark things that he liked most, such as outboard motors, fishing equipment, sleeping bags, or some tool or gadget he fancied. That Christmas she had Bob Vom Cleff of Bullock's Wilshire design some beautiful silk pajamas with matching robe for him. They were of heavy off-white silk, imported from Hong Kong. The robe had a shawl collar and both robe and pajama coat were monogrammed. Clark loved them and had them copied year after year. She also liked to give him fine sweaters and other wearing apparel.

Clark had a most extensive wardrobe; he was meticulous in his dress and in the care of his things. His shoes were all handmade in England, and Martin kept them shined to perfection. Whether he was in dinner jacket or blue jeans, Clark wore his clothes magnificently and was certainly one of the best-dressed men in films.

He loved his work and hunting clothes, and was greatly attached to his old hats. Immaculate and impeccable in his attire in every respect, he had one clothes "quirk": he would never permit one of his hats to be cleaned.

Clark took a keen interest in women's clothes, and Carole dressed to please him. She had great style and an unerring instinct for the right thing, and wore her clothes with grace and *élan*. Her wardrobe featured the colors she knew Clark liked best—white, beige, gray, black. Her furs were of sable, mink and silver fox, the latter very fashionable that year. Her jewels and accessories were exquisite. She knew when to underplay and when to overplay for effect.

Carole was mad about hats, the crazier the better. I've seen her buy a dozen or so at one time at Bullock's Wilshire.

"I'll probably never wear them," she'd say. "I just want to take them home to make Pa laugh."

CHAPTER SIX

SOON AFTER New Year's, *Gone With the Wind* had its Hollywood premiere at the Carthay Circle Theater. Clark and Carole invited Russ and me to go; they arranged for a special car pass and tickets for us. It was to be a full dress affair and we were very excited.

Before I had time to even plan what I'd wear, Carole ordered a beautiful black velvet evening gown with matching cape for me. And she had Bucket out at the ranch to do her hair and mine that afternoon before I went home to dress.

The Atlanta premiere had been patterned after our own Hollywood premieres, which were put on with a great deal of fanfare. Bleacher stands in front of the theater were erected a day or so in advance and the fans began arriving at dawn on the day of the opening. They came equipped with blankets, cushions and lunchboxes, cards and reading material, and staked-out a seat or vantage point along the curb to wait patiently all day to share in the evening's excitement and catch a glimpse of the stars.

The theater was always decorated inside and out in keeping with the background and theme of the film. Huge searchlights probed the sky, bands played, streets were roped off and uniformed attendants held back the crowds as the police permitted only those cars with passes to draw up in front of the theater.

A long flower-decked canopy extended to the sidewalk and a master of ceremonies stood there to welcome the stars, announce their names over a loud-speaker and guide them towards a battery of microphones and cameras where they paused to extend their greetings as camera flashbulbs popped and the fans shrieked their approval. Then they proceeded down the canopied walk into the theater.

When Russ and I arrived, I was a step ahead of him after we left our car. The flashbulbs were blinding and I lost him in the crowd, partly because my long velvet cape billowed out so far he couldn't reach me and partly because I was trying to avoid the cameras. We didn't find each other until we reached the entrance, which seemed an interminably long time for me. For months after, Russ accused me of "going Hollywood" and trying to shake him, so I could "make an entrance."

Clark and Carole's car was right behind us. Irene had designed a princess-like gold lamé evening gown and cape for Carole and she was breathtakingly lovely in it. Pandemonium broke loose in the stands when the fans caught sight of the Gables, and they were mobbed by the cameramen. They posed with Marion Davies and Raoul Walsh.

Father Gable, Edna and Pinkie were there too, but Father Gable, who refused ever to wear a tuxedo, preferred to arrive quietly and occupy the seats Clark had reserved for them without being identified. *Gone With the Wind* was the only premiere Clark's family ever attended.

Howard Strickling, Gable, and Lombard at Hollywood premier of
GWTW. COURTESY OF MGM

It was an unforgettable evening. Every star in Hollywood was there, and I've never seen a more glittering array of gowns and jewels, for everyone comes to "see and be seen." Russ and I felt very elegant.

Of course I thought the picture was wonderful and Clark superb. But there was so much going on that I actually enjoyed the picture more when I went back later to see it for the second time.

Clark's mail, after the film was released, was tremendous. To his fans he was Rhett Butler. One woman wrote Clark to please tell her how it all ended. "What really happened to Scarlett and Rhett afterwards?" she inquired. It was so real to her that she refused to believe they were just picture characters.

Although Clark's contract had another year to run, it was rewritten. Beginning January 25, 1940, he would receive seven thousand, five hundred dollars a week for the next five years. He was now one of the highest-paid contract stars in motion pictures.

Clark was nominated for Best Actor in the 1939 Academy Awards Sweepstakes, but lost out to Robert Donat, who had starred in *Good-bye Mr. Chips. Gone With the Wind* won ten Academy Awards, and Clark was so gratified over Victor Fleming's Oscar for Best Direction that I can honestly say I don't think he minded not winning one himself.

"After all," he said, "one's enough for any man."

(Years later, when Fieldsie's son, Richard Lang, was about twelve, he was out at the ranch and saw the Oscar Clark had won for *It Happened One Night*. He admired it so much that Clark gave it to him. Not that he valued it any the less, but he knew Richard wanted it and he loved the boy.)

Whenever possible, the Gables went hunting. Both were excellent shots. Carole had done a lot of skeet shooting in learning to use a gun, and she now enjoyed hunting as much as Clark did. She was very quick, but she was accurate.

Harry and Nan Fleischmann owned a duck club south of Bakersfield, and Clark and Carole spent a lot of time there. The Fleischmanns built a cabin for them which they shared with the Kenny Watters from Santa Barbara.

The cabin was comfortable and fully equipped. "We furnished it in Early Sears Roebuck," Carole used to say.

The three couples were all sitting around one evening when Clark turned to Harry and said, "Harry, why don't you give us a half-acre of land here?"

Harry turned to Nan, "Nan, I think maybe we should. How about it?"

"I'm not giving a half-acre to anyone, especially Gable," Nan replied. "Let him buy his own land."

Carole was so amused over Clark's getting his come-uppance that she collapsed on the ground with laughter.

"That will teach you to open your big mouth," she told Clark.

The Gables loved to go to their special hideaway, La Grulla Gun Club in the mountains below Ensenada, which is about sixty-five miles south of the Mexican border. The gun club had very poor phone service and it was almost impossible to get a call through to them.

Late in January, Clark and Carole and the Fleischmanns went down to La Grulla in Clark's station wagon. They didn't get any duck, so decided to go farther south to Hattie Hamilton's Club to try for Brandt geese.

Hattie and her sister were two

elderly women and their club was a primitive place, with a dining room where they served meals of a sort. A few tiny cabins were scattered about which they rented to hunters.

The party stayed there two or three days but bagged no birds. On February 1, Clark's birthday, they decided to head back to La Grulla. When they departed that morning, Hattie produced a fearful and wonderful-looking birthday cake she'd made for Clark.

"It looked pretty terrible but we had to take it along," Nan says. "As we left our cabins, Carole snatched up one of those thick white candles they furnish you for light and stuck it in the cake as a gag."

They'd driven only a few miles when it began to rain, which soon became a downpour. The station wagon got stuck in the mud on the narrow mountain road. Try as they would, Clark and Harry couldn't get it out, so the party decided to make the best of it until the rain stopped.

An old Mexican happened along with two cooked lobsters he was taking to his village. When he realized their predicament, he insisted on giving them the lobsters, and the foursome settled down to a birthday dinner of lobster and cake. Carole lit the candle and they all sang "Happy Birthday" to Clark.

"The lobsters were tough and stringy and the cake was wicked, but we ate all of it," Carole told me later.

When the Gable party did not return to La Grulla on schedule, someone sent word to Ensenada and the news that they were missing was phoned to Hollywood. There were big black headlines, and the phone at the ranch rang incessantly as newsmen tried to check with me on the story.

The studio and I tried to get in touch with the Gun Club but the phone service was, as usual, so poor that we couldn't get through. Howard Strickling told Otto Winkler to fly down at once and investigate.

Meanwhile, the foursome in the station wagon had climbed into sleeping bags, and slept the night through. Next morning the rain stopped, and two men came along in a truck and pulled them out of the mud. They returned to La Grulla just as a very worried Otto Winkler was about to start out with a search party.

People always marveled how Carole had changed, how she'd made herself over as a rough-and-ready man's pal for Clark; but no one, except very intimate friends, was aware that Carole in turn was changing Clark.

She was so vital, so full of the joy of living, that she carried everything and everybody along in her light-hearted wake. The atmosphere of love and companionship, the "Clark comes first" attitude in all her thinking, had its effect—for Clark was inclined to reflect the prevailing mood of those around him.

"Until now Clark had never quite believed in his success," a friend summed it up. "He always acted as if it might all disappear in a flash and he'd be back doing day labor. With Carole he began to relax, to be free, to shake off the old fears and depressions."

In the spring of 1940, Clark started shooting *Boom Town* and was happy to be reunited with Claudette Colbert for the first time since their big hit, *It Happened One Night*. The cast included Spencer Tracy, Frank Morgan and the beautiful Hedy Lamarr. They all had a lot of fun and it meant a great

Carole sitting on a rail fence which surrounded the ranch property. (1940)

Clark, Carole, and Harry Fleischmann at La Grulla Gun Club in Mexico. (1941)

Carole and Clark celebrate their first wedding anniversary. (1940) COURTESY OF MGM

deal to Clark to be playing again with Spencer Tracy, whom he admired so much.

The story had an oil field background and they went on location for a while at a nearby field. Clark took a deep interest in observing the difference between a big company's drilling operations and techniques as compared to the wildcatting conditions under which he had worked in Oklahoma years before.

"Things have sure improved since Dad was operating on a shoestring and I was on the work gang," he said. "In those days we couldn't afford a geologist. We just went out and drilled by guess and by gosh."

Clark had a free day on their first wedding anniversary, March 29, and he and Carole celebrated by going to the races at Santa Anita near Arcadia. Neither of them was inclined to gamble

heavily, so they never got beyond the two-dollar window.

Clark came home a winner with thirty-six dollars and eighty cents; Carole lost ten dollars. "I try to pick 'em by studying the racing sheet," Clark said. "Ma bets on a horse if she likes the color of the jockey's silks."

By the time Clark finished *Boom Town,* Carole was busy in the film version of Sidney Howard's Pulitzer Prize play *They Knew What They Wanted,* at RKO.

Carole played the role of Amy, the discouraged hash slinger who married Tony, the simple and kindly Italian grape rancher in the Napa Valley. Tony was played by Charles Laughton and William Gargan played Joe, the ranch foreman to whom Amy is attracted.

Garson Kanin directed and he took his company up to the Napa Valley for two weeks' shooting. Clark went along to be with Carole. The cast and crew stayed at hotels, but Carole and Clark were invited to be guests at a local home, which insured complete privacy for them.

Napa is in the heart of California's "wine country" and the Gables had a fascinating time visiting the various wineries, and sampling different vintages.

"Carole thought they still stomped the grapes in vats," Clark teased, "and she wanted to come home with purple toes."

Their wine hosts were so charmed with them that soon after they returned to Hollywood, many cases of fine wine were shipped to the ranch as gifts from the various wineries.

The Gables' liquor cabinets were well stocked with the finest brands of all descriptions and Clark liked to dispense with Martin's services and take over the bartending duties himself when they had guests. Both the Gables enjoyed a nightcap.

When they'd remodeled the house, a small Early American wall cupboard was discovered in Clark's bedroom suite. Carole fitted this up with glasses, an ice bucket and the "makings." Each night when the servants brought carafes of ice water upstairs, they always filled the ice bucket in "Clark's bar" in case he wanted a bedtime drink.

"I have to wait on my old man, you know," Carole said, "and it saves having to patter downstairs for it."

Occasionally, Clark broke his rule about no end-of-the-picture gifts and gave his stand-in or make-up man a bottle of fine liquor.

Aside from their small informal dinners, the Gables did little entertaining, but once a year there was a formal dinner for eight or ten of the studio executives and other bigwigs in the industry.

And every summer Carole staged a "fun" party for about twenty of their most intimate friends. As soon as she finished *They Knew What They Wanted,* she began to plan one of these.

A small dance floor was built in the patio, and garden and patio were enclosed in walls of heavy cellophane, the whole area illuminated by cleverly arranged floodlights.

Small tables decked with red checkered cloths and kerosene lamps were scattered about the patio. An attractive bar, buffet and gaily decorated hot-dog stand were put up. A small orchestra was engaged to play during dinner and for the dancing afterwards.

Bob, the head chef at the Brown Derby, catered and was on hand in his tall white cap to supervise the serving of dinner. Carole was one of his favorite patrons and he liked to handle her parties himself. Among his speci-

Clark intended to someday build a house on this spot in the Napa Valley.
(1941) COURTESY OF AL MENASCO

79

alties were tiny, succulent, piping hot steaks, served as hors d'oeuvres.

Available at the hot-dog stand and buffet were a wonderful stew, steaks, roast turkey, baked beans, salads, and Clark's favorite homemade ice cream and chocolate cake.

Carole's brother Stuart was as witty and fun-loving as she and between them they kept things on a hilarious plane. It was all very gay and friendly.

"We never do anything much," Carole explained to me when I inquired as to the evening's festivities, "but we have a lot of laughs and Pa is relaxed and happy."

Clark hated night clubs and they seldom went out socially themselves except to small parties at the homes of close friends.

One evening they were at the Fred MacMurrays in Bel Air. Irene had created a lovely long white "souffle" evening gown for Carole, who was crazy about it and was wearing it for the first time. During the evening, she got to romping around the swimming pool and fell in. Nothing daunted, she spent the rest of the evening happily sheathed in a MacMurray dressing gown.

Next day she called Irene and told her about it.

"Anyone else would have been disturbed over ruining the dress," Irene says, "but not Carole. She thought it was a big joke on herself. I told her to bring it in and let me look at it, but it was beyond repair. Carole laughed and ordered another."

Clark joined the Citrus Association soon after the move to the ranch. Under this arrangement, the Association sends in workers to pick the fruit, and it is graded and marketed. The first season, the yield from the original trees was large and we eagerly awaited the payment from the Association. Months later the check came. It was for six dollars and twenty-eight cents. The Gable fruit had been graded as "culls"!

Clark was terribly disappointed, for the orchard was his pride. Care of the critus was stepped up. The new trees were growing nicely and Clark himself did much of the pruning, spraying, and fertilizing, working with Fred the caretaker. Irrigation was carefully controlled.

The second season the trees were attacked by an infestation of red spiders. We called a pest-control company, and the trees were all covered with heavy tarpaulins, then sprayed. This proved highly effective, but much of the fruit was lost. The third year, an unexpected freeze destroyed the crop. Reluctantly, Clark came to the conclusion that the citrus was not going to pay off and he abandoned the idea of making a profit from it.

We just relaxed and enjoyed it, along with the peaches, plums, apricots and figs from the rest of the orchard. The Gables gave away fruit to various friends and the family and sent the remainder to their favorite charity, the Children's Hospital.

The chickens were another venture. "We'll sell the eggs and the chickens will pay for themselves," Clark said.

Howard and Gail Strickling were of invaluable aid in this project—for they raised chickens themselves, very profitably. Howard supervised the building of the pens and the runs and recommended a proper feed mixture.

Carole designed an attractive cream-colored egg box featuring a brown egg and a chicken wearing a tiny crown. They were labeled "The King's Eggs" and she ordered several

While clowning around at a party, Carole fell into a pool. She was wearing this dress designed by Irene. (1941) COURTESY OF JOHN ENGSTEAD

thousand made up. Clark bought six hundred New Hampshire Red hens, and we were in business.

Fred and his wife were conscientious poultry tenders, but somehow the hens didn't lay as expected. Conferences were held with Howard and other experts, the situation reviewed. The feed formula was changed but that effected no improvement. Next it was decided that perhaps the lights in the pens weren't being switched on at the right time in the morning.

"Let's get those lazy hens up earlier," Clark said. So various experiments with the light schedule were made.

Since this was a business project, I'd set up accounts for the poultry venture. The feed bills were enormous. My records showed that even when Clark Gable, chicken farmer, sold dozens of eggs to Clark Gable, movie star, at the current market price, he didn't come anywhere near making a profit.

When the figures were analyzed, I estimated that the eggs were actually costing about a dollar apiece. In the face of this example of diminishing returns and as Clark's business manager, I was forced to recommend that he abandon the egg project as a commercial proposition.

The egg boxes were stored in the barn and we gradually used them up over the years.

Clark next got the idea of raising beef cattle as a source of meat for the ranch, the meat to be stored in the walk-in freezer. This, too, was to be part of the self-sustaining farm program.

A couple of steer calves were bought to raise. The calves had big velvety brown eyes and white faces, and everyone fell in love with them.

Their feed bills were also astronomical; but it was gratifying to watch them thrive and grow.

Finally the day came when they were to be butchered. Fred was to do the job. He tried to bring himself to the point but chickened out. "I just can't kill them," he told Clark.

Clark had to hire a professional butcher to come in and slaughter the calves and dress the meat for the freezer. Serving of the first steaks was to be an occasion.

"Just think, we're going to eat our very own home-grown meat," Carole said when she planned the menu.

When we sat down to the table, however, the idea wasn't nearly so appealing. Everyone stalled at first, then confessed that he couldn't touch his meat.

"I can't help it," Carole said. "I keep thinking about those big sad eyes!"

Clark sent the remainder of the meat to the Children's Hospital and that was the end of the grow-your-own meat movement.

We did have one project that paid its way. Clark bought two Jersey cows, then built and equipped a completely modern milk room with a cream separator, churns, and other essentials, so Fred and his wife could take care of the milk and make butter. The cows were good producers; we had an abundant supply of rich milk, butter and buttermilk, and cream so thick you could spoon it up.

Because they had a ranch, Clark and Carole were the recipients of many gifts of livestock from their friends. We had pigs, goats, rabbits; and there were the doves, of course, in their special aviary.

The doves were Clark's pride. Their story dates back to the time before his marriage to Carole. There have been many versions of this story in print, but this is the real one.

Carole was volatile by nature, and her high spirits had clashed with Clark's Dutch stubbornness and they'd had a spat. Clark had returned to the Beverly Wilshire Hotel, where he was living at the time, and gone to bed.

Carole began to feel contrite and wanted to make up. She bought as many white doves as she could locate, took them to the hotel in a cage, and bribed a bellboy to introduce them into Clark's room while he was asleep.

When Clark woke up the next morning, he found himself the central figure in a dove cote. "There's nothing like having a dove sitting on your chest, staring you in the eye the first thing in the morning," Clark laughed when he told me of the incident.

He knew the birds were from Carole, so he had them caged and sent them to her house in Bel Air, where they remained until the move to the ranch, when he had a special pen built for them.

Clark loved the doves. They multiplied, of course, and bigger and bigger pens had to be built. But he would never allow any of them to be killed. He said one of the sounds he liked best was their cooing in the mornings and evenings.

Clark and Carole jealously guarded their personal privacy. It was necessary at times for publicity purposes to permit studio and news photographers to take pictures of them at the ranch, but these were all outdoor shots. No taking of photographs was ever allowed inside the house.

There was a great demand for personal interviews with them. These were carefully screened and set up by the studio publicity departments and now and again various newsmen and columnists came out. Both Clark and Carole avoided personal publicity, per se, but Carole was regarded as a very astute judge of news values in connection with the exploitation of their films and was always very cooperative for that purpose.

Her last picture before their marriage had been *Made for Each Other*, for David Selznick. A week before the film started she went to Russell Birdwell, Selznick's publicity director, and announced: "I have a spare week before my picture begins. I'd like to work here that week and see what goes on in a publicity department."

Birdwell turned his press bureau over to her and instructed his staff to give her every cooperation. Carole took the place by storm, called idea conferences, made assignments and by the end of the week had personally "planted" or placed seventy stories with news editors. This resulted in an outstanding publicity campaign on the film.

Despite their efforts, however, the matter of privacy at the ranch became a real problem. Although the place was twelve miles from Hollywood and twenty from Los Angeles, people of all types began coming in at all hours. Sightseeing buses even swept up the curving driveway to stop in front of the house, while the driver proudly announced to his passengers that they were at the home of Clark and Carole Gable.

Clark finally had to install fences and an electric gate which was controlled from the house. Visitors announced themselves via a bell and a loudspeaker.

At first the fences were the split-rail type. Clark dug many of the postholes himself. But people, mostly women, still climbed through and came to the house. Children perched on the gate and threw the electric circuits out of order, so that I was constantly calling the repair man.

Eventually, Clark installed a chain-link fence around the front of the property, so that it could not be entered from the road except by way of the electric gate. Mermaid roses were planted along the front fence. They grew very thick, and their thorny branches helped make the fence an impenetrable barrier.

The gate bell rang in my office and I was able to screen all callers. Most of them were fans, solicitors or strange women, demanding to see Clark. When I informed them that Mr. Gable was not at home, it was sometimes amusing—often infuriating—to hear their comments about me, which came in over the loud-speaker.

Teenagers often camped outside the gate for hours, hoping to catch Clark and Carole as they drove in or out. Martin, the butler, and I had to keep a close watch, frequently threatening to call the police in order to get them to leave.

Even with the chain fence and gate, people climbed through the split-rail fences somewhere else on the property and came to the front door.

Martin and I became very proficient at persuading hapless females that it would be impossible for them to see their idol, Mr. Gable. We worked as a team, for Clark's attorney, W. I. Gilbert, Sr., had cautioned Martin and me to act as witnesses for each other in dealing with these people and under no circumstances to touch the intruders in any way for fear they might claim abuse or injury. We were always careful to be polite, but firm.

One day Clark, who'd been out in the paddocks, came rushing into my office, wild-eyed. "There's a woman behind me!" he said, slamming the door.

Calling to Martin, I rushed out to meet the trespasser, who had climbed through the fence on the upper property and come down through the fields.

She was a bleached and blowsy blonde in a riding habit who insisted that she must see Clark. We could not induce her to leave. She made herself comfortable in one of the patio lounges, lit a cigarette and calmly announced: "I'm not leaving until I see Clark."

I called Howard Strickling at the studio and he instructed Whitey Hendry, Chief of Police at MGM, to send a couple of the studio police to help us.

The situation had its comic aspects, for when the police arrived, the lady decided on a game of hide-and-seek among the trees, with the police giving chase. She was finally tagged and persuaded to leave.

Clark never scorned his fans, was always smiling and cooperative, happy to give autographs, and was pleased over their attention; but he'd had some unfortunate and embarrassing experiences with hysterical women and he felt that this invasion of his privacy at the ranch was intolerable.

Clark got volumes of mail at the studio, which was handled by the studio fan mail department, but the home mail was almost equally heavy despite the fact that the address and phone number were unlisted.

I had to screen this mail carefully because much of it was from lovelorn, hysterical women, from crackpots of all kinds, and there were many solicitations for funds—few of the causes worthy. Much of the mail was salacious. There were many "repeaters," some of them threatening harm, and these I turned over to the postal authorities. Clark never saw them.

There were several instances where perfectly nice girls, holding responsible jobs, went off the deep end in their impassioned love letters to Clark. One of these became such a nuisance that the postal authorities had to intervene.

There were many honest and sincere letters, of course, and Clark was happy to read them. It was a source of great satisfaction to him that so many *men* wrote him, men who admired him, his tastes and hobbies and the things for which he stood.

Both Clark and Carole got many small gifts of all kinds from their fans—handkerchiefs, pipes, book ends, even clocks. These were all given to charitable organizations, the donors receiving thank-you notes from Clark, written by me.

Besieged and harassed as they were, Clark and Carole began thinking of a larger ranch, far out in the country, beyond the reach of fans and tourists. This ranch would be self-sustaining and would form the nucleus of a small private colony. Here they would have true privacy.

Whenever possible, Carole and I began scouring the countryside. We covered all the area around Bakersfield. The main problem was to find a place with an adequate water supply, for irrigation is a major concern in California.

While we were looking, Clark suggested that we begin laying in food supplies for the ranch-to-be, storing them in one of the waterproof barns.

Carole bought sugar in hundred-pound sacks, and lined shelves in the barns with cases of tomatoes and canned foods of all kinds, olive oil and molasses.

Among her new purchases were ten new garbage cans of galvanized metal, four feet high. These Carole filled with beans of all varieties.

"Why on earth did you buy so many beans?" I asked in amazement.

"Pa likes his baked beans," Carole replied. "We must never run short!"

Soon it became apparent that the stored beans were spoiling. Now we had to get expert advice on how to avoid this. Carole ended up buying soda in hundred-pound sacks. Thereafter the beans were stored between layers of soda, which acted as a preservative.

"Why not look over some of the Arizona ranches, see how they operate? You might like that country," Al Menasco suggested in late summer.

So Clark and Carole joined Al and his wife on a weekend trip to the O-W Ranch, high in the Arizona mountains halfway between Globe and Holbrook.

The ranch was owned by Ken Jay and was a real "working spread" with a full complement of ranch hands, no fancy frills and not a dude in sight.

Haying and other fall work was in progress and Clark's foursome pitched in to share in the activity. Mrs. Jay did all the cooking and laundry for the family and the hands. "Clark and I helped with the haying and I wish you could have seen the girls doing the washing," Al says. "The only piece of modern equipment was a hand wringer, and Carole tangled with that. She got herself soaked as she wrung out the Levis. When the clothes were dry, Clark loaded them into a basket, placed it on his head and carried it to the house."

In romping around the place,

With Ken Jay at his ranch, the O-W, in Arizona. (1941)
COURTESY OF AL MENASCO

These four snapshots were taken at the O-W Ranch.
COURTESY OF AL MENASCO

Carole stepped on a rattlesnake, letting out a bloodcurdling scream and jumping aside just in time.

"Clark and I began banging away at point-blank range but it took twenty-two shots to kill it," Al says. "This was pretty bad shooting and we both felt terrible. We were using Frontier forty-fives and just the day before had demonstrated that we could hit anything in sight, deadeye. Clark had killed a rattler at fifty yards' range with just one shot."

Clark skinned the snake and hung the skin on the barn door to dry. They brought it back to the ranch to show me.

Both were bubbling with enthusiasm over the Arizona location, full of plans for buying a ranch similar to the O-W, modernizing it, and "really making it a paying proposition."

"When we find our place, Jeanie," Carole said, "you and your old man are going to come up and live with us. We'll be just one family and have a lot of fun."

Fred, our own ranch hand, was cutting hay when they got home. The next afternoon Carole called to me: "Come and see what my old man is doing."

I looked out and there was Clark riding the hay rake pulled by Judy, the mule, raking the hay Fred had cut. He was the picture of contentment.

Off and on during the next two years, we investigated ranch properties. We never located the ideal ranch the Gables had in mind, but Carole never gave up hoping.

Boom Town was released early in September. The critics said that the studio was trying to exploit the Gable-Tracy combination with a mediocre story, but the fans loved it and the film was a box-office success.

Clark never read reviews of his pictures, and he left the selection of his stories to the studio. "They know more about it than I do," he said.

A month later *They Knew What They Wanted* was released and these reviews Clark *did* read, for the critics were unanimous in their raves about the picture, the director and the cast, particularly Carole. Her performance was rated "extraordinarily fine" by the *Herald Tribune* reviewer; "distinguished," commented another, the consensus being that "Miss Lombard has established herself as an excellent dramatic actress."

Once again that fall I was making the rounds between two studios and the ranch. The fan mail on Hedy Lamarr in *Boom Town* had been so large that MGM decided to make her Clark's leading lady in *Comrade X*, with Oscar Homolka. Clark played an American reporter in Russia who falls in love with Hedy, a beautiful streetcar conductor.

Clark wore a full beard in this picture and had to be at the studio very early each morning, for it took Stan Campbell, his make-up man, a full hour to put it on.

Clark thought Hedy was beautiful, liked her very much, and ribbed her unmercifully because she spent so much time on her face and clothes. "Come on," he'd say to her, "forget your face—let's do some acting."

"When she arrived in the morning without make-up," Stan says, "she was so beautiful that I felt it was a shame to have to make that face up."

Hedy was new to American picture methods, and was still very unsure of herself. Clark and director King Vidor were very patient with her, trying to put her at her ease.

Things were much livelier over at

RKO, where Carole was making *Mr. and Mrs. Smith* with Robert Montgomery and Gene Raymond under Alfred Hitchcock's direction.

The gay comedy script was by Norman Krasna, and Carole had howled when she read it, for the story revolves around a young couple who discover—after three years—that their marriage isn't really legal. Robert Montgomery, the husband, wants to woo and wed his wife (Carole) all over again; but she has different ideas, and spurns him at first for his law partner (Gene Raymond), then leads him on a merry chase.

There was one hilarious sequence in which Carole had to shave Robert Montgomery with an old-fashioned straight razor. She took lessons from the studio's head barber, but this didn't reassure Bob, for Carole kept "breaking up" during the filming of the scene.

"I was afraid I'd wind up without any nose," he said.

During the shooting of the picture, Bucket, the hairdresser, had a birthday. So Carole gave a party on the set for her and, as usual, pulled all sorts of gags. She ordered ice-cream cones for everyone and had them filled with cold cream, then snapped pictures of the expressions on the faces of the guests as they tasted them.

Alfred Hitchcock always appears in one scene in each of his pictures. It is usually nothing more than a walk-on, or he is one of a crowd. In *Mr. and Mrs. Smith,* he elected to appear in front of an apartment house, tip his hat to Robert Montgomery and bid him good morning. Carole nagged him into letting her direct it.

Naturally, she made the most of her opportunity and Hitchcock realized too late that he'd let himself in for something. Carole was very fussy about the scene, criticized Hitchcock's make-up, his voice, his walk. She shot the bit over and over before finally announcing that she was satisfied. The story made all the local newspapers and was picked up by the wire services. *Life* gave it a big picture spread.

The cast and crew had so much fun that, when the picture was over, one crew member said: "It broke my heart to see it all end. We'd never had such a good gang together, never had such laughs."

Clark was always impatient when work caused him to miss the opening of the hunting season—as it did this year. He finished *Comrade X* before Carole was through at RKO and wandered the ranch during the day, lost without her.

"Hurry it up, will you, Ma?" he said one morning as she was leaving. "We've got to get going."

"What's on your mind, Pa?" Carole asked.

"Ducks," Clark replied, grinning.

The hunting party at La Grulla that fall was a gay and congenial one. Clark and Carole and the Fleischmanns arrived in Clark's station wagon. They were joined by Buster Collier and his wife Stevie, who also drove down, as did Eddie Mannix of MGM. Phil Berg and his wife Leila flew down in a small rented plane that Phil was thinking of buying. He called it "the Puddle Jumper."

They didn't get any duck at La Grulla so they decided to go high in the mountains to Laguna Hanson, a lovely little lake, where they thought they might find some canvasbacks. Phil's plane was too small to carry the entire party; and Carole refused to let Clark fly in it, anyway, as Phil had scraped the treetops with his wings coming in for a landing at La Grulla.

"Let's get Paul down here," Clark suggested. "He'll take us to the lake."

He put in a phone call for his old friend Paul Mantz, and Paul flew down in his Sikorsky S-38 Twin Engine Amphibian, which the gang called "Nellie the Goon." Paul loaded the whole party aboard with their hunting and fishing gear, food and other camp supplies, and flew them to Laguna Hanson.

They found they had the lake to themselves, and commandeered an old hunting cabin. They put up their stove, cooked their own meals and had a wonderful time hunting and fishing. At night they slept outside in their sleeping bags.

"Clark and Carole were real down-to-earth people and I was so glad to be a part of their gang," Paul says. "They didn't act like movie stars and I loved being with them."

Carole ran afoul of a swarm of yellow jackets on the last day. "Everyone stood around advising her to keep still, not to slap them and they'd go away," Nan recalls. "Poor Carole did her best but she was wearing short hunting pants and socks and one of the yellow jackets zeroed in on her bare leg and she got a bad sting."

When they were ready to leave, Paul had a little difficulty getting them out, for the lake was small and ringed with trees right down to the water's edge.

"It was as smooth as a mirror," Paul says, "so I taxied in a circle in order to rough it up and create a few waves. We were carrying two cases of ammunition and a heavy battery, however, and when I'd reached the point of no return, I 'aborted' the take-off and we had to start over again.

"This time we unloaded the ammunition and the battery and Clark said he'd send a jeep back for them. I guess I'm ultraconservative, but maybe that's why I'm still flying. We made it the second time."

"It was very exciting," Nan recalls, "for Nellie the Goon just barely missed the treetops. Carole, who was never afraid of anything, turned pale and said to Clark, 'Please, let's never travel in separate planes. Whenever I fly, I want you with me.' "

Clark spent his time working on his car. Everything seemed to be wrong with it and he kept complaining about it every day.

"My old man tickles me," Carole said one morning when we were driving into town. "He thinks he's fooling us, but what he's really doing is building up to a new car. The 1941 models are out and he won't rest until he has one."

She was right. Within a week Clark decided his only recourse was to trade in his old model for a new one. Carole solemnly agreed that this was indeed a wise move.

"You know, Jeanie," she commented to me in private, "it's ingrained in Clark's nature—a sort of guilt about spending money, a fear that he's going to be without it. To justify buying the new car, he had to convince *himself* that he *needed* it."

Comrade X was released in December. The critics claimed it was a bad imitation of the successful *Ninotchka*, and that only Clark's personal popularity would carry it at the box-office. They said he'd done nothing worthwhile since *Gone With the Wind* and speculated as to the effect a series of mediocre pictures would have on his career.

Carole planned the usual quiet family Christmas party at the ranch.

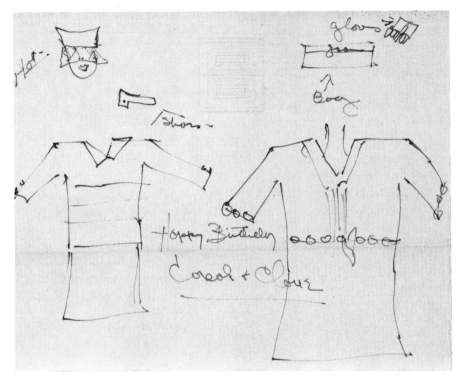

When Clark and Carole gave me gifts, they were always complete outfits, as this drawing indicates. When the presents weren't ready for my birthday, Carole drew this as an I.O.U. (1941)

Their present for me that year was an exquisite platinum and diamond wrist watch, with their signatures engraved on the back, and again a generous bonus check. Clark's gifts to Carole were a lovely ruby and diamond ring and a mink cape. She gave him a new fishing rod and some English hunting boots.

Clark was seldom ill and, though he never complained, we all knew that he'd been having trouble for some time with a shoulder he'd injured while filming *San Francisco* in 1936.

Aware of the impossibility of getting treatment in Hollywood without a great deal of publicity, Carole persuaded him to go East to Johns Hopkins to have the shoulder checked.

They left right after Christmas, during the usual holiday hiatus at the studios, and went to Baltimore by train. They managed to get in and out of the city without attracting undue atten-

tion, although according to Carole, Clark's presence at Johns Hopkins created a major upheaval among the nurses.

The doctors' recommended treatment for the the shoulder was deep massage and a series of exercises which Clark began to follow carefully. Otherwise they gave him a clean bill of health. Carole phoned me the good news and was in a seventh heaven of happiness, for she had secretly been concerned about him.

With the shoulder worry out of the way, Carole was ready for fun. She had never been to Washington, D.C., and the Shoreham Hotel there was their next stop. Carter Barron, then division manager for Loew's Theaters, was their unofficial host and plotted regular sight-seeing tours of the city for them, managing to keep publicity at a minimum.

They visited the Capitol, the White

House, the Lincoln Memorial and the Washington Monument. I got a string of postcards of the "Having a good time, wish you were here" type.

Carole had the best time of all at Mount Vernon, where she went into ecstasies over the antique furniture. The guides at Mount Vernon are well trained, steeped in historical data, and have the lore of the place at their finger tips; but Carole stumped one of them. She spotted a chair she liked particularly and got into a friendly debate with the guide as to whether or not it was of English or American manufacture. The attendant was sure it was English. Carole was positive it was Early American. "I've got one like that at home," she said.

A search of the records was made. Carole was right—the chair had been made by an American craftsman.

"Ma was a gracious winner," Clark said. "She complimented the guide on having such a wonderful knowledge of the period."

As they left, Carole told Clark that Mount Vernon had given her some new ideas for the ranch house.

"I like it the way it is," Clark replied, "but go ahead. I knew this was going to cost me money."

Here and there they were recognized, and fans pushed close for autographs. Carole always signed herself "Carole Lombard Gable." She was proud of her husband and her name.

Word of their presence in the city reached the White House. President Roosevelt was about to give one of his famous fireside chats. He invited Carole and Clark to sit with a group of guests in his study while he went on the air. This was a proud moment for both of them.

Afterwards the President had them remain for a visit, questioning them closely about the film industry and their careers. He was most interested, for he was aware of the publicity Carole had garnered in 1937 when she paid 85 per cent of the four hundred and sixty-five thousand dollars she earned that year in state and federal income taxes and announced that she was glad to do it because she was proud of being an American. "I enjoy this country," she had declared, at the time, "and I like everything the government does for its citizens."

Carole was still excited about the White House visit on her return. "Just think, Jeanie," she said, wide-eyed, "Pa and me sitting there pretty as you please—talking to the *President of the United States!*"

They Met in Bombay began shooting early in the spring of 1941. Rosalind Russell, who had made such a hit in *The Women* and was now one of Metro's top stars, played opposite Clark.

Clarence Brown directed and Peter Lorre and Jessie Ralph had supporting roles in this story of a couple who were partners in a series of jewel thefts in the Orient. To escape the police, the man Clark portrayed donned a uniform and impersonated a British officer, and when World War II broke out he distinguished himself in action and won the Victoria Cross. Clark thought Rosalind was a fine actress and respected her very much.

The Gables' second wedding anniversary, March 29, occurred during the filming of *Bombay*. Carole staged a surprise party for Clark on the set. She had the Brown Derby send over champagne, roast turkey and all the trimmings, and assisted in serving the cast and crew. Everything was in pairs or doubles—presents, refreshments, gags—because they'd been married two years.

Russ and I started building our own home in March 1941. Until this time we'd been living in Westwood, and Russ, a Bell and Howell executive, had a long drive into Hollywood while I had the trip to the San Fernando Valley each morning and evening. This commuting was time-consuming and not very practical for either of us, so we acquired a lot in Sherman Oaks, high in the hills overlooking the valley as the site of a home that would be close to both our places of work.

Because I'd fallen in love with the Early American atmosphere of the Gable home, Russ and I designed a modest gray shingle Cape Code house and engaged Kersey Kinsey, a good builder, to do the construction work.

When Clark saw the plans, he was so intrigued that he decided to build a similar home for Father Gable on nearby Ethel Avenue in North Hollywood, and asked Mr. Kinsey to handle this also. Both houses were less than five miles from the ranch.

The construction of the two homes went forward simultaneously and Clark and Carole drove up every Sunday to check progress on both.

Father Gable's house was larger than ours and featured a huge living-dining room, which opened into a playroom and thence to a patio. There were three bedrooms, two baths, a kitchen and pantry. A lovely sycamore stood on the front lawn. Carole had the painters paint the exterior of the house the exact shade of the gray of the tree. She also selected the color scheme for the interiors, the drapes and carpets.

Father Gable was delighted with his house, though he was never one to show enthusiasm. He insisted on doing all the landscaping himself and Edna and Pinkie could hardly wait to move in.

Our house was designed so that each room afforded us an imposing view of the valley. A huge white fireplace dominated the raftered living-dining room, which was flanked on one side by a breakfast room and kitchen and on the other by two bedrooms, dressing rooms and baths. Beyond the house, and in view of the living room, we built a covered patio and barbecue of white brick.

Carole said she'd like to make a film record of the Garceau's building problems, as so many amusing incidents arose—although they didn't seem amusing at the time, at least not to us.

Russ and I had made a pact that we had to agree before we made any important decision about the house or the decorating. Morning after morning I'd arrive at work in a quandary because we couldn't decide whether the hood over the stove was to be of wood or metal, or if the period wallpaper should be yellow or green. Carole frequently acted as referee, and made the decisions for us. She had exquisite taste and a real flair for decorating.

I had insisted on a spacious bathroom and the Gables helped make ours glamorous by giving us the white marble for the counters.

When we moved into the new place in July, Clark and Carole sent us our dining room furniture: Early American sawbuck table, hutch and chairs, all made by Rennick, a noted period furniture expert. They also sent us a set of pink English dinnerware for the hutch.

Carole remembered moving day at the ranch and had the Brown Derby send us our dinner that night. Never has anything been more welcome to two tired people. The fireplace was so beautiful that after dinner we could not resist building a fire in it, although the summer evening was extremely warm.

It was soon so hot in the house that we couldn't bear it and had to go outside. Clark and Carole drove up a little later to inspect the new home and found the Garceaus peering in the windows at the charming firelit scene, exclaiming over and over, "Isn't it wonderful!"

Father Gable and family moved their own loved and familiar home furnishings into their place on Ethel Avenue a short time after, and Carole had a gay housewarming for them.

"Pa had such a bad time of it with Father Gable when he was a boy," Carole told me, "it's a joy for him to be on good terms with his Dad."

For some time Carole had been unhappy with her representation by the Myron Selznick Agency. She felt that Myron was not doing his best by her and she asked for a release from her contract. Myron refused.

Carole then asked Clark's lawyer, W. I. Gilbert, Sr., to handle the case for her. Mr. Gilbert tried to effect an amicable settlement of her contract, but Myron was adamant; so the case went to an arbitration court.

Carole and I attended the hearings, which were held before three arbitrators and stretched over a period of several weeks. One amusing incident came to light during the proceedings. There was a quirk in the contract Carole and Myron had signed. At the time of signing, Carole, as a gag, had inserted a clause giving *her* 10 per cent of *his* earnings; Myron had signed it without noticing.

The case was finally decided in Carole's favor, and she obtained her release. Under the terms of settlement, Myron was still to collect a percentage of Carole's earnings for films he had negotiated for her, but had no claim on her earnings thereafter.

The case was widely acclaimed, as it set a precedent in the industry and was the first time a star had ever been able to break an unsatisfactory agency contract.

It was a joy to watch Mr. Gilbert work. At first I was worried, for he seemed to doze frequently and to be oblivious to what was going on around him. But let a vital point arise and he was on his feet in an instant, hotly challenging his legal opponent. He was a noted lawyer and had handled many important cases. Shortly after Carole's case was settled, he passed on; his son, W. I. Gilbert, Jr., took over the Gables' legal affairs.

Thereafter Nat Wolff became Carole's agent. Nat had once been a member of the Selznick staff, but was now in business for himself. Carole felt he was a "go-getter" and both she and Clark liked him and Edna Best, his wife.

Metro-Goldwyn-Mayer had a script called *Honky Tonk*, the story of a fascinating, fast-talking con-man-about-town in the West who falls for and marries a beautiful but proper Boston belle. Clark was beginning to be concerned over the roles given him since *Gone With the Wind*, and decided that the character of the hell-raising gambler in *Honky Tonk* was made to order for him; the studio bosses, however, did not see eye-to-eye with him on this.

"I'm sticking my neck out, I know," Clark told Carole, "but I want this role and I'm going to fight for it." He had his way, but there were still misgivings on the part of the studio brass.

Lana Turner, then a rising young star, was assigned to play opposite him; Frank Morgan and Claire Trevor were also in the cast, which was directed by Jack Conway. Chill Wills was engaged to teach Clark the card tricks required in his role as a gambler. Clark became very proficient at these and used to entertain friends at the ranch with his "the hand is quicker than the eye" card routines.

The film, a mixture of comedy, sex and the Wild West, was shot in record time. Lana was very nervous when the portrait stills were shot; Clark and Stan, his make-up man, and the still-cameraman clowned to make her laugh and relax enough so they could shoot the pictures.

There were no tennis courts at the ranch, so while Clark was busy at the studio, Carole played tennis with Alice Marble in Bel Air. Carole had taken lessons from Alice's tennis coach, the famous Eleanor Tennant, and both enjoyed their games together.

Clark liked to fish as well as hunt, and he and Carole frequently went up to the Rogue River in Oregon with the Fleischmanns to visit Clark's old friends the Gibsons, who owned the famous We Ask U Inn sportman's lodge. The Gables had always occupied a favorite cabin down by the river, but their trip this year was spoiled by the young people of the vicinity who surrounded their cabin at night, knocked on the windows and were very noisy and objectionable.

Clark decided to leave the next morning, so they drove the Fleischmanns back to Bakersfield and then he and Carole went on to Lake Meade, near Las Vegas. There they rented a cabin cruiser and went on a three-day fishing trip, preparing their own meals and sleeping aboard the boat.

Honky Tonk was previewed in mid-September. Clark and Carole rarely went to previews, but they attended this one.

"If I'm wrong about this picture, I want to be there and face the music," Clark said.

He and Carole held hands all during the showing of the film. The reaction to the picture was sensational. Everyone agreed that the studio had a hit on its hands and that Clark and Lana were the newest and hottest "love team" on the screen. All the executives congratulated Clark.

When the film went into general release, the public confirmed the verdict of the preview cards. The trade journals described the picture as "box-office dynamite."

Carole was greatly intrigued with the script of *To Be or Not To Be*, which she signed to do that fall for United Artists. The background was Warsaw, and the story had a strong anti-Nazi theme. Carole was to play a Polish actress, the wife of a "ham" actor, Jack Benny. Together they outwit the Gestapo, escaping Poland and parachute to safety in England.

Robert Stack, Lionel Atwill and Sig Ruman were in the cast, Ernst Lubitsch was to direct, and Carole felt that the role was a challenging one and would be important in her career.

That fall, the Gables invited the Fleischmanns to fly to Watertown, South Dakota, for the opening of the duck and pheasant season. Carole had a new mink-lined hunting jacket Irene had made her which she was dying to wear, and it was packed along with all their other gear and the guns. Clark bought corsages for both girls and they were a gay foursome at the take-off.

"Everything that could happen, happened," Clark told me later.

First, their plane was grounded by bad weather in Albuquerque. The airline put them on a train for Kansas City, where they were to make other plane connections—but by the time they got there, they had missed that plane.

They were taken to the Muehlbach Hotel in Kansas City, where an indifferent hotel clerk assigned them two very small rooms. They had barely settled down when the hotel manager appeared, wringing his hands and apologizing. The room clerk had belatedly realized that he had *the* Clark Gable and Carole Lombard as guests. The manager insisted on moving them to the bridal suite, with an adjacent luxury suite for the Fleischmanns, and ordered a magnificent dinner sent up. Clark threatened to leave if the manager notified the press.

"We had a waiter standing behind each of our chairs at dinner," Carole said, "and you know how Pa hates formality."

Clark was very impatient at the thought of missing the opening of the season, so he called the airline and said, "You've *got* to get us out of here tonight."

Nothing was available except a huge transcontinental plane, which was put at their disposal. The four flew to Omaha, "rattling around like mad," as Carole described it. There they changed planes, reaching Watertown at two in the morning.

Arriving at the private home where they'd made arrangements to stay, they rushed into their hunting clothes,

were driven sixty miles, and were in the duck blinds at daylight when the season opened. They all shot their limit of ducks that morning.

The pheasant season was to open at one o'clock that same day. By that time it was raining hard, and Clark thought they ought to call it off, but Carole refused. "We came here to shoot pheasants," she said, "and that's what we'll do."

They trudged all day in the downpour.

"Did you see that?" Carole would squeal when she knocked a bird from the sky.

"She could hit and retrieve like a pro," Nan says.

"What a girl!" Clark said admiringly. It pleased him that she liked to rough it right along with him. All four got their limit of pheasants.

That night the word got around that they were in town and the townspeople surrounded the home where they were staying. They were trapped. "The phone rang all night and all day, until finally we took the receiver off the hook," Carole told me.

Back in Hollywood, a columnist put out the story that Clark was off hunting alone—that he and Carole had separated. This made the headlines. I was besieged at the office by calls from all the wire services and local reporters.

I tried to get through to the Gables at Watertown, but the receiver was off the hook. The Watertown operator and I went round and round in argument. Finally I asked her if there wasn't some sort of a buzzer she could use to attract attention to the phone.

"It'll make a terrible noise," she warned.

"I don't care," I replied. "I've got to get through."

It worked. Soon I had both Clark

and Carole on the line and told them what the headlines were saying.

They both laughed. "Forget it," Clark said.

They decided it was better not to deny the story—just to let it die of inanition; and so it did. This taught me a lesson. Thereafter I was never disturbed over false news stories, especially when I knew the facts.

It continued to rain in South Dakota, so the party decided to ship their luggage, hunting gear and the birds and fly directly home.

With luggage gone, they discovered all the planes were grounded. Clark solved their transportation problem by buying a Ford, and they started home with nothing but the clothes they wore and their toothbrushes.

En route they stopped for the night at motels. Harry was the "front man" and engaged rooms for the four, then Clark and Carole slipped in quietly. Their meals were sent in and they managed to avoid any publicity along the line.

When they got home Clark and Carole made a sudden decision. They were fed up with trying to maintain a degree of privacy at home and abroad.

"Let's put the ranch up for sale and take our chances on finding the place we want by the time we sell it," he said.

CHAPTER SEVEN

CLARK and Carole were having a quiet Sunday at the ranch when the news of Pearl Harbor was flashed by radio on the morning of December 7, 1941.

Russ and I had just come home from church when they phoned us to know if we'd heard the bulletins. "We're going to write President Roosevelt, offering our services wherever needed," Clark told me.

Carole was in the final stages of shooting *To Be or Not To Be* and had left for the studio when I arrived at the ranch Monday morning. Clark dictated his letter to President Roosevelt and we dispatched it by air mail. A few days later, a reply came. The President expressed his gratitude for their offer, but reminded the Gables that entertainment was a vital factor in wartime morale. "You are needed where you are," he wrote.

Clark and Carole were both disappointed. The United States was mobilizing on all fronts and they wanted to have an integral part in this, do something more specific than "just keeping on doing what we'd do anyway," as Clark put it.

The war did put a stop to the plan to sell the ranch, however. We'd had two tentative offers, both of which Clark refused to consider, and he now asked me to take the property off the market.

Soon requests for Hollywood stars and personalities to appear at various bond rallies, camp shows, and patriotic functions of all kinds all over the nation began pouring in.

A Hollywood Victory Committee, composed of the Screen Writers Guild, the Screen Actors Guild, and various other guilds and talent agencies in the motion picture industry was organized to coordinate these activities. William Dover of Famous Artists Agency was drafted to set up the mechanics of procedure and to direct activities. Clark was appointed chairman of the Screen Actors Division.

"Jeanie, will you volunteer and be my secretary at the meetings, help me handle the work?" he asked. I was glad to comply.

The first meeting was held in mid-December at the Hollywood-Roosevelt Hotel in Hollywood, and the turnout was tremendous. All the stars were there. I found myself as thrilled as any tourist at seeing all my favorites.

Clark, as chairman, made a speech, outlining the work of the committee and his hope that every star would pledge his services. Enthusiasm was high, and the meeting was most successful.

The planning and paper work for the committee was considerable, and Christmas was upon us before I knew it. Clark and Carole conferred with me over their Christmas lists. Both felt that this was no time for the usual presents and celebrations.

"We'll just send out cards, notifying people that we're making a gift to the Red Cross and other charities in their names," Carole said. "We won't do any Christmas shopping this year."

Naturally it was a great surprise

when a handsome bedroom set for our new home was delivered Christmas Eve, as a gift from the Gables. Carole had ordered Rennick to make twin New England beds, night stand, desk and corner washstand of the "Beehive" type, to complete our Early American decor.

Accompanying the furniture were individual plaques to be hung over the beds. One read "MERRY CHRISTMAS— Jean, 1941, from Carole and Clark." The other was similarly inscribed to Russ.

"You and Russ are part of our family, Jeanie," Clark said when I protested this generosity in wartime. "We wouldn't think of cutting out presents to you."

His gift to Carole was a pair of diamond and ruby clips to match her ring and her ruby heart. Carole was thrilled over them and wore them constantly. Her "special" present to him was a very elegant, very thin gold cigarette case, engraved with a personal message. It became Clark's favorite case.

Clark's new picture, *Somewhere I'll Find You*, with Lana Turner, was scheduled to begin in mid-January. Before starting, he decided to go to Washington to discuss his personal situation with General "Hap" Arnold of the Air Force. He was still not satisfied at being "sidelined," and he thought possibly he could get into the service in some useful capacity. Carole, of course, thought he should be commissioned as an officer immediately.

"She won't settle for anything less than a colonel," Clark said.

Before he left, a request came in to the Victory Committee concerning Carole. She'd been born in Fort Wayne, Indiana, and, as a native Hoosier, she was asked to star in the nation's first war rally in Indianapolis on January 15, to launch the Indiana campaign for the sale of Defense bonds being sponsored by the governor, the State Defense Bonds Committee, and the United States Treasury Department.

Carole was eager to have Clark go with her, but this was impossible if he was to make the Washington trip as planned and still start his picture on schedule.

"Bessie's a Hoosier, too," he said. "Why not take her along? I'll ask Otto Winkler to go with you in my place, just to keep an eye on you dames," he grinned.

I was dying to go too, and while plans were being discussed I asked if I might be included. Carole thought it would be unwise to take along a "retinue," since this was wartime and she was on official government business.

"Wait, Jeanie, and we'll take a trip together later," she promised. "We'll go to New York, see all the shows, buy all the clothes, and have a grand time."

We began preparations for her trip. Irene designed and made the wardrobe she would need: a slim, severe black street dress, with a coat, toque and muff of broadtail for daytime appearances and a beautiful strapless black velvet gown for the evening occasion. With this Carole was to wear a cape of silver fox.

Carole wore no other jewels except her ruby and diamond clips, with the matching ring, which Clark had given her.

Bessie was to be equally glamorous in a black daytime dress and a gray feather toque, and she, too, had a black gown and a fox jacket for evening wear.

MGM's publicity department

Inspecting an army plane at Douglas Aircraft Company. (1941)
COURTESY OF FRED PETERS

helped in the preparation of Carole's speech. We rehearsed it until she was letter-perfect.

Carole was to travel by train with special arrangements made for stops at Salt Lake City, Chicago, and way points, to permit brief station appearances, press interviews, and platform talks in support of the War Bond and Stamps sales campaign.

Unfortunately, Carole's departure was scheduled the day before Clark was to return. She hated to leave without seeing him, since this was the first time they had been separated for any length of time, and she wanted to be at home when he got there. She wrote a series of little notes, one for each of the days she expected to be away, and directed me to be sure to give him one each morning.

Carole was not overly affectionate or demonstrative with her women friends, and had never put her arms about me or even kissed me until now. But when she was ready to leave, she hugged me hard, kissed me, and said: "Take care of my old man for me, will you, Jeanie? You know you'll be working with him more and more now."

She left on a very quiet and rather sad note—which was unlike her, usually so gay and lighthearted.

Clark came home the next day and he and Carole were on the phone constantly. Carole called from Salt Lake, where they'd made a whistle stop, telling about the huge crowds that had greeted her despite the ten-below temperature.

Her next call was from Ogden, Utah, and she asked to speak to me. "I know it's peaceful there without me," she teased. "Bet you haven't a thing to do. Did Clark tell you that we really killed them at Salt Lake?"

There was a call from her when they stopped at Chicago on Wednesday. On the morning of Thursday, the fifteenth, Carole and party arrived in Indianapolis, and were immediately caught up in a whirlwind of activity, culminating in a big rally at Cadle Tabernacle, which lasted far into the night.

At four o'clock on the morning of the sixteenth, Carole, Bessie and Otto boarded a plane for Los Angeles. She wired me in midmorning from Kansas City, saying she was dead-tired and eager to get home, and wanted me to have Peggy and Bucket at the house the next morning to do her hair and nails.

On the evening of the sixteenth Clark returned to the ranch after his first day's shooting on *Somewhere I'll Find You*. He was in a state of excitement over Carole's arrival. He'd planned a wonderful homecoming; Carole's brothers, Stuart and Freddie, Freddie's wife Virginia, and Jill Winkler, Otto's wife, were invited for dinner.

When I left that evening the table was set, fresh flowers were everywhere; the place looked very gay and beautiful. Carole was due in a couple of hours.

Russ and I were at home when Clark called about eight o'clock. "Ma's plane is down," he said. "Howard and Ralph Wheelwright are picking us up and Jill and I are going out to the airport to check on it. I'll call you later."

We were not unduly alarmed, because Carole's plane had been down once before when she was returning from location. She'd laughed and made a big story out of it.

We turned on the radio. Reports were coming in that the plane was down, its location unknown. Then

Carole's brothers called—and suddenly things began to look very serious. Stuart joined Clark at the airport.

Shortly thereafter, Clark called again, with the report that the plane was down near Las Vegas.

"Howard has chartered a plane and we're all flying over there," he said. "I'll keep in touch with you at the ranch."

Jill, Stuart, Howard, and Ralph Wheelwright of the studio's publicity department were on the plane with Clark. Freddie and Virginia started the six-hour drive to Las Vegas in their car. Russ and I left for the ranch. The Langs joined us there, together with Phil Berg and the Goffs.

When Clark's party arrived in Las Vegas, they went directly to the sheriff's station. The Mayor, Howell Garrison, was there with a group of deputies, local men, and Military Police from nearby Nellis Air Force Base.

They were looking over maps of the area, plotting routes prior to sending rescue parties up the mountains to the crash. Art Cheyney, a Western Air Lines pilot, had spotted the wreck and radioed back that it was afire. No one paid any particular attention to Clark and the others, but continued their discussions as to the best route to the crash.

"How do you know the plane is there?" Clark asked one.

"Because it's on fire," the man replied. "The flames shot up two or three hundred feet."

"My wife is on that plane," Clark said quietly.

"Clark's face whitened," Ralph recalls. "I think he *knew*, then."

Their route plotted, the rescue parties started out. Clark insisted on going along, but Howard and Eddie Mannix held him back, persuaded him to wait. Eddie and Ralph would go up the mountain with the others. "We'll come back for you when we locate the plane," they promised. Clark, Jill, Stuart and Howard went to El Rancho Vegas to wait for news.

Two rescue parties of deputies, army recruits, miners and ranch men started up the snow-covered, barren, flint rock mountain side, with a pack train of horses and mules.

Eddie Mannix and Ralph tore their shoes to ribbons in the seven-mile climb over the rugged terrain. Hours later, they reached the wreckage. The transport had crashed into the Table Rock Mountain, only two hundred feet below the crest, then fallen into a steep ravine. Flames had melted the snow and scorched the trees all around. There were no survivors. Ralph and Eddie identified Carole. A charred script lay near her hand.

Eddie and Ralph started back down the mountain. Halfway down, they found a little way station hooked into a telegraph line. Ralph asked the station agent to send a telegram to Clark. The wire read: NO SURVIVORS. ALL KILLED INSTANTLY.

"I knew I had to make it plain to Clark immediately that Carole and her mother and Otto had not suffered," Ralph says.

At El Rancho Vegas, Clark had been pacing the floor like a man possessed, waiting for news. When Ralph's wire arrived, he was out on a little balcony alone, looking up at the stars. Howard took the wire to him.

For us, the group at the ranch, the suspense was dreadful. Clark had called on arrival at Las Vegas; he told us that the search parties had started out and that he would relay any further information. The servants kept vigil with us. Jessie was quite calm, but Martin and Juanita were visibly upset.

At first we all kept up a steady stream of small talk, as people do when they are desperately worried yet wish to put the best possible face on things. We kept reassuring each other that the plane would be found, that Carole and Bessie and Otto were all right. Injured, perhaps, but alive. As the night wore on, however, we slowly lapsed into a strained, hopeless sort of silence, each busy with his thoughts—and prayers.

At four o'clock in the morning Clark called.

"Ma's gone," he said simply.

My one thought was to comfort him as best I could, but it was hard to speak when my own grief was so great. Clark told me that he'd have to stay on there in Las Vegas for a day or so—until the rescue parties came down the mountain.

When Eddie Mannix and Ralph got back to the hotel they found Clark more composed than anyone in the party. "Jill was hysterical and Clark really stood by," Ralph says.

Clark questioned Ralph about Carole.

"She never knew what happened," Ralph reassured him.

"Thanks," Clark said.

At midnight, Al Menasco heard the news over the radio and called Clark in Las Vegas immediately. He talked to Howard, who urged him to come on over. "He said Clark wasn't eating or sleeping and would talk to no one," Al said.

Despite the good work of the Military Police and others at the scene, there was some looting at the wreck. The next day two gunnery school recruits approached Ralph. One of them had a newspaper picture of Carole, showing the ruby and diamond clips she wore. The soldier showed Ralph a portion of one of the clips which he'd found at the wreck. It was badly damaged, but identifiable as Carole's. He wanted to sell it to Clark.

Ralph remonstrated with him, pointing out that it was a cruel thing to try to *sell* Clark his wife's clip.

"But I ought to get *something* for it," the man said.

Ralph suggested that a jail term might be appropriate. He persuaded the man to relinquish the clip, and gave him a receipt for it.

Later, through the cooperation of the air base officers and the M.P.'s, all the articles stolen from the wreck were recovered, including Otto's watch, which had been a present to him from Clark.

When Al Menasco arrived, he found Clark sitting in his room alone, red-eyed, unshaven. Clark wanted Al, a former pilot, to help him figure out how the crash occurred.

"Why did this happen, Al?" he asked.

"I was hard-put to answer," Al recalls. "I took him for a drive in my car and let him talk. He wanted me to show him where the plane had crashed, so we drove to a point at the foot of the mountain where we could see the plane wreck from afar. I tried to explain from a technical standpoint what I thought *might* have happened. This seemed to satisfy him. We drove around for a couple of hours and then returned to the hotel. Clark ate his first meal then."

Other friends rallied around, among them Spencer Tracy and Phil Berg. All reported that as the exhausted men of the search parties came down the mountain, Clark met them and was the calmest, the most restrained, of those around him. He waited on the weary men hand and foot, ordered steaks and coffee for them, and helped serve the food.

"Grief usually makes men completely self-centered," Ralph says. "Clark was just the opposite in his agony. He was so kind, so solicitous of everyone. And so grateful to the soldiers from the air base for the way they had helped out."

One little man, a deputy coroner, had worked tirelessly. Clark noticed that he had difficulty eating because he had no teeth. Clark slipped Ralph a hundred-dollar bill and said, "Give it to that little guy and tell him to get himself some teeth."

Meanwhile the radio and newspapers carried full details of the air tragedy and the bond rally in Indianapolis.

Carole's day had begun with a flag-raising ceremony in front of the State House in Indianapolis. Surrounded by Governor Henry F. Schricker, Mayor Reginald H. Sullivan of Indianapolis, and Will H. Hays, head of Motion Picture Producers-Distributors of America, she'd reviewed a Culver Military Academy color guard.

Governor Schricker then introduced her as "The Little Hoosier girl who'd made good in Hollywood" and Carole had made her speech. "Heads up, hands up, America!" she'd cried. "Let's give a cheer that will be heard in Tokyo and Berlin!"

Moving inside to a table in the crowded rotunda of the State House, she'd started the bond sale with a gay "Let's go!" Each purchaser received a small certificate bearing Carole's autographed picture and a message from her: "Thank you for joining with me in this vital crusade to make America strong."

The crowds surged forward to buy. Young, old, many with babies in their arms, patiently waited their turn. The *Indianapolis News* reported that not one bought without a personal word from Carole.

"Glad to see you. Yes, I'm fine, and so is Clark. How many? Thanks. How nice of you. Tired? Oh no, this is fun!"

So it went, all that hectic morning.

"How are we doing?" Carole asked at noon.

"Past the million mark," was the answer.

"Let's make it two," Carole said, and went back to selling.

Late that afternoon, still gay and charming, she appeared at a tea for county and city chairmen in the Women's Defense Bond Committee and various other women's organizations.

"Your chief work is to keep up the morale, just as you maintain morale in your own homes," she told them.

Over ten thousand people crowded into Cadle Tabernacle that night, to hear Eugene C. Pulliam, Chairman of the Indiana Defense Savings Staff, introduce Carole as "Indiana's Number One saleslady," and report that she'd sold over two million dollars in bonds and stamps that day. "I hope they can hear me in Tokyo," he said.

There were concerts by the Purdue and Indiana University bands; songs, speeches; and then Carole, radiant in her black velvet gown, led the audience in singing "The Star-Spangled Banner."

When it was all over late that night, Carole was exhausted. She had but one thought: to get back to Clark and the ranch. She told Otto she wanted to fly home. They reached the airport at four in the morning. The first flight out had no sleeping accommodations. Otto suggested that they take the train, to get a good night's sleep in a pullman berth.

Carole vetoed this plan. She didn't mind sitting up on the plane. "I'm so tired I could sleep anywhere," she said, "and I want to get back to Pa."

Bessie was a devotee of astrology and numerology. Friends said later that she checked the number of the plane, the number of the flight, and other data, and then sided with Otto about the train. "Carole, we must not take this plane," she said.

Carole laughed, and overruled them both.

There were no jets in those days, and planes were much slower. Their flight reached Albuquerque, New Mexico, in late afternoon. Fifteen Air Force officers and men were waiting at Alburquerque for transportation to their base on the California coast. Four passengers gave up their seats to make room for them. Three of these were women, and the fourth was violinist Joseph Szigeti.

At dusk, the plane reached Las Vegas and took off again after a brief stop, only to crash and burn a half-hour later.

Telegrams, telephone calls, letters began pouring in at the ranch. President Roosevelt sent Clark a wire reading:

MRS. ROOSEVELT AND I ARE DEEPLY DISTRESSED. CAROLE WAS OUR FRIEND, OUR GUEST IN HAPPIER DAYS. SHE BROUGHT GREAT JOY TO ALL WHO KNEW HER AND TO MILLIONS WHO KNEW HER ONLY AS A GREAT ARTIST. SHE GAVE UNSELFISHLY OF HER TIME AND TALENT TO SERVE HER GOVERNMENT IN PEACE AND IN WAR. SHE LOVED HER COUNTRY. SHE IS AND ALWAYS WILL BE A STAR, ONE WE SHALL NEVER FORGET NOR CEASE TO BE GRATEFUL TO. DEEPEST SYMPATHY.

The *New York Times* and other leading newspapers carried editorial tributes to Carole. The *Times* said, "Like the army pilots who fell from the burning plane with her, she too died in the service of her country."

The United States Senate stopped in midmorning to hear a brief tribute paid by Senator Willis of Indiana to Carole, whom he praised as "a great actress and a loyal citizen."

In Las Vegas the bodies from the plane wreck were slowly brought down and taken to a barn, where the mayor (who was also the coroner and under-taker) held an inquest. Howard and Eddie Mannix refused to let Clark attend, so Ralph made the offical iden-tification of Carole, Bessie and Otto. Ralph cut a lock of Carole's long blond hair and put it in an envelope in case there was any question. (Ralph later gave this to me to keep for Clark.)

When it was all over, Clark and his party started home by train, with the bodies aboard. En route that night, Clark visited Ralph in his Pullman room. "I understand you have some-thing of Carole's," he said.

"I had cleaned up the clip as best I could," Ralph says. "I handed it to him. Clark took it in his hand, stood looking down at it for a moment; then, without saying a word, he went back to his own compartment."

They left the train at Colton, the station before Pasadena, and the party went to Al Menasco's house at San Gabriel to wait until it was time to go to Forest Lawn Memorial Park to make funeral arrangements.

Clark had called me from Las Vegas, asking me to meet him at the Park that morning. This was one of the saddest moments of my life. I was shocked to see the change in him. He seemed to have aged years, was hollow-eyed with grief and loss of sleep. My own feeling of loss over Carole and Bessie, who had been like a mother to me, was deep.

Because Carole had been on a patriotic mission for her country, there was an official wire from the Defense Department at Washington, offering a military funeral. An elaborate memorial service and a huge mausoleum were being urged by others. Clark was hesitant.

I was privy to Carole's will and knew of her desire for a simple funeral, with expense kept within the bounds of good taste, and no publicity. She'd even specified the order of service and the Bible texts to be read. Quietly, I outlined her wishes to Clark and he quickly vetoed all other funeral suggestions, ordering things as Carole wanted them. At that time he selected simple crypts for Carole and her mother, and one for himself.

"This is to be a private funeral for Mrs. Elizabeth Peters and her daughter Carole," he said.

The services were held at the Church of the Recessional in Forest Lawn on January 22, 1942. They were conducted by the Reverend Gordon C. Chapman of Westwood Hills Methodist Church. Only members of the immediate family and a few close friends were in attendance.

The service was as Carole had directed. No ritual prayers, no songs or hymns, no music other than the organ. The Reverend Chapman read from the fourteenth chapter of John and the Twenty-third Psalm. A four-line poem loved by Carole and Bessie was recited, followed by a simple affirmation of faith. It was over.

We all went back to the ranch with Clark. Howard Strickling, Eddie Mannix, Nat Wolff and his wife and a few other intimate friends spent the evening there. Harry Fleischmann planned to stay with Clark several days.

During the evening, I went into my office to attend to several details and Clark followed me, closing the door behind him. I still had a last note from Carole, which she'd asked me to give him if she did not arrive on schedule. I felt he should have it now.

Up until this time, Clark had borne himself with fortitude and courage, stronger than any of us throughout the entire ordeal. When he read her note, he broke down completely.

It is a dreadful thing to see and hear a strong man cry. My own heart was so full I felt it would be cruel to witness his agony. To spare him embarrassment, I turned to leave but he caught my hand and held it. All I could do was stand by his side, lending what strength and comfort I could muster until he was calm again.

That night, in my office at the ranch, we said our good-byes to Carole. After that Clark was in perfect control, his grief masked. He asked no sympathy, wanted none, was unapproachable.

Howard had told me that Clark was afraid that I might not want to stay on at the ranch now that Carole was gone.

Before we rejoined the others, Clark asked me if I would continue as before, in my capacity as his secretary-business-manager. There was no thought in my mind other than to remain and be of help to him if possible in the days ahead.

My warm and wonderful friendship with Carole was ended. Now I was to begin a close and rewarding association with Clark, one that was to last for eighteen years.

Young Sid Menasco, Al, and Clark astride motorcycles at Al's home, San Gabriel Valley. (1942) COURTESY OF AL MENASCO

Clark training at Officer's Candidate School in Miami, Florida. (1942)

CHAPTER EIGHT

OTTO WINKLER'S funeral and the desire to be of comfort to Jill put an additional strain on Clark. Harry Fleischmann had been staying at the ranch, and when it was all over, Clark drove to Harry's shooting lodge at Bakersfield and spent a few days with him and Nan. I set myself to the task of acknowledging the hundreds of letters and wires of condolence that were still pouring in.

Somewhere I'll Find You was deferred for several weeks. Upon Clark's return, he called W. I. Gilbert, Jr., his attorney, and we went about the sad business of settling Carole's estate. He waived his right to sue the airline. Clark wanted nothing for himself, but he felt there should be equitable settlements for Jill and Carole's brothers.

These were dark days for all of us, and there were many adjustments to make. I think the thing that brought Clark through this unhappy period was his kindness and consideration for others. He tried not to let his grief be a burden on us. We had many serious talks about the deeper, spiritual side of life, and I endeavored to help him as much as I could. In turn, he comforted me; for Carole had become such a part of my life that to go on without her was not easy. At no time did he seek forgetfulness or solace in liquor. In fact, he drank not at all during this period.

Clark thought at first that he should get rid of the ranch and we went through the business of looking at homes in Bel Air and Beverly Hills.

One of the houses we considered was Greta Garbo's home in Brentwood, which was up for sale. She had been the idol of my high school days and it was interesting to hear Clark tell of his experiences with her in making *Susan Lenox*. He thought she was a great artist.

We never found a house that seemed suitable, and I know that in his heart Clark could not have left the ranch, even if he *had* found another place. It has been reported many times that Clark made a shrine of Carole's room after her death. This is absolutely untrue. Clark was not a man to make a shrine of anything. He loved and grieved deeply, but there was nothing morbid in his grief. Carole's room and her things were left untouched for the simple reason that nothing could be moved or given away while the estate was in probate.

At the proper time Clark disposed of her wardrobe and personal possessions among her friends, and gave her horse, hunting clothes and hand-tooled leather saddle to Mrs. Valdez. He left her room and the rest of the house intact, for he loved his home and saw no necessity for changing anything.

Otto had wanted to build a home on property he owned across the street from the Stricklings. Clark told Jill to go ahead with the plans and he had a very attractive house built for her, which was her home for a number of years.

Carole owned forty-five acres of citrus land in the valley and had built a small but comfortable home there for the Claude Wises, a couple from Indiana, whom she and Bessie had cared for. We all called Mrs. Wise "Aunt Lottie," and one of the first things Clark now discussed with me was her well-being. Clark told her that the home was hers as long as she lived. When he sold the land some years later, he would not sign the papers until the subdividers built a comparable house on another lot for the Wises. The house was built to Aunt Lottie's specifications and we moved them in. They were both very grateful to Clark for his consideration and generosity.

Al Menasco and Clark became close friends now. Clark had a beautiful motorcycle, as did Al, and they rode a great deal together.

"We always rode toward Ventura at night," Al says, "and Clark never seemed to want to turn back even though it was often quite late and we were both half-frozen."

The motorcycle craze spread to others among Clark's cronies and he and Al frequently rode with the "gang"—which consisted of Bill Wellman and his wife, and Keenan Wynn, Andy Devine, Victor Fleming and Ward Bond.

They would roar out to Calabasas in the San Fernando Valley to a hill where the professional cyclists trained. The amateurs would sit around and watch the "pros" try to make it over the hill without a spill.

One day Keenan Wynn attempted the hill and went over the top successfully. Then Al tried it and made it. When he came around from behind the hill, he was puffed with pride, and started bragging about his riding skill. Clark and the rest of the gang pretended that they hadn't seen him do it.

"You'll have to prove it," Clark said.

"I had to do it again before they'd let me off," Al says.

"Clark wanted to make the ride up the hill," Al continues, "but he was no show-off; so he waited until we were alone— then he went over the top on the first try."

On another occasion the motorcycle gang rode over to the Goffs. Clark bragged to Andy Devine that he'd never had a spill. Ten minutes later, he hit a bad spot in the road and had a nasty fall, but was not hurt. Andy walked over and stood looking down at him, "Well, there's always a first time," he drawled in his gravelly voice.

They all bragged so much about their prowess that I began to think motorcyclists were bigger liars than fishermen and hunters.

On February 23, Clark went back to Metro to finish *Somewhere I'll Find You* with Lana Turner. Wesley Ruggles was directing the picture and had also been the director on the one picture Clark had made with Carole.

Ruggles gave cameraman Hal Rosson and the cast and crew strict instructions: "Let's not baby Clark— he's not that kind of man."

"Clark worked hard and asked no favors," Ruggles says. "Often, out of consideration for him, I'd want to quit shooting at five o'clock, but he'd say, 'Don't lay off so early—I want to work.'"

He usually got home long after six o'clock, but Jessie always had a good dinner ready for him. For the first two or three nights after he started back to work I waited to dine with him, to try to bridge the fact that he was coming home to an empty house. He saw only his most intimate friends in the evenings now, and rarely went out except to their homes.

It was touching to see how Carole's little dachshund, Commissioner, transferred his love and allegiance to Clark. Before her death, he used to growl when anyone, including Clark, approached her. Now he became Clark's dog entirely.

As the months passed, the change in Clark became obvious to us all. He seemed to tap deep reservoirs of strength within himself which carried him through. There was a new maturity about him, often an almost spiritual quality in his face, and we all felt that a stronger man was emerging from the tragic experience.

For some time Clark's desire to get into the war effort had been under discussion. Many people thought he should apply for a commission, and there is no doubt that, with his background, any branch of the service would have been delighted to give him one; but Clark was not interested.

"I don't want to sell bonds, I don't want to make speeches and I don't want to entertain, I just want to be sent where the going is tough," he said.

His picture finished shooting late in April and Clark and Al Menasco went to Phoenix, Arizona, for a few days. While there they had a chance meeting in a restaurant with Colonel Luke Smith, and it was he who encouraged Clark to join the Air Corps. They talked things over; Colonel Smith told Clark that their toughest recruiting job was for air gunners.

"Everyone wants to be a pilot," he said, "but you'd be doing a real service as a gunner. It would help to glorify the plane crews and the 'grease monkeys'."

Clark came home and announced his decision to enlist in the Air Corps. He put his affairs in order, and on August 12, 1942, Ralph Wheelwright drove him down to the recruiting office in the Federal Building in Los Angeles, where he was quietly sworn in by Colonel Malcolm P. Andruss. The time of his taking the oath had been kept secret to avoid crowds. There were photographers present, however, and Clark had to pose for pictures, although he had tried to avoid publicity.

Andrew ("Andy") J. McIntyre, a Hollywood cameraman, was inducted into the service at the same time, and after he and Clark had been given their shots, they received transportation and travel orders and Clark was put in charge to see that they arrived at their destination. "I enlist as a private," Clark said, "and find myself in charge of a two-man contingent."

Shortly thereafter I got a card from the United States Army stating that he had been accepted for active military service and was being sent to Fort MacArthur, California, and that I was not to try to communicate with him unless it was urgent.

The papers played up the story of Clark's enlistment. The fact that a $7500-a-week movie idol was going off salary and going into the service as a $66-a-month private, received much favorable comment. Army spokesmen said its effect on the morale of other servicemen was tremendous. He had many wires from various noncommissioned officers and their units, congratulating him. ("Actions like yours are actions that are gratifying to men like us.")

Within a few days I had a long-distance call from Clark, telling me that he and Andy had been advanced to the rank of corporal and were now at Officer Candidate School at Miami Beach, Florida, for a twelve-week training period. There would be no leave for the first six weeks and they had made him shave off his mustache!

"Don't fall over in a faint, Jeanie, but I'm up every morning at five o'clock and on the go every minute until lights-out at ten P.M.," he said. "Could you send me some of Jessie's gingerbread?"

Subsequent letters from him gave me details of his living quarters (three bunks to a barracks room and bath) and his grueling schedule of endless inspections, close-order drills, lengthy classes and calisthenics, interspersed with bedmaking, floor swabbing and intensive study. Clark, writing his letter in the bathroom after lights-out, indicated that the place was a "complete madhouse," but he was enjoying it. This was quite a change for a man who was accustomed to silk pajamas, breakfast in bed and a staff of servants to do his bidding!

Clark's classmates were all young men. It was somewhat difficult for a man of forty-one to adjust to the discipline—all the more so because every eye was upon him, and he had to be very careful to take what came without complaint. The weather was murderously hot, which added to the general discomfort, but Clark never wavered, and he soon won the respect and acceptance of the others.

Prior to his induction, Clark had made careful plans with me for keeping the ranch going and taking care of his business affairs while he was away. He was deeply appreciative of the loyalty and devotion of the servants, and while it was obvious that it would be impractical to keep a full staff, he wanted to make sure that they were provided for in his absence.

Arrangements were made for Martin to work in a defense plant and Jessie got another place as cook, with the proviso that when Clark returned, both she and Martin would enter his service again. Fred, the caretaker, and his wife had left us some time earlier; Roy, the new caretaker, was to remain to look after the livestock. Juanita, the maid, was also to stay on. "I'd rather lose an arm than let Martin and Juanita go," Clark said. "As for you, Jeanie," he went on, "I know your old man will be going too, and I don't want you worrying about the payments on your house. I'll take care of the balance while he's gone."

Before he left, Clark gave me the battered remains of Carole's ruby and diamond clip and asked me to have it fitted in a tiny gold case, which he wore around his neck, together with his service tags. The lock of her hair was put away in his safe-deposit box.

His farewell gifts to Howard and Gail Strickling, Jill Winkler, Russ and myself were gold identification bracelets, bearing our names and addresses.

About the time of his induction, Clark was gratified to learn that a newly recruited Indiana naval air squadron had named themselves the "Lombardiers" in honor of Carole and had adopted an insignia featuring her profile superimposed on an outline of the State of Indiana.

Howard Strickling suggested that I move Clark's personal effects from his dressing room at the studio, in case someone else might be assigned to it. I was glad that I did so, for I found a note from Carole to Clark which I put away in his safe-deposit box.

Clark either called or wrote with great regularity, and was hungry for news, insisting that I tell him every single detail of what was going on at the ranch. We had settled down on a tight wartime basis. We had only one cow now, and all but fifteen of the chickens were gone. Father Gable and I shared the milk and eggs. He came out two or three times a week and seemed to enjoy browsing around and talking about Clark's babyhood.

Mr. Valdez brought over a couple of his horses, which together with our Sonny and Melody kept the hay cropped down so there was no need to cut it. Clark wrote me to be sure to ride the horses, and "for goodness' sake use the good saddles." Russ's work at Bell and Howell had been classified as essential to defense, and the age limit of thirty-eight was now in effect, so he did not go into the service. We had some fine rides together at the ranch.

All of the food that Carole had bought and stored away, including the beans, had been sent to various hospitals by Clark; his cars had been jacked up in the garage; and he now suggested that I take over five new truck tires he had and put them on my car, turning my own tires in (as was now required) in place of the new ones. This was a boon to me and I was thus able to keep my car going all during the war.

Clark wrote to me and asked me to call all his friends and relay the news. In turn I acted as a clearinghouse for his personal mail, all of his friends sending their letters to me, and I forwarded them in packages, together with the endless business papers and checks requiring his signature. I kept him posted on ranch affairs, his father's activities, and the Hollywood and studio gossip; I advised him of Martin's high status among his fellow workers by virtue of his having worked for Clark Gable, and the fact that Jessie's new employer said she might make gingerbread in his kitchen on his time, to send to Clark, whenever she pleased!

The studio issued a steady stream of publicity stories on Clark's progress, and Howard Strickling sent several magazine writers out to the house to look around and get background for magazine articles on him.

Clark found the academic side of the training very tough but doggedly memorized the training manuals in the bathroom after hours. He and Andy had started in ten days behind their class but soon caught up.

The pressure of the last two weeks of training was intense. Clark wrote that many of the boys were being "washed out." The school had the reputation of being the toughest in the country, and he felt that they were trying to live up to the tradition.

Clark passed all his examinations and finished 700 in a class of 2600. He was graduated on October 29, 1942, and received his commission as first lieutenant from General Henry H. ("Hap") Arnold, the Air Force chief.

Clark was chosen by his classmates to reply to General Arnold's commencement address and his response was given wide publicity and later reprinted in *Education for Victory*, the bi-weekly magazine of the Federal Security Agency.

"I've worked with you, scrubbed with you, marched with you, worried with you over whether this day would ever come," he told them. "The important thing, the proud thing I've learned about us is that we are men. The discipline we have learned here has a national value, a world value today. It is proper that we should have learned it the hard way. We will keep it longer because of that."

"Soon we will wear the uniforms of officers. How we look in them is not very important. How we *wear* them is a lot more important. Multiply us by

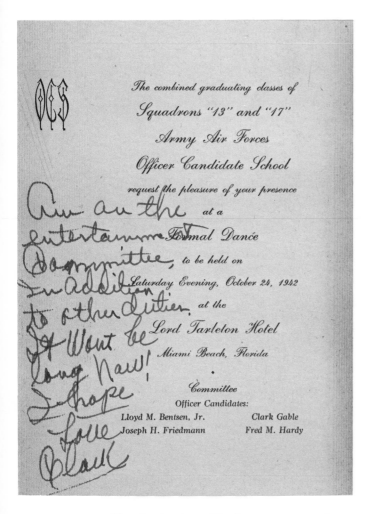

The invitation Clark sent to me for a formal dance celebrating the graduating class of his squadron from Officer Candidate School. (1942)

millions of other Americans and you have what it takes to win a war. The job is to stay on the beam until in victory we get the command 'Fall out.' "

Prior to graduation, there was a formal dance given by the graduating class. Clark was on the Entertainment Committee. He sent all of us invitations and said he would be unable to get home because he and Andy were being sent immediately to Gunnery School at Tyndall Field, Panama City, Florida. He was delighted at the prospect of getting out of the classroom, of using a gun instead of a pen!

When Clark arrived at Tyndall Field, he mailed me his OCS diploma and honorable discharge, and wired me an order for some uniforms to be made to his measurements. He had worn the GI issue all through the Miami experience in order not to be different in any way from his younger classmates. As an officer, however, he could have his uniforms custom made. He phoned me to send him his English shoes, and said he was letting his mustache grow back.

Once more he was plunged into classroom work, but as he told me, "if a man needs larnin' then larnin' is what he gets, in the Air Corps." He now began also to do a good deal of flying, which he liked very much, and said he thought he'd be able to get leave at the end of his first six weeks of duty and would come home.

At Tyndall, Clark met Lieutenant Norman Price and his wife Loulie, who lived in a bungalow court. Clark spent a good deal of his free time with the Prices. Loulie cooked dinner for them, and Clark and Norman sat about swapping service "shop talk." Norman later became a captain and he and Clark kept in touch for a while.

Juanita and I kept a steady supply

line of cookies and candies going to Clark, at his request, and he told me that he and his classmates enjoyed them very much. Early in December, he phoned me that he would be home on the eighteenth for a few days but would have to return to the base before Christmas. This was disappointing to all of us, but we decided to make the most of the time he did have at home.

Clark called me on December 18 and asked if I would meet him at the airport at eleven o'clock the next morning as he did not want anyone from the studio to meet him or to publicize his return. I was out there long before eleven and waited interminably, unable to check on the plane because it was Army and unscheduled. Finally he called home in the late afternoon, asked Juanita to page me at the airport and tell me that they were down in Texas somewhere with engine trouble and that I was not to wait for him.

I did wait, however, and he arrived at seven o'clock that night. He was happy to get home, but upset because I'd waited. He knew I was concerned particularly because of Carole's plane crash.

Clark looked wonderfully tanned and fit and said he'd begun to gain back the weight he'd lost at Officer Candidate School. Juanita had put the big pot in the little one and had all his favorite foods for dinner which he enjoyed so much. He made a tour of inspection of the place and was delighted with the way things were going.

Clark was at home only a few days, seeing only intimate friends, and we managed to get through the stacks of business matters waiting for his attention. He did take time out, though, to visit "Aunt Lottie" and satisfy himself that she was getting along all right and was well cared for.

Al had ordered two boxes of Golden Delicious apples from Wenatchee, Washington, to be sent to the house for Clark and one for Fieldsie and Walter Lang. Clark's arrived while he was at home, but the Langs' did not. Al asked Clark if he might give his box to the Langs, because he felt sure that the other would arrive any day.

"I like apples," Clark replied and that ended the matter. He kept them.

Jill Winkler planned a dinner party for Clark and called Virginia Grey to come over early and help her decorate her tree. When Virginia arrived, Clark was there. It had been several years since Clark had seen her and she had grown into a beautiful woman. This was the beginning of their wonderful friendship, which lasted many years.

When Clark was ready to leave, he asked me to drive him to his plane. He was flying in a B-17 and said that he would graduate as a gunner in January. There was some delay in the take-off, as the plane was still being checked over, so they permitted me to crawl into the fuselage. "Crawl" is the right word, for that is what I did, over mountains of apparatus and equipment. There was no space to walk or even stand up, and Clark and the other men had no place to sit except on the equipment. It was a thrill for me to see it and later, when Clark was in Europe, I was able to visualize the conditions under which he was flying.

He walked back to the car and sat with me while we waited for the plane. Clark was very quiet for a moment and then said, "Jeanie, you know I have everything in the world anyone could want but one thing. All I really need and want is Ma."

My heart sank, for I had hoped that he'd begun to be reconciled to her death. What *could* I say to comfort him? While I was frantically groping for the right words, they gave him the signal for the take-off. A hasty handshake, and he was gone.

Clark missed Christmas at home so we sent him his presents. I sent "store-bought" candy this time and a huge box of white camellias from the garden. The flowers arrived in good shape and he displayed them with pride, for many of the boys in Florida had never even seen one!

He was graduated on January 7, 1943, and received his gunnery officers wings from Colonel Warren A. Maxwell.

Just before graduation, Clark and his classmates had to pass a four-hour pressure-chamber test, wherein they were taken to a simulated altitude of thirty-eight thousand feet, in order to determine what altitude each man would qualify for.

Clark wrote Al Menasco a description of his experience in the chamber: the lightness of the air, the swelling in his body, and how various men were struck by various pains at different air levels, and had to be removed from the chamber one by one. Clark was taken out at thirty thousand feet with bends in his right leg. After being put in a reduction chamber until he recovered, he was taken up again to twenty-eight thousand feet, some of the men volunteering to go up without their oxygen masks, to demonstrate what would happen if you forgot your mask.

He reported that the man next to him began to turn blue at twenty thousand feet, was unable to solve a simple sum in addition, failed to write his name at twenty-five thousand feet and

after that began to pass out, so they put his mask on him.

When it was all over, Clark was qualified to fly at thirty thousand feet and had formed a deep attachment for his oxygen mask. Immediately thereafter he received his orders to go to Fort George Wright near Spokane, Washington, a replacement training center for B-17's and B-24's.

After several weeks of advanced gunnery training at Fort George Wright, Clark was given a special assignment by General "Hap" Arnold. He was ordered to assemble and take command of a photographic unit which would be sent to England to produce motion picture films on aerial gunners and their work, which was sorely needed at the time to simulate applications for gunnery training.

Lieutenant Andy McIntyre, Clark's classmate, was assigned to him as cameraman. Clark began a series of trips to various air bases, assembling and testing camera equipment and film, and recruiting his photographic crew.

He came home in February, this time bringing several of his fellow officers. He had asked me to meet him at Lockheed Airport in the San Fernando Valley and again I had a long wait. When his plane, a huge B-29, did come in, it overshot the field; and in taking off to gain altitude it skimmed so low that it barely missed the airport fences and the parked cars, giving everyone, including myself, the fright of our lives. They made the landing on the second attempt and Clark told me afterwards that they all had their "feet on the brakes."

Juanita had a wonderful dinner ready. I've never seen anyone eat like Clark and the men he brought home with him.

My next call from Clark came from Biggs Field in Texas, the staging area for the departure for the European Theater. Andy McIntyre had recommended Sergeants Mario Toti and Robert Boles as cameramen, and Clark had them assigned to the unit as Andy's assistants. Lieutenant Howard Voss, a sound man, and Lieutenant John Lee Mahin, a screen writer who'd worked on several of Clark's MGM films, completed the six-man crew headed by Clark. They called themselves the "Little Hollywood Group."

Clark made one other brief trip home to pick up film and camera equipment; he phoned me a few days later from Colorado Springs, where he'd gone on a few days' leave—then I heard nothing more until a regulation Form 206 government postcard arrived, stating that Lieutenant Clark Gable, 0-565390, had "arrived safely at a new destination."

The card was dated April 19, and we could see it was postmarked Presque Isle, Maine so we knew he was at the take-off point for Europe.

Thereafter I was besieged by phone calls and the oft-repeated question was, "Have you heard from Gable?"

Father Gable was the least concerned. "You don't need to expect to hear from Clark," he advised me matter-of-factly. "He left me in Oklahoma in 1922 and I didn't hear one word from him until 1928."

We were all greatly relieved to get a cable from Clark on April 24, saying that he had arrived in a beautiful country and all was well.

Of course we knew that the "beautiful country" was England and eventually we learned that Clark's unit was now with the 351st Bomber Group stationed at Peterborough Air Base, eighty miles from London. Colonel William S. Hatcher, their commanding officer, had been with them at Biggs Field and was a very special friend of Clark's. (Colonel Hatcher was later shot down, taken prisoner by the Nazis, and eventually released. Back in the United States after the war was over, he was accidentally killed while making a routine take-off.)

The 351st was a heavy bomber group and its men found, on arrival in England, that they were replacing a

This card, in Clark's handwriting, was the first news we had of his safe arrival overseas. (1943)

unit that had been virtually wiped out. Loss of men at that time was very heavy. Clark, John Lee Mahin and Andy received routine promotions to captain, Clark's getting the usual publicity splash in the newspapers.

Then for a month we heard nothing from him. Everyone worried until we decided to cable him. Back came a cable in reply, assuring us that everything was fine and that he'd written four or five letters. Sure enough, four "V-mail" missives turned up the next day in a bunch.

Censorship prevented Clark from giving details of his activities, but we heard a good deal about the English rain, the beauty of the flowers and green countryside, and his yearning for orange juice!

At first Clark's publicity created a problem for him. Once again, he had to "prove" to a group of much younger men on the base that he was not just a Hollywood star out for publicity, but a serious-minded officer engaged in an important assignment.

Clark flew his first mission as an observer in a B-17 in a raid on Antwerp in May 1943.

Thereafter, he flew four other missions in different B-17's, serving as gunner and taking 16-millimeter color film during actual combat over Nantes, Villacoublay, Gelsenkirchen and the Ruhr Valley, which the airmen dubbed "Happy Valley." On each occasion his plane was blasted by heavy fire and Clark narrowly escaped death in one raid when a shell passed within a few inches of his head.

He had refused to accept special living quarters and shared wooden barracks with the other men. After his first "baptism by fire," he became one of them, was accepted and liked. The men called him "Pappy" and would gather in his quarters to "shoot the breeze."

The fact that Clark was flying combat missions was known, of course, to the Germans. It was reliably reported all over the European theater that German Air Minister Hermann Goering had placed a high price on his head. Goering was said to have offered the equivalent of five thousand dollars in German marks, a two weeks' leave, and immediate promotion to any fighter pilot who could bring Clark Gable down, dead or alive!

The photographic unit not only recorded actual combat conditions but filmed scenes on the base, showing how the airmen lived and worked. Returning raiding crews were interviewed and photographed as well as the hospitalized wounded at Blackpool, an English seaside resort, where the Air Force maintained a rest, recreation and rehabilitation center.

"Clark worked very hard and was all business," Mario Toti recalls. "He had his whole heart and soul in it and said he was going to get the pictures he wanted even if Jerry dropped a bomb down the back of his neck."

Andy McIntyre flew a good many missions and on his return one day, his plane ran out of fuel. The pilot made a forced crash landing on the field at Peterborough.

"As they hit the runway, the plane broke in two," Toti says. "Clark and I were on the field waiting for them and we raced over. Fortunately the crew had all gone forward in the plane and none of them was hurt except the pilot, who got a clip on the jaw. They took them all to the hospital anyway, but found they were just shook up. By the time they'd lifted a few Scotches they were feeling no pain.

"Clark really loved those boys on

the base, and, when one of them he'd been using in the film was killed on a mission, he gave up a few hours' leave to stay behind and write the man's widow a letter of condolence," Toti said.

Periodically Clark took the film to London for processing and was there for two days at a time. He wrote me that he stayed at Claridge's.

"As a sergeant I expected to have to carry Captain Gable's bags," Toti reports, "but Clark would never let me do it. He carried his own."

On one occasion while Clark was in London, he wrote that he'd gotten in touch with Elizabeth Allen, an English actress who had appeared with him in *Men in White* and several other films. Elizabeth was now married and had a family.

Most of the boys rode bicycles around the Peterborough base. Clark located an old English motorcycle and went tearing around on it in preference to a jeep, for he wrote me that he was sure the jeep seats were upholstered in armor plate and when he got home he'd enjoy driving his Lincoln again.

Toti tells of an amusing incident when a driver named Pool was assigned to Clark, who did not know that Pool was just learning to operate a jeep.

"Clark usually rode with his right leg over the side of the jeep," Toti says. "They were en route to the bomber area when Pool lost control of the jeep and almost took Clark's leg off as he scraped against a tree. Clark's only remark was, 'That's the last time I'll ride with Pool.' "

During the war, RCA featured a radio program, "What's Going On around the World." The program director asked Corney Jackson if it would

Clark took 16-millimeter color film during five combat missions in 1943. The film was for Air Corp's recruitment.

be possible for him to get Clark on the program. Corney said he would try.

The Army cooperated and gave him permission to call Clark at Peterborough to make arrangements for having him "cut in" on the program at a pre-arranged day and time. Pat, John Lee Mahin's wife, asked Corney if she might sit in his office when he called Clark and perhaps say a few words to John.

Corney was put through to Clark, who agreed to do the program and was told the time and place. Then Corney asked Clark to put John on, but when Pat tried to talk to her husband, the army operator disconnected them. Corney had no chance to confirm the date with Clark and everyone assured him that there'd be a slip-up and Clark wouldn't be "standing by" on schedule.

Naturally, we were all excited at the prospect of hearing Clark's voice and I alerted everyone, including Aunt Lottie Wise. We all gathered around our radios at the appointed time, and heard Don Ameche, the master of ceremonies, say, "Now we take you to England, where you will hear from Clark Gable."

We held our breaths. For an instant it seemed as if he were not coming on. "The suspense was awful," Corney says. Then, suddenly, there was Clark's voice, telling us of wartime conditions in England, the film he was making, and the boys of the Air Force. "They are the greatest men in the world," he said, "and every one of them is doing a fine job, risking his life daily for us all."

At the ranch, Juanita was tuned in on the kitchen radio. Clark's dogs were asleep when the program started, but when they heard his voice they woke up, became terribly excited, and raced all over the house looking for him.

At the NBC station, Corney received congratulations for having engineered this radio "scoop." The program director got up on the studio stage and shined his shoes, while the rest of the crew bowed low.

I kept Clark posted on news on the home front and the Encino ranch. We were busy with ration books and standing in line for the many hard-to-get items. Father Gable decided to start a victory garden at the ranch and I went into partnership with him on the project. We both wore ourselves out, but were very proud of our corn, string beans and watermelons. We also acquired a mother hen and twenty baby chicks to raise, so that when Clark came home he'd have "eating" poultry.

The berries that year were wonderful. Blackberries, raspberries and currants grew in profusion in the hollows at the foot of the hill. And we had a large crop of grapes. Juanita made the most delicious berry cobblers, and we thought we'd preserve as much of the berry crop as possible so Clark could enjoy them on his return.

Neither of us had ever done any preserving, but we followed the directions to the letter (or so we thought) and the finished jars looked beautiful. Something went wrong, however; one morning Juanita and I heard a machine-gun-like series of explosions in the pantry and discovered that the berries had fermented and "blown their tops."

Because of the food problem, suddenly everyone in Hollywood became interested in buying ranches, particularly Clark's. Raoul Walsh tried his best to buy the place back, and Teresa Wright had her agent call to see if Clark was interested in selling; but he told me to advise any and all bidders that it was not for sale. I recommended some necessary painting, to which he agreed at once, and he also gave me the "go ahead" on raises for Juanita and Roy, in the light of the ever-mounting wartime cost of living.

About this time, Father Gable had to have a suit. Clark asked me to attend to this for him, as he paid all of his father's expenses. We went out to Bullock's in Pasadena and I thought I was in for a long "trying-on" session.

I was agreeably surprised to have Father Gable walk up to the racks, without hesitation put his hand on a suit, and say, "This is the one I want."

His selection was very good, and was one of the most expensive suits in the store. Here was one Dutchman who knew his own mind and wasted few words in coming to the point!

Richard Lang, Fieldsie's son, was four years old that summer. He used to watch the papers for pictures of Clark. One day he saw a picture of Tyrone Power on the inside pages, while Clark's was on the front page.

"Uncle Ty looks so tired, and has such a little picture," he commented to his mother, "but Uncle Clark is on the front page and there is a lot of writing about him."

I wrote Clark that loyal eyes were watching out for his "billing"—even at four years!

In August 1943, Clark wrote that he was trying to finish shooting, but the delays were endless because most of the men he was using in the film were flying and the movie crew had to fit their time to the flight schedule. Sound recording was difficult because of the constant roar of the airplane motors, and aerial photography presented problems, for the cameras often froze at thirty thousand feet and Jerry refused to pose! He also reported that it was always either raining, or had just stopped raining, or was about to rain.

At the end of October, the crew had shot fifty thousand feet of color film and were ready to return home. Clark received orders to fly direct to the Pentagon in Washington and report.

The film and all the equipment was shipped home by boat, in care of Sergeant Toti, who was to continue by train with it to California.

Prior to Clark's departure from England, he was awarded the Air Medal for "exceptionally meritorious achievement while participating in five separate combat bomber missions." The citation also stated that "his courage, coolness and skill in five missions reflected great credit on him and the Armed Forces."

Clark reported that his plane ride to the United States was very exciting (by that day's standards). "I had breakfast in Scotland, lunch in Greenland, and dinner in New York," he told me later. He sat up all the way home, having given his berth to a man who was ill.

Proceeding to Washington, he reported on the completion of his photographic mission, then found that the War Department had arranged a press conference for him. Stenographers in the Pentagon lined the corridors six-deep to watch him walk by. One hundred reporters were waiting for him in the conference room, and Clark said that it was an ordeal—for they treated him as if he were a "hero," and he was very conscious of the fact that, comparatively speaking, "other men had done so much more."

He arrived in California on November 1, by train. Howard Strickling sent a studio car to pick me up and I joined him and Ralph Wheelwright at the station in Pasadena, where a few

Ralph Wheelwright and Howard Strickling of MGM accompanied me to the station to meet Captain Clark Gable, U.S. Army Air Force, upon his return from European service, November 1, 1943. PRIVATE COLLECTION OF HOWARD STRICKLING

newsmen and photographers and a crowd of about three hundred people had gathered to welcome him.

Clark looked very handsome in his uniform with the Air Medal and campaign ribbons on his chest and was wildly cheered as he stepped from the train. I thought he seemed thinner, but very fit and poised. The touches of gray at his temples gave him a new air of maturity.

The studio car took us all straight to the ranch. Clark was so thrilled to be home again he was like a small boy—dashing around trying to see everything at once, returning now and again to a huge pitcher of fresh orange juice we had waiting for him. Finally, he gave up and carried the pitcher with him as he made the rounds of the place.

Having arrived home ahead of Toti and the film, Clark, John Lee Mahin and the rest of the crew had a few days to rest before reporting to "Fort Roach," the headquarters for the photographic division of the Air Corps, at the Hal Roach Studios in Culver City.

One of Clark's first visits, of course, was to MGM, where his appearance in the studio commissary created a sensation. The huge lunchtime crowd rose to its feet and broke into thunderous applause. Old friends crowded around his table, and it was a true "welcome home" party.

The studio promptly rewrote his contract for another seven years at seven thousand, five hundred dollars a week, part payment to begin immediately although Clark was still in the Air Force. This contract contained the clause that Clark had long wanted. Hereafter, he could quit shooting at five o'clock in the afternoon. In addition, he was to have four months' vacation after completion of each film. This fabulous contract established him once and for all as the top star in the movie world.

Clark's agent was still Phil Berg, who was in association with Bert Allenberg, forming the Berg-Allenberg Agency.

The one sad note to mar Clark's homecoming was the sudden and unexpected death of his old friend Harry Fleischmann from a heart attack on November 28. Clark and I drove up to the hunting lodge at Bakersfield to comfort Nan and attend Harry's funeral. All of Harry's hunting "pals" were there, and Clark's grief was deep, for he had loved Harry as a brother.

While waiting for his film, Clark spent many hours working around the ranch. At that time he thought perhaps he would be sent to the Pacific theater after he had finished the training films, so we continued with the same household staff and Juanita did the cooking.

"I don't want to miss even one of Juanita's meals," Clark said. And after hearing about English cuisine, I could hardly blame him. "I hope I never see another Brussels sprout as long as I live," he said.

Soon after Clark arrived, our lone cow went up the hill, somehow got through the split-rail fence, wandered into the nearest neighbor's Victory Garden, and managed to demolish it before she was discovered.

Clark was terribly embarrassed and went up to apologize. He offered to reimburse the owners, who were charming about it, insisting that it didn't matter in the least. Thereafter Clark periodically sent them baskets of fruit and vegetables from the garden Father Gable was cultivating.

He spent his evenings with Fieldsie and Walter Lang, and all his old friends, including Virginia Grey. Commissioner the beloved little dachshund, died while Clark was overseas and Clark missed him so much that Virginia wanted to find a replacement. She and I drove to a kennel in the Valley where she bought a brown "docksie" puppy for Clark, who named him "Rover," and became utterly devoted to him. Later, Clark bought a male, whom he called "Noodles."

Clark always smoked a pipe when we were attending to business matters. During these times we had opportunity for quiet talks about his war experience and his future.

"I saw so much in the way of death and destruction," he told me, "I realized that I hadn't been singled out for grief—that others were suffering and losing their loved ones just as I lost Ma."

"I love the quiet here," he said on another occasion. "The only thing I really want now, Jeanie, is peace—peace and a quiet life in my own home with those I trust and love around me."

At Christmas, Clark surprised me with a generous bonus check. "I'm very happy over the way you managed everything while I was away," he said.

"You've done a hell of a good job, Jeanie, and I'm grateful."

He spent Christmas Day with the Langs and early in 1944 reported at Fort Roach to begin work on his films. Paul Mantz, now a lieutenant colonel, was his commanding officer there. When Clark went into his office, he started to salute, but Paul said, "Na-a-ah, sit down and relax!"

Although Fort Roach was technically "headquarters," and his orders were always sent there, Clark actually cut and edited the film at MGM, the studio having turned all of its facilities over to him and assigned Blanche Sewell, an experienced film editor, to the project. Blanche had worked on many of Clark's feature films and was a long-time friend of whom he was very fond. Later she became ill and Clark often went to see her, standing by when she passed on. Other editors were assigned to him at various times.

"There was a wonderful feeling about Clark at the studio," a friend says. "Everyone wanted to be of service to him." Clark renewed his friendship with Eddie Mannix and they became very close again. The studio had to assign a special policeman to remain on duty outside Clark's unit to keep away a constant stream of visitors so he could get some work done.

On January 15, 1944, Clark was asked to make a speech at the launching of a Liberty ship, to be named in honor of Carole by the California Shipbuilding Corporation at their Terminal Island docks.

More than fifteen thousand shipyard workers and guests were present at the ceremonies, which were presided over by Louis B. Mayer, head of MGM studios. This event marked the opening of a War Bond sales campaign, and Carole's own record of having sold more than two million dollars in bonds in one day was cited by Mr. Mayer.

Russ and I had received passes and were on the platform with Clark. I felt so sorry for him when it was time for his address. He clenched his fists tight to keep control of his emotions as he spoke briefly of the Liberty ships and the importance of the work being done in the shipyards. When Irene Dunne formally christened the ship the Carole Lombard, Clark's rigid self-control snapped. News photos taken at the time show the tears that streamed down his cheeks.

Supervising the editing and narration of the fifty thousand feet of film he brought back was quite a challenge for Clark. In the end, he produced five training and educational films from the footage. The first of these, Combat America, was designed to encourage gunnery enlistments; the second, Be Careful, was for combat fliers alone. It took a combat crew through a routine check of their plane prior to going into action, showed what to watch for when airborne, what to do when they were under fire, explained and taught techniques that must be learned in order to react automatically, fight and live. The other three dealt with various phases of the training program and life in the Air Corps.

John Lee Mahin wrote the script for the narration, which was done by Clark, who also was seen occasionally in the film. The real "stars" of the film were two Air Force sergeants with the similar names of Huls and Hulse.

In May 1944, Clark was promoted to the rank of major, and was honorably discharged on June 12 of that year, being placed on the Army's inactive list subject to recall. His Report of Separa-

June 1944

Clark, Ward Bond, and Victor Fleming loved to roar around the San Fernando Valley on their motorcycles. (1944)

tion was signed by Captain Ronald Reagan of the Air Corps Personnel Office, Culver City.

Although he was now out of uniform, Clark continued his work on the training films, which were completed in September. He flew to Washington to deliver finished prints in person to the War Department. The Pentagon announced its complete satisfaction with the films, which became an integral part of the Army's recruitment and Training Program. It was stated that the films would not be released to the general public but would be made available for showings at bond rally drives, war plants and club meetings.

From Washington, Clark went to New York for a well-deserved vacation. While dining at the Stork Club, he met and renewed his acquaintance with an old friend, Dolly O'Brien, whose former husband he had known for years. Dolly, a chic and fascinating hostess, invited Clark to her West Palm Beach home for a pre-Christmas house party.

That fall, Clark spent a lot of time hunting at the Fleischmann lodge in Bakersfield. When Nan decided to sell the Club it almost killed him, for he loved the place, which was a refuge and a retreat for him. Some of his hunting friends urged him to buy it himself, but Clark was never one to invest in real estate, so passed up the opportunity.

Nan moved to Pacific Palisades and Clark's friendship with her continued. He loved Nan, who was a loyal friend, knew all of his faults and foibles, and always gave him a frank opinion. Clark frequently spent an evening with her, talking over old times, meanwhile calling the ranch every half-hour or so asking them to hold dinner for him.

Just before Christmas, Clark spent two weeks in West Palm Beach at Dolly O'Brien's house party, but returned to the ranch for Christmas, which he spent with the Stricklings.

For the first time in over two years, he was ready to resume his career, and the studio immediately began the search for a good story which would herald his return to the screen.

CHAPTER NINE

MARTIN and Jessie came back to us right after New Year's. With Clark at home and the domestic staff up to full complement, affairs at the ranch returned to normal routine.

"I know it's an imposition," Clark said, "but would you continue to manage the household for me, Jeanie? It would help me so much." He had been so generous and considerate that I was happy to say, "Of course, Mr. G— ."

The adjustment to private life, after months of hectic activity in the Air Corps and the long hours spent in preparation of the training films, was somewhat difficult for Clark. He missed Harry and the shooting lodge at Bakersfield. The war was still on, and Al Menasco and many of his old friends were away in the service. The studio had no story ready for him. Suddenly he had nothing to do, and he was bored and lonely.

We were all delighted when he began going out socially. Although he hated night clubs, he was seen at Ciro's and Mocambo and other night spots with a series of lovely ladies. Among these was Kay Williams, a beautiful blond divorcée. Kay was under contract to MGM. She was witty and amusing, and Clark was with her a great deal.

Another charmer was Anita Colby, the former Powers and Conover model, who'd been brought to Hollywood in connection with Columbia's film *Cover Girl* and stayed on to become fashion consultant for the David O. Selznick organization.

Anita had style and beauty. She was known as "The Face" because her photograph had been on the cover of over seventy magazines in one year. Her sister Francine was visiting her at her Brentwood apartment and both girls were out at the ranch frequently.

Clark also continued to see Virginia Grey, and that spring he met Betty Chisholm while on a trip to Phoenix. Betty was a widow who had lost her husband under tragic circumstances, and she and Clark became very good friends. Her home was on the Arizona Biltmore estates and Clark frequently went to Phoenix to see her, staying at the Arizona Biltmore so they could ride and golf together, for Betty played an excellent game.

Clark had joined the Bel Air Golf Club during his marriage to Carole, and he now reactivated his membership and began to play again. His golfing companions were Eddie Mannix, Howard Strickling and Billy Grady, the MGM casting director.

"Gable was not an aggressive golfer, but had great potentialities as a star player," Joe Novak, the Bel Air "pro" says. "He was powerful in build and loved to 'play the big ball.' "

Another of his golfing partners was Adolphe Menjou. Joe recalls one occasion when the match was very close and Menjou, nervously concerned with the result, began to coach Clark. When Clark overdrove the cup by several feet, Menjou exploded.

"For heavens' sake, Clark," he said, "this is a matter of mind and judgment, *not* a matter of muscle and force!"

Late in March, Clark had a freak automobile accident one night on a traffic circle in Brentwood. He was rushed to Cedars of Lebanon Hospital, and Howard Strickling and Dr. Myron Prinzmetal were called. Clark's injuries were minor, but the doctor thought it wiser that he remain there a day or so for "observation." Clark insisted on returning to the ranch, however; and, to prevent this, Howard took all of his clothes away.

Clark stayed in the hospital for a couple of days, wandering around visiting the children's wing and looking in on other patients, among whom was Susan Peters, the young and lovely actress-wife of Dick Quine. Susan, paralyzed as a result of a hunting accident, was a model of courage and optimism.

On the third day Clark called me. "Jeanie, will you bring me some clothes?" he said. "I've *got* to get out of here. I can't stand it any longer."

I took him an outfit and, while he was dressing, the doctor came along and signed a release for him, so we drove back to the ranch together.

Clark continued to visit Susan at the hospital and sent her flowers. As part of her therapy, she was doing some writing, and Clark let her interview him for a magazine article. It was the first interview he'd permitted since getting out of the service.

Peggy Gibson of We Ask U Inn, near Grant's Pass, Oregon, called that spring to tell Clark that a beautiful tract of land along the Rogue River was on the market and she thought he might be interested in it.

Clark couldn't get away just then, so he suggested that I go up and look it over. "If you like it, use your own judgment and buy it for me," he said.

Of course I went directly to the Inn to stay with the Gibsons. Rainbow had passed on sometime before and Peggy was running the place herself with the help of her daughters and a guide named Popkins, who beached the boats and piers in the winter and was noted for his fried fish. The girls, Sybil, Carol and Vee, were grown now. Vee was at college in Portland.

We tramped over the property, thirty-eight acres of the most beautiful land I've ever seen, right on the Rogue River. The trees—madrona, pine, fir and cedar—were magnificent, and the undergrowth was lush green. I called Clark that night and raved about it, so he told me to buy it. I stayed over another day to make arrangements and sign the necessary papers.

Clark began shooting his first postwar film, *Adventure*, at the end of May. Much care and thought had gone into the preparation of the picture, which was produced by Sam Zimbalist with Clark's old friend Victor Fleming, of *Gone With the Wind* fame, directing.

The screenplay was written by Frederick Hazlitt Brennan and Vincent Lawrence, based on the novel *The Anointed*, by Clyde Brion Davis. Greer Garson was to co-star, Joan Blondell and veteran Thomas Mitchell were in the cast, and Joseph Ruttenberg headed the camera unit. With that lineup, success seemed assured.

Before starting, Clark asked Don Roberson if he would like to be his personal make-up man. Don had started at MGM as a messenger boy, was in the Publicity Department for a while, and was now in make-up. He and Clark had been friends for years, Clark having met him through Jean

Clark and his friend, Betty Chisholm, with their friends, Ann and Hubert Merryweather, in Nogales, Mexico. (1946) COURTESY OF BETTY CHISHOLM

Harlow, who was Don's cousin. Naturally Don was delighted with the assignment.

"Clark was jittery the first few days of shooting but finally settled down," Don says. "He never complained, just kept his feelings to himself, would be a little moody for a day or so—then suddenly it would pass and he'd be the same old Clark again."

They had a lot of fun on the set and Victor Fleming jokingly complained that there was too much "drinking" going on, for Greer had to have her tea every afternoon, Joan wanted lots of coffee and Coca-Cola, while Clark brought in jugs of milk from the ranch. (He couldn't seem to get enough fresh milk and orange juice.)

Despite the glittering talent array, the picture was wrecked by a poor script and heavy-handed direction. The novel had recounted the adventures of a philosophical sailor named Harry Patterson. The script made Harry a handsome, daring, open-shirted bo'sun on a merchant marine freighter. The philosophy was handled by an Irish deck hand, played by Thomas Mitchell. Together they go to a library in San Francisco to do a little research on the Irishman's soul. Greer Garson was the cool and conservative librarian who fell for Clark.

The spiritual overtones were lost under Fleming's direction, and some of the scenes, particularly where an obvious dummy baby was used, were ludicrous. The studio got out a big promotion campaign on the film, built around the slogan "Gable's back and Garson's got him!" Clark loathed the whole idea. When *Adventure* was released the following Christmas it got dreadful reviews. Clark thought it was worse than *Parnell*.

The fans all rushed to see their idol, home from the wars, however, and the picture was a box-office success in spite of the bad notices. His two years' absence from the screen had not dimmed Clark's popularity with his public.

He had to take an awful ribbing on the golf course from his three pals, Howard Strickling, Eddie Mannix and Billy Grady. If Billy was losing, all he had to do when it was Clark's turn to play was say, "I just saw *Adventure* again," and Clark would blow the shot.

"We'd also kidded him about being the star of stage, screen, and radio, but *not* TV, because *they* saw you in *Adventure*," Billy says.

When Clark finished *Adventure*, he went up to Oregon to inspect the land I'd purchased and was highly pleased. He enjoyed seeing the Gibsons again and almost lost his heart to Carol, now a tall, willowy brunette who was a splendid sportswoman.

Popkins, the guide, had at least a dozen children and was a devotee of hillbilly jazz. Clark liked him immensely and frequently sent him jazz records.

While he was up there, he and Carol and a group of friends made a trip to Gold Beach at the mouth of the Rogue River to do some salmon fishing. The party stayed at one of the resort hotels. A feature of the salmon fishing was that one could have his catch canned and individually labeled on the spot. A few days later I got a case of canned salmon, each can bearing the label, "Jean Garceau Salmon."

Z. Wayne Griffin had replaced Corney Jackson in the radio department of the Berg-Allenberg Agency when Corney went to the J. Walter Thompson organization. Wayne, a former singer, was married to Elinor Remick Warren, the composer-pianist.

He and Clark became friends and Wayne suggested that Clark do some radio work. He offered him a "Cavalcade of America" show, and said that Du Pont, the sponsor, was willing to pay him seven thousand, five hundred dollars although their top price then was five thousand.

"There's really no use my doing this," Clark told him. "I can't keep any of the money and I'm not worth it anyway."

Wayne persisted, however, and showed him the script of *Take Her Down*, the story of a wartime submarine skipper. The submarine surfaces, the skipper is on the bridge, and enemy planes appear. He gives the order to "take her down" immediately, loses his own life but saves the submarine and his men.

Clark read it and said, "I can't do it—it would make me nervous, before, during and after the broadcast."

Wayne got him to do the show by putting it on a patriotic basis, convincing Clark that it would do much for public morale. But Clark warned him that it would be the last radio show he'd do.

It was a standing joke between them about money and how pinchpenny they both were. Clark often said jokingly, "I don't like money—any more than the air I breathe!"

As I was Clark's business manager, his attitude toward money was a real problem to me. Unlike other stars, who invested in race horses, baseball clubs and other less glamorous business enterprises, Clark preferred to keep his money in a checking account at the bank. Not only that, he hoarded large sums in cash in a safe deposit box and always carried several thousand dollars in cash on his person. This worried me.

"But Mr. G———, it isn't safe for you to carry that much money," I'd protest. "Let me get you a personal checkbook and you can write checks for cash as you need it."

I also pointed out that the cash in the safe deposit box earned no interest.

"I don't care," Clark would say. "I like my money where I can get my hands on it right away."

I finally persuaded him to let me invest some of his funds in blue-chip stocks (which later proved extremely profitable), and he consented to put some of the surplus cash in a savings account, after I'd assured him that he could get it out without delay. I never did educate him to carrying a checkbook. All the bills were paid from the office checkbook, and when he needed "carrying money" I'd get a check cashed for him. He never would permit me to make it out for less than five hundred dollars, and often it was for a thousand dollars.

Clark never gambled, never speculated on anything. His only extravagances were English-made shoes, fine luggage and expensive sports cars.

About that time, many of the big stars were setting up their own corporations in order to avoid heavy personal income taxes. There was much discussion about whether or not Clark should incorporate, but he felt that he was personally unable to handle all the details incident to such an enterprise, nor did he want the responsibility.

Clark hated detail of any kind, never even wanted to write a letter. And I must confess that letter writing was also my bête noire. Inevitably, I'd have to pin Clark down to the important dictation; and then there was always much reading back on my part with Clark making change after change before we arrived at a satisfactory result.

Clark was single, attractive, a war hero and a big star. Women swarmed after him. We used to have a standing bet between us as to how long it would be before some gossip columnist linked our names together. Russ and I had insisted from the first that there was to be no publicity on either of us, that our private life was to be kept completely apart from my work with Clark. As a result the general public was not aware that I was happily married.

Women used to rush up to me at parties or on the studio lot and say, "How can you *stand* being around that divine Clark all the time? I'll bet you're in love with him."

My stock reply was, "I have a handsome husband at home, whom I love very much."

Clark's fan mail reached staggering proportions, and so much of it that came to the house was from love-lorn women that we started a "Frenzied Female" file. This file contained letters from "repeaters," women who wrote in time and time again and were of the type we considered potentially "dangerous." The postal authorities could do nothing about these unless there was an actual threat in the letter, but we were legally advised to keep them on hand, in case trouble of any kind developed.

It became impossible for Clark to travel freely under his own name, so he adopted my husband's—Russel Garceau—when wishing to remain incognito. When in New York, he stayed at the Waldorf Astoria, registered there under Russ's name to avoid publicity.

Sometime later, Russ's nephew was in New York and checked in at the Waldorf. The desk clerk recognized the name and said, "Oh, that's the name Clark Gable always uses!"

When he first bought the ranch Clark had not wanted a swimming pool, but now that he was entertaining a good deal he thought it would be nice to have one for the use of his guests.

He decided on a site north of the house, which entailed cutting away part of the hill and doing some extensive landscaping. The pool construction began in early fall and for one reason or another there was a series of maddening delays before it was completed. That was one of the few times I ever saw Clark upset. Usually he took things as they came, but these delays irritated him. The pool, an enormous one, was finally finished in November, and an attractive green-awninged cabana erected.

Just before Christmas, Clark came home one night to find a regulation-size dinghy in his living room, cellophane-wrapped and tied with ribbon—a present from Anita Colby. It was painted white, and the name *The King III* was neatly lettered on her bow.

Anita said later that she "didn't have the nerve to let the salespeople think that Clark Gable didn't have *at least two other boats!*"

Clark left the boat in the living room until he could have it moved outside to the pool. Father Gable came in a day or so later and saw it. "That's just what I need," he said. "It will make a wonderful fishing boat for me."

"Oh, no you don't," Clark replied. "That's *my* boat." He had two moorings built in the swimming pool, and for a time it was a novelty for Anita, Francine and his other guests to row back and forth across the pool. (The boat took up a lot of room, however, and Father Gable eventually inherited it.)

Clark liked to sit around the pool but swam very little. Later on he gave it up entirely.

He continued to hunt a great deal, but did not do much riding, for his horse, Sunny, was now quite old. Clark sent both Sunny and Melody up to Wayne Griffin's ranch in the mountains near Gorham to be put to pasture. He sent Melody with him, because Sunny was crazy about her and he didn't want to separate them. Later, Wayne told Clark that he'd had Sunny's teeth fixed and he was "smiling at all the other horses."

Clark read a good deal, and was constantly in search of a story for himself. While not too disturbed over *Adventure*, he was nevertheless aware of the fact that bad scripts would eventually affect his career. When he read for "fun," he liked mystery stories.

Clark was not happy when he learned that his next picture was to be *The Hucksters*, based on the Frederic Wakeman novel about Madison Avenue advertising agencies. His chief objection was that the heroine was an adulterous wife. All the censorable elements were eliminated in the final screenplay, however, and the heroine became a genteel English widow.

Deborah Kerr was under consideration for the role, which would be her first in an American film. Clark made tests with her. Understandably nervous, Deborah was put completely at ease by Clark, the tests were good, and she got the part.

Clark's role was that of an advertising man trying to please a soap sponsor. On the first day of shooting, Anita Colby sent him a huge flowered horseshoe and a case of soap of every conceivable variety, including dog soap.

When the film was released, *Photoplay* magazine voted it the best picture of the month, and Clark felt that it compensated somewhat for *Adventure*.

For years Al Menasco had been trying to get Clark to go to the Indianapolis races on Decoration Day. Clark always hesitated, saying it would look too much like "grand standing," and he dreaded the publicity. In May 1947 Al, now out of the service and divorced, persuaded him to make the trip. They went by train and Al's friend Wilbur Shaw made all arrangements for their entertainment, with a minimum of fanfare.

Clark loved meeting the racing drivers and pit crews, all the "man talk" about motors, and the race itself. When it was over, he went on to New York for a few days while Al left for Detroit to pick up a new car. Clark met him in Detroit, and they started driving west with some fishing at Guaymas, Mexico, as their next objective.

The first night out was spent in Decatur, Illinois, where they were unable to find a hotel room and had to settle for a third-rate motel on the outskirts of the town.

"The place was dirty, the bath unspeakable," Al recalls.

After unpacking, they decided to return to the hotel for dinner. By that time the hotel manager had learned they had been turned away and was horrified when he heard the name of their motel. He told Clark he'd turn the hotel upside down to find him a room, even offered his own quarters; but Clark said, "We are very happy where we are," and refused to move.

Reporters picked up the story; the

next day, when Al and Clark stopped at a town a hundred miles south, they read of their experience in the headlines.

Clark and Al took turns driving. The car gave them a good deal of trouble. One day in Arizona, Clark (who was at the wheel while Al slept) gunned the motor as he approached a little hill, went flying over the top, and was promptly tagged by a traffic officer, who claimed that the car was out of control.

Clark protested, explained that he'd deliberately sped up because the car was not functioning properly and he wanted to make the hill.

The officer was very matter-of-fact. "When *all four wheels of a car are off the ground,* Mr. Gable," he explained, "the car is out of control."

When they got to California, Al decided to forgo the fishing trip, so Clark went up to We Ask U Inn alone, instead of to Guaymas.

On June 28, Al married again and Clark drove to Reno to be best man at the wedding. He gave a small reception for the newlyweds in his suite at the Riverside Hotel, ordering special flowers and vintage champagne.

Another old friend of his married that year. In July, Corney Jackson married Gail Patrick, the beautiful movie actress, who later became a successful TV producer.

Following his four months' vacation, Clark went into *Homecoming,* teamed again with Lana Turner. Anne Baxter played second lead. Clark played an army doctor married to Anne. He has a tragic love affair with a nurse (Lana), while overseas during the war. *Photoplay* named it the "Best Picture of the Month" when it was released, and noted that Clark was "the most popular man in the world."

Clark now went to New York on a holiday, visiting Rocky (Mrs. Gary) Cooper's stepfather at Southampton. Here he met Millicent Rogers, the Standard Oil heiress. Millicent was a slender, exoic beauty with enormous style, and Clark liked her very much. Later that year Millicent came to Hollywood for a visit, and she and Clark had many dates together. Millicent was a friend of the Adrians (Janet Gaynor) and fell in love with their pet monkey. She bought one for herself and used to go everywhere with the monkey perched on her shoulder or draped around her neck.

Women are women the world over, and, as Clark's secretary, I was frequently "courted" by those who were interested in him and hoped to glean information that would be useful. Millicent Rogers now invited me to lunch at Romanoff's, and we did a little polite fencing over the chicken *en gelée* as she tried to find out what Clark thought of her. I was at my blandest and most obtuse. (Imagine my surprise at the end of the meal when Millicent produced a long, delicate *gold* toothpick and put it to use!)

Millicent's hobby was the creation of jewelry from eighteen- and twenty-four carat yellow and green gold. She called it "sculptured" jewelry, and gave each piece a name—such as Tree Face, Golden Pool, Magic Stalk and so on. For Christmas that year she sent Clark a buckle, cuff links, shirt studs and a ring. She also sent me a green-gold ring called Green Leaf, with her name and the date engraved inside. It was a charming bauble but extremely heavy, and I found it difficult to wear. Later, she wrote asking me to lend it to her for an exhibit of her jewelry at the Philbrook Art Center in Tulsa, Oklahoma. She returned the ring, together with a program listing her collection. She had shown some fifty-four rings, necklaces, bracelets, pins, clips and other articles.

That fall Clark went up to Grant's Pass to fish for steelhead and he and Carol Gibson made up a party to go downriver by boat to Gold Beach. They took two boats with two guides in each, because some of the gorges through which they passed were so narrow that it took two men with oars to keep the crafts from smashing into the cliff walls.

They had a wonderful time, stopping at night at farmhouses along the riverbank, feasting on the fish they had caught during the day. Bathing facilities were limited, and it took hours for the water to heat so everyone could have a bath, but no one seemed to mind, according to Clark.

At Gold Beach, the party was met by the guides' wives, who'd driven down with boat trailers. The boats were loaded aboard and the group went back to We Ask U Inn by car.

Clark spent Christmas with the Stricklings. Early in 1948 he started *Command Decision,* wherein he played the part of a conscience-torn Air Force officer who has to send his men on bombing missions, knowing that their chances of survival are practically nil.

Van Johnson was in some sort of difficulty at the studio and was being disciplined. Clark wanted him in the picture and went to bat for him. "I've got to have this boy," he said, "he has talent." He had his way, and Van made the picture with him.

Clark, Howard and Gail Strickling went to New York when the picture was finished and on the way home

Clark suggested that they stop in San Francisco and phone Carol Gibson to come down and spend Easter with them.

Carol arrived in San Francisco wearing a green suit, with a pair of Levis in her bag just in case there was a fishing trip in the offing.

"They were wearing colored hose that year," she says, "and I'd left in such a hurry I snatched up only one spare pair. They happened to be blue, and, with my green suit, I looked like an Easter egg myself!"

Carol had never been in San Francisco, and Clark wanted her to see everything. They made a gay foursome touring the city, dining at the Fisherman's Wharf, riding the cable cars.

"Clark sat on the outside," Carol says, "and it was fun to watch cars drive by and people doing double takes as they recognized Clark and shrieked, "There's Gable!' "

Saturday night, after everyone had retired, Gail slipped out to buy some Easter eggs for Easter Sunday. Apparently Clark had the same idea, for when she went to hide her eggs in the hotel sitting room, Clark was there hiding those he'd bought!

Later that spring Eric Tyrell-Martin, the noted polo player, and his wife were Clark's house guests at the ranch. Clark told me that they had complimented him on his beautifully managed household. "I want you to know how proud I was to hear this, Jeanie," he said. Naturally, I basked in this unexpected praise.

Clark was making plans for a vacation trip to Europe when Edna, Father Gable's wife, had a heart attack and became quite ill. Clark was very considerate about going down to see her.

Edna died June 19. Clark, Father Gable and I attended her very quiet funeral at Hollywood Cemetery. Clark refused to look upon Edna in death. "I want to remember her as she was," he said simply.

Father Gable was very depressed at her passing, and on the way home reminisced about the old days in Hopedale when he was superintendent of the Methodist Sunday School and Clark was in regular attendance there.

Pinkie, the aunt who lived with Father Gable and Edna, was a very elderly woman who got about with difficulty. It was necessary to arrange for someone to stay with her and Father Gable, so I got Mrs. Dyson, my former housekeeper, to move in with them and take charge of the household.

Clark was due to sail on the *Queen Mary* on July 9, and left for New York a few days before. Anita Colby was there at the time, and he saw her, as well as his old friend "Slim" Hawks, now divorced from Howard Hawks, the director, and about to be married to Leland Hayward. Slim was a fascinating woman, on the "Ten Best-dressed Women" list. Clark was very fond of her, and was godfather to Kitty, her three-year-old daughter.

His friends staged a gay farewell party for Clark, and the pier officials had to hold the *Queen Mary* half an hour for him while he bade his charming companions good-by.

Clark sent me the passenger list from the *Queen Mary* and reported a wonderful voyage over. His frequent dinner companion aboard ship was the lovely actress Marilyn Maxwell.

The Stricklings were in Europe on a business trip and Howard met Clark at Cherbourg. They went directly to the Hotel du Golfe in Deauville for several days, then on to the George V Hotel in Paris to join Gail. Howard had made arrangements for a press reception for Clark, leaving Gail in charge of it while he returned to London on important business.

Clark admired Katharine Hepburn greatly and, when he learned she was at the hotel, he invited her to join him at the press reception, which was held in one of the rooms off the hotel lobby. Katharine arrived early and was obviously nervous, so Clark suggested a glass of champagne, which she accepted, although she ordinarily did not drink. Clark asked her if she could speak French and she said "No."

Three hundred and fifty of the press showed up for the conference, all demanding autographed pictures. Katharine was seated at one table and Clark at another. After a while, he glanced over at her and found she was chattering like mad in French.

"Thought you couldn't speak this lingo," he teased.

"I was having so much trouble understanding *their* English that I thought I'd try my French and I'm doing just fine," she replied. Thereafter, she spoke French throughout her stay in Paris.

The conference was a great success. Howard sent me photographs of Clark and Katharine, together with clippings from the Paris press.

Immediately afterwards, Clark bought a Mercury convertible, hiring a man to drive and also serve as his valet, for he planned to do most of the driving himself. He went to the south of France, and there met Dolly O'Brien and Elsa Maxwell, the famous party giver. They had a gay time, for Clark had often said that Dolly was "the

At the door of his dressing room, during production of Command Decision, *1948. The film won Gable an award from the U.S. Air Force for outstanding contribution to the cause of peace through air power.* COURTESY OF MGM

funniest and wittiest woman I have ever known in my life." Elsa introduced Clark to the Duke and Duchess of Windsor, and he played golf with the Duke.

Before leaving, Clark asked me what I'd like as a present from Europe. Tentatively, I mentioned perfume. Clark was exasperated. "I mean something special, like a Paris gown," he said. "What size do you wear?"

Naturally I was thrilled at the prospect. Clark had exquisite taste in clothes. I gave him my measurements and waited in happy anticipation.

At the end of July, he phoned me from Paris and said he'd been making the rounds of the couturiers—Jacques Fath, Dior, Balmain—but was too late for the spring collections and too early for the fall. "All of these hemstitchers leave town for the month of August," he said, "and none of them will even promise to make you a dress by the time I sail at the end of the month." I told him to skip it and have a good time.

Clark was in love with Europe. He said he'd expected to find France war-torn, the people half-starved. He was amazed at the marvelous cuisine, and raved about a little Seine restaurant where he'd enjoyed thick steaks and wild strawberries with clotted Devonshire cream.

He told me he was starting on a motor tour and would send me his itinerary. He wanted to hear every single detail of what was going on at home, and I thought I detected just a tinge of homesickness.

We were busy at the ranch; necessary painting was in progress, plus a thorough housecleaning, and I was interviewing and trying out cooks, for Jessie wanted to stop work for a while.

Father Gable, who was now seventy-eight, continued to come out two or three times a week but was not very well. Of course, he still missed Edna. He passed away suddenly on August 4, of a heart attack. I had no idea where to reach Clark, so called Howard in London. He was able to locate him in Switzerland, and Clark cabled me that he was sailing with the Stricklings aboard the *Queen Mary* on August 7. All funeral arrangements were held up pending Clark's arrival.

Gail told me later that Clark was very quiet on the trip home, taking no part in shipboard activities. They arrived in California by train and I met them at the station.

Father Gable had requested simple and very private funeral services, and only Clark, Howard and I attended.

Clark told me many things about his early life with his father, and seemed comforted by the thought that he had made his declining years happy and comfortable.

Pinkie now went East to live with relatives, and Clark decided to sell the house on Ethel Avenue. Russ had recently gone into business for himself as a realtor, so Clark asked me to have the house painted and redecorated, and he commissioned Russ to handle its sale.

Russ priced it at its real worth, but it didn't move right away. Clark got impatient and suggested a price reduction, way below market value. Of course it sold immediately—and for cash, which was gratifying to Clark, who always wanted his money at once.

This was Russ's first real estate deal. Thereafter, he was in a position to advise Clark of some good property investments, but Clark was never interested. "You can't get your money in a hurry if it's tied up in real estate," he said. I never pressed him, for fear it would seem that I was taking advantage of my position as his business manager to recommend deals that would be profitable to my husband.

I *was* able, the following spring, to persuade Clark to invest in some California tax-free bonds.

I did not see much of Clark that fall, as he did a great deal of hunting and had resumed dating various belles about town. Joan Harrison, the English beauty who was associated with Alfred Hitchcock, was one of his steady companions, and he was also seeing Anita Colby, Virginia Grey and Carol Gibson.

When the duck season opened, Clark, Carol Gibson and a party went up to Klamath Falls near Keno, Oregon, for some duck and goose hunting. They stayed at the home of Dick Morgan, a guide.

Carol had never slept in a feather bed and went home convinced that they were ideal for the freezing weather they found there.

"It was so cold," she recalls, "that when the dogs went out in the water to retrieve the ducks, icicles formed on their coats."

The shooting was excellent, and Clark shipped his ducks home to be plucked and stored in the freezer. (How the servants hated the plucking!)

The guide business wasn't too good for Dick that year and Clark wanted to help him. He bought a Black Labrador bitch and left her with Dick, paying him to train her to retrieve. "Clark gave me half the dog—the rear end," Carol says. The Labrador proved to be very nervous, however, and Dick was unable to train her.

A little later, Clark bought another Labrador, named Joe, for Dick to handle. Dick reported that Joe was doing very well and would make an

Virginia Grey and Clark on the set of The Homecoming, *1948.* COURTESY OF MGM

excellent hunting dog, but for some unknown reason Joe died suddenly one day.

Clark had a magnificent recipe for pressed duck which he'd got from Bob, the chef at the Brown Derby. We had a duck press, and whenever there were to be special dinner guests Clark always ordered pressed duck as the *pièce de resistance* of the meal.

Now a duck press is a tricky thing. It must be extremely hot before you put the duck in, otherwise the juice coagulates and the press is very difficult to open. We had a new cook at that time and, when I'd ordered the dinner, she said she knew all about pressed duck. Unfortunately, she failed to heat the press; her attempts to open it failed, the duck was ruined, and a hasty substitution of steaks was made at the last minute.

Russ and I had a harrowing experience with a snow goose Clark shipped to us. When it arrived, it looked so wonderful I rushed to the phone and invited guests to dinner. When we set about plucking the goose, however, we couldn't budge a single feather, no matter how many times we doused the goose in scalding water. We'd heard that paraffin sometimes did the trick, so our next step was to give Mr. Goose a melted paraffin bath. This was ineffective. Finally Russ and I both wrestled with the feathers, getting to the point where we actually anchored the goose underfoot and really pulled. Not a feather came off!

In despair I called Clark, outlining our problem. Clark groaned. "It's all my fault," he said, "I forgot you have to pluck a snow goose the minute it's killed."

We wound up skinning the goose, which got rid of the feathers but left us a very unappetizing looking fowl to cook and serve to our expectant guests.

Ordinarily, Clark's Christmas gift to me was a handsome bonus. That year he gave me an additional present—an order at a smart Beverly Hills couturier for a suit. He had not forgotten his failure to bring me the promised Paris gown!

Russ and I usually had Clark's scripts bound in leather as our present to him. His name and the name of the film were engraved on the cover. We also gave him semiclassical records and scores from current musicals, which he liked very much.

Clark said that one of the best presents he got that year was the Redbook Award for *Command Decision*, which was a top-grossing film.

Dore Schary became a power at MGM at a crucial time in Clark's career. Clark was very much dissatisfied with the stories being offered him, including a script called *Any Number Can Play*. Schary asked him, as a favor, to do this story about a reformed gambler and promised in return that he'd put MGM's entire facilities to work to come up with better stories for him. Clark made the picture, but it was not a success.

Free now for the four months' vacation prescribed by his contract, Clark spent a couple of weeks at the Arizona Biltmore playing golf with Betty Chisholm, then returned to go into discussions with Z. Wayne Griffin, who had left Berg-Allenberg in 1946 and was now producing pictures independently.

Wayne owned a script called *Genius in the House* which he suggested as a possible vehicle for Clark. Clark liked it, and bought a two-thirds interest in the story. Wayne went to MGM to sell them on the idea of buying it and letting him produce it with Clark as the star.

Dore Schary offered Wayne one hundred and thirty-seven thousand dollars for the story rights, with Wayne on salary as producer and Clark receiving his regular salary to appear in it. Clark turned down the offer for the story rights, saying it wasn't enough, and told Wayne to go back and demand more. Wayne said he felt he might get the offer up to two hundred thousand dollars but Clark said, "I won't do it unless I get half a million out of it."

"That's impossible," Wayne replied. "I know they'll never go for it."

"Aw, go on," Clark needled. "You know you can do it."

"Schary practically collapsed when he heard Clark's demands," Wayne says, "but said he'd consult Nicholas Schenck, Chairman of the MGM Board."

The deal fell through entirely, and Wayne bought back Clark's interest in the script.

Clark continued to enjoy his vacation. He had sold the Mercury convertible in Europe and now acquired one of a limited number of new Jaguar XK-120 sports roadsters. The car, light gray with red upholstery, was shipped to him from England. Clark was assured it had a top speed of 128.6 miles an hour, and was dying to try it out. He asked me one day if I'd like a ride and, all unsuspecting, I went with him.

Clark drove out to the desert and opened the car up. I was scared half out of my wits when we got up to ninety miles an hour, and was simply congealed with fright when the speedometer registered one hundred and fifteen. I didn't look after that, being too busy invoking the Deity, but Clark told me later that he'd hit one

hundred twenty-five miles an hour. I was barely able to totter to my old Chrysler when we got back to the ranch, and more than willing to eschew Jaguars!

Clark's moods were mercurial. When Juanita took him his breakfast in the morning, she reported that he was always happy and bright; but there were days when he'd be quiet and moody, often spending hours just sitting in his room. I knew he was lonely. Then the mood would pass, and he'd be out playing golf again, or squiring one of his girl friends around.

Now and again he would see Joan Crawford, his friend of long standing. He asked me to arrange a dinner party at the ranch for her birthday in March and order a special birthday cake. The next day I had a lovely note of thanks from Joan, who was very pleased and happy with the party. Although my own birthday was not until August, Joan, as a gag, sent me a birthday cake with the inscription "Happy Birthday to you too, Jean dear."

About this time, Al Menasco bought two new Mossbergs and gave one to Clark. These guns were triggered to discharge clay pigeons, whereupon the hunter could shoot them with the same gun while they were in the air. Clark was crazy about his, and promptly loaned it to someone who failed to return it. He complained so bitterly that Al brought his out for Clark to use.

When Clark was away on a trip, Al phoned and said he'd like to come out and get his gun, which he did. Clark insisted that the gun was really his and needled Al, hoping to get it back, but Al would never let him have it again. "Let him get his own gun," he said.

Sometimes Clark was a bit of an "Indian giver." He gave me a set of

Clark drove 215 yards for a hole in one. (1949)

matched golf clubs, then borrowed them one day to lend to a friend, and that is the last I ever saw of them.

His own golf game improved to the point where he became a sought-after partner. One day he was playing a foursome at Bel Air with Tom McKearnan, Les Kelley and Roy Bargy and scored a 215-yard hole-in-one on the thirteenth hole.

"I was playing in the foursome just behind and saw him do it," Billy Grady recalls. "It was a fly shot, and he hit so hard it bent the staff."

"This game's a cinch," Clark said airily.

(In later years Fred Astaire, Fred MacMurray and Howard Keel all made holes-in-one on the thirteenth hole, which is now known at the Bel Air Club as "the actors' hole.")

Wayne continued to discuss story possibilities and independent produc-tion with Clark, who was beginning to talk now about retiring from the screen. "I just want to hunt and ride and fish," he said.

"You'd never do it, you'd get too bored," Wayne said. "You've got to keep working. You can't just sit down and count your money."

Privately, I thought the business about retirement was all talk on Clark's part. Deep in his heart, I knew he didn't mean to retire at all. No matter how much money he had, he never felt he had quite enough, and seven thousand, five hundred dollars a week was not to be passed up lightly.

Wayne owned a script called *Key to the City* which he was trying to promote for Clark at MGM, with Wayne producing. Clark and I both read it and liked it very much. But the studio was hesitating, because they wanted Clark to do *Quo Vadis* and Clark was bucking it.

"Why don't you test for it?" Wayne urged. "We can do my picture later."

But Clark refused. He objected to *Quo Vadis,* for he was sure he'd look silly in the robes of the period.

Wayne finally got the go-ahead to produce *Key* with Clark and Loretta Young, who played a serious-minded young New England mayor who meets Clark—a tough, self-made man—at a convention in San Francisco. Frank Morgan was also in the cast.

Wayne recalls an amusing incident in connection with a scene between Loretta and Clark which was supposed to take place on a park bench in San Francisco. Fog machines poured fog all around the bench on the sound stage. The action called for Loretta to edge toward Clark. In order to avoid her, he edged away along the bench as she moved in on him. Clark miscalculated the length of the bench and fell off the end.

"He disappeared entirely in the fog," Wayne says. "Then suddenly we heard this ghostly voice saying, 'Guess we'll have to have a longer bench!' It broke everybody up!"

When the question of working beyond five o'clock arose, Clark stubbornly insisted on enforcing the clause in his contract which allowed him to quit at that time. Loretta objected because it meant that, in shooting her closeups, someone else would have to "feed" Clark's lines to her. To keep peace, Wayne told George Sidney, the director, to close down the set each day at five o'clock.

Soon after completion of *Key,* Loretta and her husband Tom Lewis gave a party which Wayne and Clark attended. During the evening, it was announced over the radio that Frank Morgan was dead. Frank was a great friend of Clark's and they'd just finished some retakes together on the picture the Sunday before. Clark and Wayne left immediately and went up to the Morgan home to see if they could be of any assistance to Alma, Frank's widow.

Minna Wallis gave a dinner party during the summer of 1949. Among the guests Clark met Lady Sylvia Ashley, whom he'd known when she was married to Douglas Fairbanks, Sr., who had died in 1939.

Sylvia was ten years Clark's junior, English, blond and beautiful. She had been married three times, divorced twice, and was an important figure in international café society, noted for her gaiety and wit, her clothes, jewels, and *savoir-faire.* Clark found her interesting and amusing.

Born Sylvia Hawkes in England, she'd made her first appearance on the London stage in the famous *Midnight Follies* with her friend Dorothy Field. Billed as *Silly and Dotty,* the two girls sang songs, played ukeleles, and were the rage of London, according to a contemporary.

"She also appeared in *Tell Me More* at the Winter Garden in 1925," a friend recalls. "Sylvia was extremely pretty, with a wonderful, slim figure and fair sleek hair which she always washed herself. Those were the Roaring Twenties. We all knew everyone, were all a bit crazy, and mad about the Charleston."

Although she'd been married to Douglas Fairbanks, Sr., and subsequently to Lord Stanley, a commander in the Royal Navy, Sylvia still retained the name and title of her first husband—Anthony, Lord Ashley, son of the Earl of Shaftesbury.

Sylvia's sister Vera was married to Basil Bleck, and had two teen-age children, Loretta and Timothy, whom Sylvia adored. The Blecks lived in a beach house Sylvia had inherited from Douglas Fairbanks, and Sylvia made it her headquarters when she visited Hollywood.

Clark dated Sylvia many times that fall, but he was also dating Joan Harrison, Betty Chisholm and others, so I had no idea that he was deeply interested in her. They were together at a dinner party Saturday night, December 17, at the home of Charles Feldman, a prominent agent. Sunday, Clark asked Sylvia if he might see her again.

Monday morning, December 19, he telephoned me before I left my house. "Are you sitting down, Jeanie?" he said. "I have something to tell you."

I assured him I was comfortably braced for anything he might wish to reveal.

"I'm going to be married," he said.

I gasped in surprise. "Who to?" I asked, most ungrammatically, several names flashing through my mind.

"To Syl," he replied.

(This *was* a surprise, for I'd thought another beauty was way ahead in the running.)

"I'm so happy for you, Mr. G——," I said. "I know Sylvia will make you a wonderful wife."

I knew he was lonely, that he loved his home and wanted to share it with someone. Sylvia was wise in the ways of the world, had been married before, and I felt that she would bring charm and color into his home and life and make him very happy.

"I'll call you later," Clark said, and hung up.

He called Howard Strickling next and asked him to make arrangements for a quiet wedding right away, with as little publicity as possible. Howard set the wheels in motion by calling his friends Lynn and Patsy Gillham, owners of Alisal Ranch, an exclusive guest resort near the Danish colony of Solvang, about thirty miles north of Santa Barbara. The ranch was ideal for privacy, far removed from the public eye. The Gillhams took over, saying they'd arrange for the wedding and a minister.

Without revealing any identities, Howard bought a narrow gold wedding band from John Gershgorn, a Beverly Hills jeweler, and phoned Clark that everything was in readiness for the wedding to take place the next day, Tuesday, the twentieth.

Monday afternoon Clark drove down to Sylvia's beach house to pick her up, and they started for Alisal Ranch that afternoon. Howard, together with Jim Mahoney of the MGM publicity staff, and Eddie Hubbell, a still photographer, also left for Alisal Monday afternoon, as did the Blecks and their children.

Tuesday morning, the party went to nearby San Luis Obispo, where the marriage license was obtained from the County Clerk at noon. The wedding was set for three o'clock.

Before leaving, Clark had asked me to drive up for the wedding, so Tuesday morning I picked up Gail Strickling and Mildred Kelly, one of Howard's assistants, and we started out.

I was so excited that when we stopped en route for gasoline I unwittingly remarked aloud to Gail, "Did you ever think, when we were going to school in Seattle, that someday we would be going to Clark Gable's wedding together?"

The minute I said it, I was horrified, fearful that the gas attendant had heard me and that the secret Clark was trying to keep from press and public was out! But the man at the pump gave no sign of having heard me and, weak with relief, we drove on. We were late getting to the ranch, but Clark held the wedding until we arrived.

The Gillhams had decorated the ranch living room with palms, evergreen boughs and white chrysanthemums, and a crackling fire in the huge stone fireplace made a bright and cheerful setting for the simple Lutheran ceremony, which was performed by the Reverend Aage Miller. Recordings of western music played softly in the background.

Sylvia, who was hatless, wore a soft wool dress of navy blue with white collar and cuffs and had a corsage of white orchids from Clark at her belt. Clark wore a dark suit with a white carnation in his buttonhole. Basil Bleck gave the bride away; Howard was Clark's best man and Vera Bleck the matron of honor.

The Gillhams had provided champagne and a wonderful four-tiered wedding cake, decorated with a miniature bride and groom. We had a very gay party. Clark and Sylvia cut the cake with an ancient Spanish sword, and Sylvia was so nervous she spilled champagne over her orchids and Clark had to help her dry them off.

A reporter had seen Clark and Sylvia in San Luis Obispo and was now phoning around the area, trying to locate them. To avoid him, it was decided that the newlyweds would leave in Howard's car and drive to the Strickling home, where the wedding party would rejoin them.

Mildred Kelly, Eddie Hubbell and I left ahead of them, but I got lost and we reached the Strickling ranch after Clark and Sylvia had arrived. Gail had

With his fourth wife, Lady Ashley. I took this photo of them at the entry to the main house of the ranch. Sylvia is holding Minnie, her Manchester terrier. (1950)

phoned her servants, Marge and Harry Wallace, and asked them to ice champagne for the bridal party and to keep any reporters out. They both got so excited that when we arrived, they would not let us in, because they thought we were from the press!

Howard finally rescued us, and the wedding party continued while Howard called the wire services and press and broke the story on the marriage.

Before leaving that morning I wanted to order a wedding cake for that night. I took Martin into my confidence as he was to pick it up, and since he was known at our usual caterer's, I had to make several calls elsewhere before I could locate one who would prepare the cake on such short notice.

When Clark brought his bride home later that evening, a wedding supper, the wedding cake and champagne were waiting in the firelit dining room.

The ranch was like a madhouse for the next two days. We were swamped with telephone calls, wires, cables, flowers and gifts. (Douglas Fairbanks, Jr., wired his best wishes; he told newspaper reporters, "We adore her and Clark is one of our best friends.")

Reporters and photographers laid siege to the place until a special guard from the studio had to be posted at the gate to keep them out. The newlyweds were to sail on the *Lurline* the night of the twenty-third, to honeymoon in Honolulu. But Sylvia's clothes were all at her beach house. How to get her out of the gate without being stopped was a problem we solved by hiding her on the floor of the car with an auto robe over her, while Martin drove through.

Howard Strickling arranged for the press to meet the bride and groom at the ranch just before they left for the drive to San Francisco, where they were to board the ship. It was like a mob scene for a while, with reporters and photographers everywhere. The resulting publicity was tremendous. The Gable wedding dominated the headlines, and there were photographs and feature stories about them for several days after.

In San Francisco they had to fight their way through hundreds of fans to the *Lurline*, which sailed at midnight. Clark and Sylvia had the Lanai suite— two bedrooms, sitting room and private deck.

Their presence aboard ship caused a great deal of excitement. On deck, they were pursued by excited women; and at the big Christmas Eve party the ship's Santa Claus, who was distributing gifts, had to intervene, begging the passengers not to mob the Gables. "I'm not giving Clark away," he said.

Christmas Day the Gables attended church services and the ship's chef baked them a five-foot wedding cake for dinner. They called me from the *Lurline*, but Russ and I had driven to Death Valley for the holidays and missed the call.

Having seen Clark and Sylvia off to San Francisco, the Stricklings flew to Honolulu. There they engaged a romantic "honeymoon house" with a private beach, and had it in readiness when the Gables arrived on the twenty-seventh. (Gloria and Jimmy Stewart had occupied the house the year before.)

Howard went out on the pilot boat to meet the *Lurline*. As the ship docked, Clark and Sylvia tossed coins to the diving boys in true tourist fashion. When Clark ran out of coins, he grabbed Sylvia's.

It took almost the entire Honolulu

police force to hold back the ten thousand waiting fans. Reporters and photographers were on the dock, and Howard permitted each photographer to take just one shot; then Clark and Sylvia gave brief interviews. Asked by a reporter if the crowds bothered him, Clark replied, "I like people. I'll begin to worry when they *don't* meet me."

A phalanx of guards rushed the couple through the mob to a waiting car, which took them to the house. As they walked in, a record player was playing "The Hawaiian Wedding March" and a luscious island meal was waiting on a table decorated with huge shells and *ti* leaves from the garden.

Nora, a small Japanese girl, came with the house. She was an efficient cook, maid and social secretary, and expert at monitoring telephone calls.

The newlyweds received many invitations from local people. "Nora would say, 'So and so called, but you don't have to call them back,'" Sylvia told me later. "Or, 'These people from wonderful family, you must call them.'"

Howard and Gail stayed at the Royal Hawaiian Hotel, and Clark and Sylvia joined them occasionally to sun on the beach or go for rides in the outrigger canoes. Sylvia wore shorts but protected her fair skin from the sun with hat and gloves.

They called me on New Year's Day and said they were having a wonderful time.

Clark played a good deal of golf. Sylvia did not play, but walked around the course with him. Ed Pauley, the oil millionaire, offered them his island as a hideaway, but they preferred the honeymoon house. They did go over to the island, however, for a picnic Mr. Pauley gave for them.

The Gables returned on the *Lurline* two weeks later and were met by the usual crowds in San Francisco. The ship docked in the morning and the Gables, driving down from San Francisco, reached the ranch in the late afternoon. Both were radiant. Clark was deeply tanned, and looked relaxed and happier than I had seen him in a long time.

Of course there were adjustments to be made now that the manor had a new mistress. When Sylvia made inquiries about the household routine, I was relieved to have Clark say, "Jeanie will be so glad to have you take over, Syl"—as indeed I was.

Sylvia's maid Elizabeth, a German girl, moved in, bringing with her Sylvia's little Manchester terrier, Minnie. Sylvia's English household furnishings, which had been in storage, were brought out and stored in the stables.

After a survey of the establishment, Sylvia decided that a guest house would be necessary and felt that the servants should have a sitting room added to their quarters. Since there was really no room in the house that could be called hers except her bedroom, she suggested that my office be made into a sitting room for her.

Clark asked me if I'd like to have my office at home, and said he would pay for the addition of a room to our house for that purpose. This was a simply heavenly arrangement as far as I was concerned; and Russ was delighted, for it would give us more time together. Bids were obtained and the same contractor engaged to complete all three building projects.

After a month's work at home under the new system, Clark phoned me one night and said, "This is no good, Jeanie. I need you here on the spot and so does Syl." He said he wanted my office in the new guest house. So I moved back to the ranch and the office at my home was turned into a sitting room.

The guest house had an entry hall, two bedrooms, two baths and a dressing room. One of the bedrooms became a delightful office, with soft green walls, white carpeting, yellow linen draperies, a yellow leather chair and a beautiful pine highboy. The files, intercom system and my big desk were moved in and I was back in business!

The only other changes Sylvia made in the house were in her own bedroom. The walls were painted pink, the sofa reupholstered in white quilted material, and some of her English antiques were introduced as occasional pieces.

New chintz draperies and a few pieces of her English furniture went into her sitting room, along with a priceless collection of rose quartz. The rest of the house remained as it was.

Sylvia planned the menus, managed the household. The ranch meals became quite Continental in flavor, and she introduced many typical English recipes.

Clark asked me if I would help Sylvia handle her business matters, which was an interesting experience for me. Her various legal and business affairs were so complicated that she was in constant correspondence with a battery of English barristers, and the muddle was compounded by the fact that her funds were "frozen" in England.

I found English legal terminology and some of the spelling and everyday idiom fascinating. Frequently I had to go to Sylvia with a letter and ask, "What does this mean?" Then she'd interpret the King's English to me.

Sylvia's accent, diction and choice of words were delightful. I said to her one day, "I love to hear you speak, Mrs. G———."

"All English children are thoroughly trained in proper speech manners," she replied.

Sylvia always addressed me as "Jean." I called her "Mrs. G———," and her favorite name for Clark was "Bird." He called her "Bird" also on occasion, but most of the time she was "Syl."

Sylvia had the true Englishwoman's love for flowers. It was not long before she was planning four large rose gardens at the ranch. This was quite a project, as the soil in the areas she chose was very poor and all new soil had to be brought in, but when the landscaping was done and the roses planted, the gardens were beautiful. Thereafter, we had glorious blooms all year round, which pleased Clark very much. While she was developing the rose gardens at the ranch, Sylvia had a similar garden planted at our place, which delighted us.

Mrs. G——— loved clothes. She had some handsome English country walking suits and shoes that were perfect for the ranch. She also had exquisite evening attire. Clark went with her to Adrian's showing of his spring collection and selected many beautiful things for her.

Her jewels were fabulous, despite the fact that a large portion of her collection had been stolen in Europe the year before. Additional insurance on them became necessary, and the insurance appraisers took hours going over the collection. I was simply agog. I've never seen anything comparable except the crown jewels in the Tower of London.

Their social engagement book was

crowded that spring, for everyone entertained for them. Many of Sylvia's friends were from Hollywood's "European set" and included Sir Charles Mendl, the Ronald Colmans, the David Nivens, Charles Boyer, Louis Jourdan, the Fred Astaires and the Douglas Fairbanks, Jrs.

Although they did very little home entertaining, the Gables were often with the Tyrone Powers and the Gary Coopers, or with Gloria Swanson, or Clifton Webb and his mother, or Sonja Henie and her husband Winnie Gardiner. Among their friends were also Charles Feldman, Cole Porter, Joan Fontaine, the Adrians, the Ray Millands, and Pat Kennedy.

In the middle of May, Clark and Sylvia left for Indianapolis, where Clark was due to start shooting *To Please a Lady,* in which he played a racing car driver. Barbara Stanwyck took the part of a sports columnist. Hal Rosson was the cameraman on the picture, which was shot against the actual background of the annual Decoration Day race itself.

The camera crew was right down on the race track. "I shot the line-up of the cars, with the pace car out in front, just before the beginning of the race," Hal says. "We had the King [Clark] in one of the cars as the driver for the scene we'd use in the film.

"Filming the whole fabulous drama of the race in front of that tremendous crowd of spectators is an experience I'll never forget," Hal continues. "Barbara Stanwyck was chosen Queen of the Race, and at the finish she kissed the winner—Johnny Parsons."

Clark really enjoyed making this picture, for he was crazy about sports cars. Sylvia set up housekeeping on a

hot plate in their suite at the Hotel Marott to make it more homey for him and his old friend Al Menasco with his son Sid—who were there for the big race—as well as for Timothy Bleck, Sylvia's eighteen-year-old nephew. (Hal Rosson is Timothy's godfather.)

Immediately upon completion of the picture, Sylvia left for Europe to straighten out some of her business affairs. She wanted Clark to accompany her, but he refused. "It won't be any fun for me if you're sitting around with all those legal lights," he said.

Sylvia took Timothy Bleck with her, and Clark came home with Al Menasco and his son.

Sylvia returned from Europe in three weeks and we began making plans for their location trip to Durango, Colorado, where *Across the Wide Missouri* was to be filmed.

The Gables left on July 28 for Durango. Clark drove across the desert to the location, while Sylvia went by train with the luggage and her dog Minnie, who was always with her.

The cast and crew stayed at El Rancho Encantado, occupying small guest cabins. Sylvia set up housekeeping in the Gable cabin; she had grass turf brought in and laid around it and flowers planted.

The entire company ate together ranch-style at long wooden tables. Sylvia always brought Minnie to the table with her, and Clark was embarrassed when the crew ribbed him about the dog.

Clark did a great deal of fishing. Sylvia made several attempts at it, but finally confessed that she was no Izaak Walton. Thereafter she and Minnie merely sat by while Clark fished.

Sylvia loved needlepoint and spent endless hours on it. In Durango she made Clark a pair of slippers and later a beautiful rug for the fireplace, repeating the hollyhock design from the living room draperies in it. She was also a rather clever painter; she had brought her easel along and did a bit of painting.

Wayne Griffin went up to visit Clark and drove with him to the location each day. Wayne said later that he sensed all was not well in the Gable menage even then, although things seemed perfectly calm on the surface.

Clark and Sylvia returned to the ranch in mid-September and we settled down to our usual routine. Sylvia gardened, did needlepoint and painted. She did a picture of herself and Clark in a pony cart with the three dogs. It was a marvelous likeness of both of them, and that Christmas she had it reproduced on their Christmas cards.

Sylvia had made no changes in Clark's staff of servants—in fact she liked them all very much, especially Martin, the butler. Clark, however, could not accustom himself to having the maid Elizabeth always hovering in attendance, so Sylvia finally had to let her go.

"It's not that I dislike her," Clark said. "It's just that she's always *with* us."

There was the usual round of social activities, but Clark frequently drove up to Wayne Griffin's horse- and cattle-ranch alone, to ride and practice lassoing. He was good at it, too. He loved to travel light on these occasions, usually carrying just a small plastic bag containing toothbrush and razor, and sleeping in his shorts.

That fall Wayne and his wife Elinor invited the Gables to have dinner with them and attend the opening night of the San Francisco opera season in Los Angeles. Sylvia was delighted, but Clark, while he loved being with the Griffins, was not much of an opera buff.

According to Wayne, Sylvia was "really ravishing" in a garnet-red velvet dress, white mink and diamonds. With Clark in white tie and tails, they made a very handsome couple.

The opera was long and dull. Clark promptly went to sleep. He had on an alarm watch, and during one of the lulls in the music, the alarm went off. Clark woke up with a tremendous start. Sylvia was amused, Clark embarrassed.

When Sylvia told me about it, I said I knew how Clark felt, for Russ is an opera devotee while I have slept through more of them than any wife I know.

"Perhaps I should take Russ to the opera next time," Sylvia laughed, "while you and Clark go to a music hall."

Al Menasco bought a ranch in the Napa Valley that year, and he and Julie invited Clark and Sylvia to come up for Thanksgiving. Sylvia, who was not the outdoor type, was not eager to go, but Clark thought it would be fun. "Your carriage will await you at five A.M., my lady," he said.

Sylvia said nothing, but when Clark came down with his bags the next morning, he found her packed and waiting in the car.

"She really was a good sport about everything, and we had a very relaxed time of it," Al says, "even though a big bullfrog kept her awake all night."

Clark loved Al's ranch, and when he found that the property next to it was for sale, he told Al to buy it for him if he could get it for seventy-five thousand dollars.

"Do you think Sylvia will like this quiet country life?" Al asked.

"That won't make any difference," Clark replied.

Another of my snapshots of Clark. Here he is in my office with Riquet, the poodle Sylvia sent him from back East. (1950)

Sylvia painted this scene and then had it made into Christmas cards. Of course, my husband Russ and I received one with a personal inscription. The card shows Clark, Sylvia holding Rover, and Bobby and Minnie alongside the buggy. (1950)

This was the first indication Al had that things were not going well in the Gable household.

In December, the Gables left for Nassau to spend Christmas as house guests of the Carl Holmes's. Russ and I were in Honolulu for the holidays and I did not see them until they returned to the ranch in mid-January.

Neither Clark nor Sylvia looked particularly happy, and I sensed an undercurrent of some sort, but thought nothing of it—for to outward appearances everything seemed fine.

Clark was interested in building a more substantial cabana out at the pool, to replace the awninged one. He and Sylvia came up to our house to see ours, and liked it so much that they built one very like it. The finished cabana had a lovely view of the rose gardens and the pool.

On Clark's first birthday after their marriage, Sylvia had had a formal dinner party for him, the guest list made up of her Continental and café society friends. For his birthday in 1951, she told me she wanted to give him a party with *his* friends, and his kind of food. She asked me what I thought he'd like most of all.

"Stewed chicken and dumplings are not exactly party fare," I said, "but they are Clark's favorite dish."

"Then that's what we'll have," Sylvia replied.

We were breaking in a new cook, and when Sylvia mentioned the party to Clark, he said, "Syl, I think you ought to wait until we see how this cook works out."

Sylvia thought the cook could handle chicken and dumplings, however, so she ordered the dinner and invited the Menascos, the Stricklings, the Adrians, the Griffins and Merle Oberon.

That evening the house looked very beautiful, with fires burning in all the fireplaces and fresh flowers everywhere. Dinner was announced and the meal began.

The cook had prepared the chicken the day before, but had not refrigerated it properly, and it had spoiled. She did not discover this until it was ready to serve, then panicked and sent it in anyway by Martin. As he entered the dining room with the platter, Martin became aware that something was wrong. But the guests were at the table, so he could do nothing but serve the slightly odoriferous mixture.

Soon several of the ladies brought out perfumed handkerchiefs to dab at their noses. Nothing daunted, the men began to eat the chicken—all except Clark, who rose from the table, went to his room, and did not put in an appearance until later in the evening. By that time the humor of the situation was paramount, and the guests were slightly hysterical with laughter as they vied with each other in recounting similar *contretemps* of their own in an effort to put the embarrassed Sylvia at her ease.

You can imagine how I felt the next morning when Sylvia called me on the intercom to tell me that the party had been a hilarious fiasco: *I* had suggested the chicken!

Together we confronted the cook.

"If you knew the chicken was spoiled, why on earth didn't you tell me?" Sylvia asked. "At least I could have phoned the Brown Derby to rush out Chicken Tetrazzini as a substitute!"

"Oh, Mrs. Gable, I was too scared!" the cook replied. "I can't handle this job—I'm quitting." And pack her bags she did.

Naturally we had to get a new cook, and Sylvia asked me to find one.

Juanita took over in the kitchen while I interviewed several prospects. Finally I hired Fanny Wakefield, who was to be with the Gable household until 1958.

Despite its authentic background, *Across the Wide Missouri* suffered in the editing and was not a good picture.

Clark and Wayne Griffin were still discussing the formation of their own company, to produce pictures which would be distributed through MGM. Borden Chase found an original story called *Lone Star,* and Dick Powers, Borden's agent, asked Clark to read it. He liked it, and he and Wayne thought they might buy it and make it the initial production of their company, which Clark wanted to call "Sylvia Productions." The company was to be a three-partner setup, with Clark, Wayne and A. Morgan Maree.

Griffin thought he could buy *Lone Star* for forty thousand dollars, since it was a rough, unfinished synopsis. Clark said, "These are my friends and we have to pay a fair figure." They paid one hundred thousand dollars for the story, which included Borden Chase's services in writing the screenplay.

Clark changed his mind, however, about forming his own company, so the story was finally sold to Metro, with Wayne as producer and Clark as star. Ava Gardner was the female lead, and Clark's old friend Lionel Barrymore was in the cast, which pleased Clark.

The picture was scheduled to start in May, and in early April Clark entered Cedars of Lebanon Hospital for a complete physical check-up. Sylvia checked into St. Johns Hospital at the same time for minor surgery. She came home a day ahead of him.

By this time rumors were flying about the status of the Gable marriage. Hedda Hopper called Sylvia and quoted her as saying, "I'm stuck on the guy and always will be."

Sylvia had a long private talk with Wayne at his office, telling him that her marriage was failing that she'd do anything in the world to save it. Naturally, I knew all of this was going on, but it was still quite a shock to have Clark tell me that he had asked Sylvia for a divorce and that he was sorry it had turned out that way.

I was very much disturbed, because I had so hoped for happiness for both of them. Yet they were two people as far apart as the poles when

Clark took Sylvia to a special showing of designer Adrian's collection, where he brought her a beautiful wardrobe. Adrian is seated with them. (1950) PHOTO BY HIGGINS/ENGSTEAD. COURTESY OF JOHN ENGSTEAD

it came to the fundamentals. Their concepts and approaches to life, people, and the business of living, their likes and dislikes, were so radically different that the break-up of the marriage was inevitable, although both had tried hard to make a go of it.

In April, Sylvia left for Nassau, still insisting to reporters that all was well and that she was going over to look at some property she and Clark were considering for possible purchase. She returned in May, and by now the rumors had become public gossip.

On May 31, 1951, Sylvia filed for divorce in Santa Monica court and left the next day with her friends the George Vanderbilts aboard their yacht *Pioneer*. They were on a six month's marine exploration voyage to the South Seas, and Sylvia was to leave them at Honolulu.

Meanwhile Clark started work on *Lone Star,* which was being directed by Vincent Sherman. Broderick Crawford was the "heavy" in the film and he, Clark, Wayne and Sherman had a lot of fun together.

One night the four had dinner in a private room at Dave Chasen's restaurant and decided to rehearse the film's big fight scene between Clark and Brad. Soon Wayne and Sherman got into the act, and the four men really tore the place to pieces.

"Dave Chasen was wonderful about the whole thing," Wayne says. "Of course we paid for the damage, and the next day Dave sent us each a pair of cuff links fashioned like boxing gloves."

Clark and the set technicians cooked up a gag on Wayne by wiring his new Cadillac, but when Wayne started the car the resulting explosion was worse then they'd planned. The blast sounded like a 75mm howitzer, broke all the spark plugs, and buckled the hood. Black smoke poured out and Wayne was covered with oil and soot.

Clark was torn between laughter and remorse. "I wish you could see your face," he told Wayne, and laughed so hard he had to lie down. After it was all over, however, he felt terrible and had the car towed away for the necessary repairs.

Clark was increasingly unhappy about the type of stories he'd been making and we had many discussions about his career. We both began to feel that perhaps a change of agents would be helpful. Clark talked the matter over with Wayne Griffin.

"I like Allenberg," Wayne said, "but if you're going to make a change, why not consider MCA: they're big and powerful, and I feel they'd do a good job for you."

Clark agreed to talk with them, so Wayne called Lew Wasserman and George Chasin of the MCA office, and a meeting was set up out at the ranch. Over the lunch table, the deal was made. Clark made the necessary arrangements to pay the Allenberg agency the commissions he still owed them, and MCA became his representatives.

Sylvia returned from Honolulu early in August and joined the Blecks at the beach house. Clark suggested that she come out to the ranch and get her things, but she delayed. Every so often he'd call her and she'd promise to attend to it right away, but nothing happened. This went on for weeks.

Clark became impatient, and moved to the Glenbrook Lodge at Lake Tahoe, Nevada, to establish residence in that state. He filed his own suit for divorce in Las Vegas early in October.

CHAPTER TEN

CLARK enjoyed the life at Glenbrook Lodge. The golf and riding were superb, and he asked the Griffins to bring his guns up to him so he could do some hunting. En route, their Cadillac sedan caught fire and burned completely. Fortunately, Wayne got their luggage and the guns out in time, but they had to thumb a ride to Carson City, where Clark met them.

A few days later Clark phoned for his saddle and we drove up to the lodge with it, passing the charred frame of the Griffin's Cadillac on our way. Russ and I spent several days at Glenbrook, enjoying the wonderful food and lodging and the beautiful mountain country.

We drove East on our vacation and were on our way home early in October when Clark (who had our itinerary) called us in Salt Lake City and asked us to meet him in Reno. We spent some time at a dude ranch there because Clark wanted Russ's advice on ranch properties; he was very serious about purchasing land in that area. He had changed his car license and established a bank account, for he wanted to become a resident of Nevada. We looked at any number of places, but never found one that suited Clark.

In late fall, when the Glenbrook Lodge closed for the season, Clark moved to the Flying M.E. Ranch at Carson City, which became his official residence. He came back to California just once after that, with the Griffins. They dropped him at his bank and

Howard met him there. Clark withdrew all his funds, in cash, and put them in a suitcase he had with him, and he and Howard left immediately for Carson City. By moving his funds to Nevada, he thus eliminated any possibility of legal attachments in connection with the divorce.

Early in December Clark had me buy him a Cadillac convertible, and Russ and I drove it to Phoenix, where he met us. We all stayed in Clark's bungalow at the Arizona Biltmore and had a wonderful time. Betty Chisholm entertained for us, and was charming. Russ and I flew home and Clark returned to the Flying M. E. Ranch for Christmas. He'd met Natalie Thompson, a young divorcee, there and found her very attractive.

During the entire time that Clark was living in Nevada, I was the intermediary between him and his legal counsel, W. I. Gilbert. Clark would call me and discuss various matters, then I would call Bill Gilbert, then call Clark right back. This went on night after night, tying up our telephone for hours, while my patient and long-suffering husband sat by. This was a very difficult time for me, for I found myself in the middle of a situation not of my making, pressured on all sides by both Clark's and Sylvia's friends. My office and home telephones rang all day and far into the night.

Meantime, Sylvia, through her attorneys Jerry Geisler and Barry Brannen, obtained an injunction against Clark's Nevada divorce action and left for Nassau. Because of certain legal technicalities Clark, on advice of counsel, announced that he would abide by the injunction. Then, since it was no longer necessary for him to remain in Nevada, he returned to California after Christmas, to wait until the divorce came to trial.

Natalie Thompson arrived in Beverly Hills to visit her mother and Clark squired her everywhere. She was young and gay and terribly enchanted with him.

Clark worked around the ranch, and began to do some spring plowing with the tractor. Wayne came out one day and found him stuck on the hill. "You'd better get somebody to pull you out or you'll cut your foot off trying to move that thing," he advised.

"Never mind, you run your plow and I'll run mine," Clark replied, but in the end he did have to have the tractor pulled out.

Clark had nothing planned for his February 1 birthday and seemed so lonely and concerned about the forthcoming divorce action that a friend and I decided to make him a coconut cake, which was one of his favorite desserts.

The friend had a fabulous recipe, involving fresh grated coconut and the coconut milk. It is very complicated and requires a great deal of work, but she helped me and together we produced a masterpiece. Clark was so touched and pleased!

He left the next day for New York to meet Sylvia, who was returning from Nassau, so they could discuss the divorce settlement.

The Griffins accompanied him, Wayne to stand by to render any help necessary. Sylvia had broken her ankle in an accident in Nassau and went directly to Doctor's Hospital. Clark and Wayne called on her the night of her arrival, and found her in a wheelchair.

"Syl was such a good sport," Wayne says. "She and Clark greeted each other like two old chums. They had many laughs and Clark kept calling her 'Bird' ".

They called on her again the next afternoon, and she and Clark were so friendly that Wayne could hardly get Clark away. "I felt sure there was going to be a reconciliation," he said.

When they arrived in New York Wayne had been asked to use his influence to get Clark to appear at a Madison Square Garden rally being staged for the purpose of persuading General Dwight Eisenhower (who was still in Europe) to run for President. Clark always felt that as an actor he should stay out of politics, and refused. Wayne persuaded him, however, that he should work for this great American—and Clark finally said, "All right, we'll do it."

On the afternoon of the rally, Clark and Wayne went to see Sylvia again. She had had a nasty fall from her wheelchair and was not feeling too well, but was very happy to see them. She and Clark began on the same old intimate footing, calling each other "Bird."

Time passed and no mention of settlement had been made. So Wayne said, "Now, Syl, this is all very jolly, but I think you and Clark should get down to business."

"I really don't want to cause any trouble or get involved in a lot of legal difficulties," Sylvia replied. "I just want to work out a fair settlement, so I can get along. Why don't you all talk to Barry Brannen and work out something? Whatever is right and proper is all right with me."

It was now so late that Wayne suggested they leave, but Clark and Sylvia were having such a fine time, laughing, joking and kidding each other, that Clark said, "You go along. I'll see you later at the hotel."

Wayne waited at the hotel for some time, then called the hospital, reminding Clark that it was nearly time for the rally.

"Don't worry about your nephew, Uncle Waynsie, I'll be there," Clark replied.

"I know," Wayne said, "but when? You've had no dinner, and you have to dress."

Clark finally put in an appearance. He ate a sandwich while changing to another suit, and he, Wayne and Elinor Griffin sped to the rally in the special limousine provided by the program committee.

They were all seated on a platform in a ring, along with various political dignitaries, other movie stars, and Fred Waring's band. The highlight of the rally was to be the broadcast of a conversation between Clark and General Eisenhower, who was standing by on a transatlantic telephone hookup. The program committee had provided a long script for Clark. He read it and said: "I can't use this. You'll have to let me say it in my own words."

Here I am with Clark in his dressing room at the MGM studio. (1950)

At the appointed time, the master of ceremonies announced: "This is being beamed to you, General, to let you know that the people want 'Ike' for their leader." Then Clark spoke.

"General, I'm sure that if you were here at this rally," he said, "there'd be no doubt in your mind that your fellow Americans want you as their next President. If you decide to run, that's the way it will be, for you will win."

Ike laughed, said something about being grateful for the demonstration but feeling he could not make a definite decision at that time.

Everyone commented on the fact that Clark's laugh, tone of voice and manner of speech were exactly the same as Ike's, and that it was difficult to tell which one was speaking.

Clark and the Griffins returned to California, the divorce settlement was discussed, and an out-of-court agreement reached.

Wayne, at Clark's request, accompanied Sylvia into Santa Monica court on April 21, 1952. Sylvia received an uncontested interlocutory divorce decree and the judge awarded her the equitable settlement agreed upon.

His sixteen-month marriage at an end, Clark was once more a free man, restless, bored, definitely at loose ends. *Lone Star* was released and received bad notices. Wayne and I were concerned about Clark's recent pictures and felt that in the future we must insist on better stories and direction for him—in fact, demand them.

MCA now negotiated a deal whereby Clark was to make *Never Let Me Go* for the studio in England. Clark's first European trip had been cut short by his father's death. He decided to leave a few weeks ahead of the film's starting date, visit France and see some of the things he'd long wanted to see.

He sailed May 6, 1952 on the *Liberté*, after a gala send-off in New York, with all the officials of the French Line on hand.

He called me on his arrival at the Hotel Lancaster in Paris, reporting that the city was "gay, warm and beautiful." The studio had given him the script of *Mogambo*, which he'd read on shipboard. He was enthusiastic about it, particularly since MGM was negotiating to have John Ford direct it.

In Paris, Clark met Schiaparelli model Suzanne Dadolle, a tall and beautiful Basque, and wrote that she was taking him sight-seeing, introducing him to many wonderful restaurants, and that it was delightful having such a charming guide and interpreter.

When *Never Let Me Go* was due to start, Clark moved to the Dorchester in London, bought a new Jaguar, and asked me to sell the one he'd left at home, as he planned to bring the new one back with him.

The picture began shooting in mid-June at MGM's Boreham Wood Studios, with Gene Tierney as Clark's leading lady. Clark played the part of an American correspondent married to a Russian ballerina. The correspondent impersonates a Russian officer in order to rescue his wife, the ballerina, from behind the Iron Curtain.

The "rescue" scenes were filmed in Cornwall, and Clark wrote from a town called Mullion that the countryside was as grim a place as he'd ever seen and the cold rainy weather was holding things up. Baths and hot water were a major problem. Clark was happy, however, at having Gene playing opposite him, and he liked Delmar Daves, the director, very much.

Before he left Hollywood, Joan Harrison told Clark she expected to be in England while he was there and he suggested that they get together for a date.

When she arrived, Clark phoned her from Cornwall and said, "I have only one more scene down here and then I'll be back in London. Let's have a date tomorrow night."

He called the next day and said that "rain had delayed things and that he couldn't make it until the day after," Joan says. "Every day it was the same story until it got to be a gag. Clark didn't actually reach London until the following Monday, when we made a definite engagement for dinner and the theater that evening.

"He called later in the day," she continues, "and said they were scheduled to shoot all night outside Covent Garden. So our first date in London was for a breakfast of English bacon and eggs at a Lyons tea shop in Covent Garden, after Clark's all-night session before the cameras."

It was now definite that Clark would waive his usual four months' vacation after completion of the picture and proceed directly to East Africa for *Mogambo*. Sam Zimbalist, the producer, suggested that he have his *Mogambo* wardrobe made in London, so Clark was busy with fittings between scenes on *Never Let Me Go*.

The weather in London was miserable. Howard Strickling's assistant, Morgan Hudgins, came over to arrange some publicity, and he and Clark rode home together every night, for both lived at the Dorchester.

"Clark had a fireplace in his suite,"

Morgan says, "and when we'd get home, he always said, 'Come on in, let's cut the fog with a tall one.' We'd sit around in front of the fire, have a few drinks and reminisce. They were quiet but pleasant times."

Never Let Me Go ran behind schedule. After Morgan left, Clark found London somewhat dull and began flying to Paris for the weekends. He was there for Bastille Day on July 14, France's big national holiday, and he and Suzanne Dadolle joined the revelers, dancing in the streets until dawn, then having hot onion soup in the famous Halles market.

Clark was delighted to have Betty Chisholm spend a few days in London, and when she sailed for home, he called to tell me that she'd rented her home in Arizona and would be in Hollywood that fall. He wanted us to put out the welcome mat and extend the ranch's hospitality to her. (Betty spent a month at the ranch and was a delightful guest.)

Meanwhile, we were busy on the home front. Because Clark was to be away for some time, we had let Fanny the cook go, with the understanding that she was to return when Clark came home. Martin and Juanita were keeping things going at the house, and I was involved with Clark's business affairs. I sold the Jaguar and his motorcycle, as requested.

Clark asked me to send him some candy, as it was rationed in England at that time. The first box was sent from Beverly Hills. After that I made arrangements with a shop in New York to forward regular shipments.

He also wired me to send him certain of his suits. His closets contained a bewildering array of apparel, but Clark knew exactly when and where he had purchased each article, even

158

though it might have been years before. When requesting a suit he would give me the date on it and all I had to do was check the dates inside his suits and I could locate the right one at once.

Clark left London on September 20 and had the Jaguar flown across the English Channel to La Touquet, then began a leisurely drive south, stopping at little inns along the way where, with his French dictionary, he managed enough French to insure his having food, wine and a good bed.

He phoned me from Biarritz that he expected to reach Rome on October 10, and would be at the Grand Hotel until he left for Nairobi.

He crossed the border into Switzerland at Geneva, drove through that country's breathtaking scenery and had a thrilling ride through a blinding snowstorm on the top of the Saint Gotthard Pass, where a Swiss guard by the roadside informed him in German that the road was impassable and he could not proceed.

Clark knew enough Pennsylvania German to ask for directions. He was told that he must go back about fifteen miles and put his car on a train that would take him through a tunnel beneath the pass, from which he could go on into Italy.

Once through the tunnel, Clark got his car off the train and drove down the mountain, ending up on Lake Como at the famous Villa d'Este. He'd intended staying two days, but liked the place so much he stayed for three weeks, even phoning London and having his golf clubs flown over, so he could play the magnificent golf course.

He arrived in Rome on October 17, and called me again to say that he was "acting like a tourist, seeing more churches, ruins and historic landmarks than I ever hope to see again."

Sam Zimbalist wired him to leave Rome on October 31, without fail, as an early start on the picture was advisable due to the Mau Mau situation, which was getting touchier every day.

Clark stored his Jaguar in Rome, flew out via British Comet on October 31, and arrived in Nairobi on November 2. MGM headquarters were at the New Stanley Hotel, where he met John Ford, the director, who'd been there for some time, supervising production arrangements.

While waiting for the rest of the cast to arrive, Clark and Ford flew upcountry sixty miles to Mount Kenya, to inspect an animal compound owned by Carr Hartley, a South African white hunter and trapper, who furnished a great many of the animals for American zoos and circuses. Carr had trapped and trained many of the animals for use in the film.

Clark had asked MGM to forward his guns and Carr took him out shooting. Clark got a number of birds. East Africa is a hunter's paradise; Clark was crazy about the place. He wired me for some of his own hunting clothes and his movie camera, and indicated that two cartons of American cigarettes a week would be most welcome.

Mogambo was to be a remake of *Red Dust,* which Clark had made in 1932 with Jean Harlow. He was to repeat his role of the white hunter engaged to take a British scientist and his wife on safari. Grace Kelly was to play the part of the wife, and Ava Gardner was to be the stranded American showgirl who turns up unexpectedly in Clark's camp.

Ava and Grace arrived on November 7, together with Frank Sinatra,

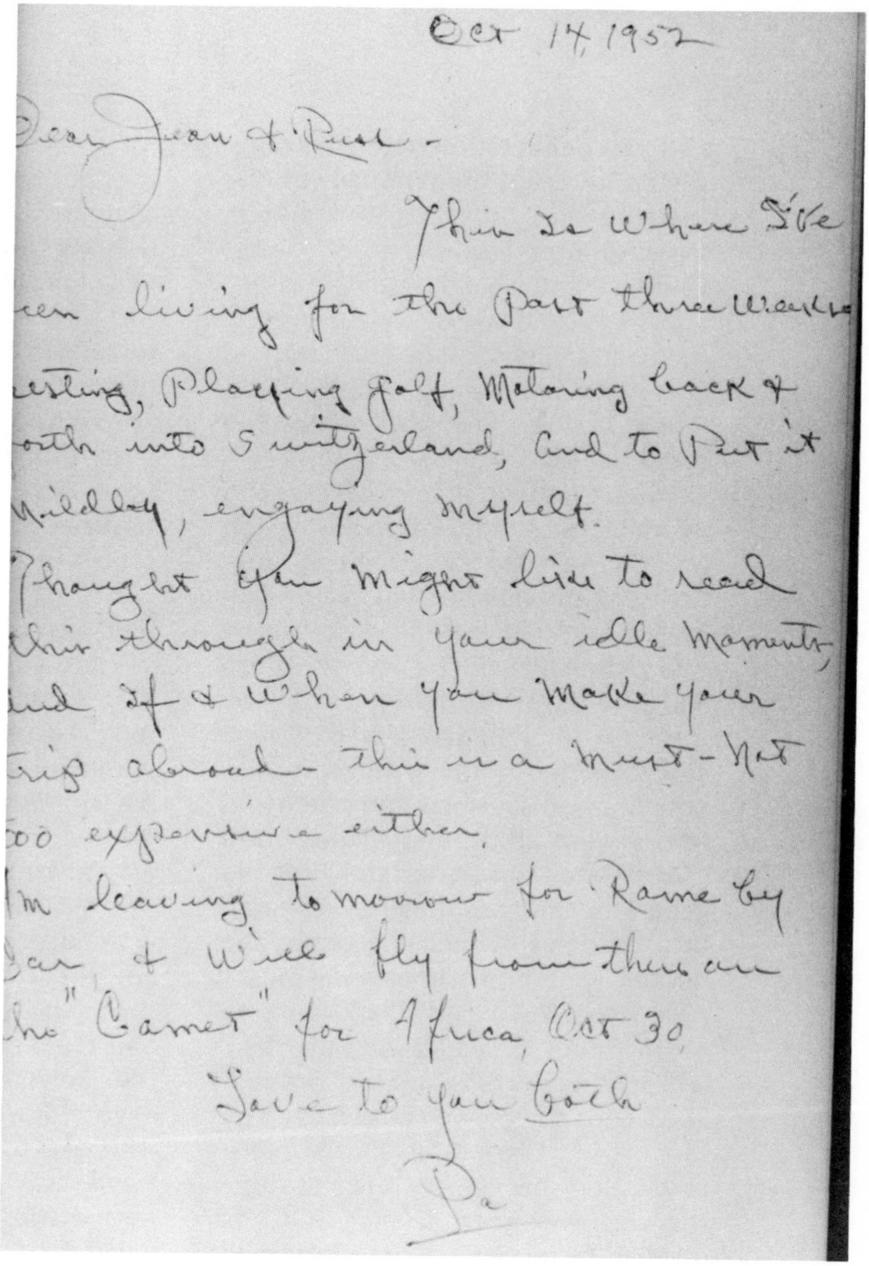

Oct 14, 1952

Dear Jean & Paul —

This is where I've
been living for the past three weeks,
resting, playing golf, motoring back &
forth into Switzerland, and to put it
mildly, enjoying myself.
Thought you might like to read
this through in your idle moments,
and if & when you make your
trip abroad — this is a must — Not
too expensive either.
I'm leaving tomorrow for Rome by
car & will fly from there in
the "Comet" for Africa, Oct 30,
Love to you both
Pa

This letter was written by Clark to me and my husband on the flyleaf of a book from the famous hotel, the Villa D'Este on Lake Como, Italy. (1952)

Eileen Thomas, an MGM secretary and Morgan Hudgins. They were tired after the long flight; but it was Ava's and Frank's wedding anniversary, so they staged an informal party in their suite and Clark met Grace for the first time.

November 12 was Grace Kelly's twenty-third birthday, and Clark got together with Morgan Hudgins to prepare a surprise birthday party for her in the hotel dining room. They got their signals mixed, however, and it wasn't much of a surprise; but they all had fun.

Meanwhile preparations were made for the entire company to take off on safari to Tanganyika, where a camp had been set up on the Kagera River. The schedule called for four weeks' shooting in this location. MGM spared no expense in organizing the expedition, which was to be the largest safari in the history of Africa.

The British Government put out

a special bulletin describing the camp and its location. The company of one hundred and forty-nine whites and three hundred Kenyans lived in tents. There were two hospital tents, a dance floor, a recreation tent, a movie tent. A full-size airstrip had been hacked out of the jungle, and supply planes shuttled back and forth between the camp and Nairobi.

Clark had the time of his life. This was his kind of country, and the ten white hunters attached to the production spoke his kind of language. Clark became very friendly with Bunny Allen, the chief of the white hunters, and whenever he could get away, he went on hunting safaris with Bunny and the other hunters. Lions, hippopotami, hyenas, zebras and other wild beasts were all around in the bush. Clark was not interested in killing big game; the only shooting he did was to bring in game to feed the camp. The hunters shot mostly impala for food.

Grace Kelly and Clark became great friends. Grace called him "Ba," which is the Swahili word for "Father." She frequently got up at dawn to go on safari with Clark and the hunters, taking along her camera. Clark thought she was a wonderful sport, but was puzzled by her enjoyment of the wild country and the rough going of the hunt.

"What is there about this that you like?" he asked her one day.

"It's the excitement and the strangeness of it all," Grace replied. "I want to be able to tell my children about it someday."

After the first day's camera work, Clark became a John Ford fan. He felt that Ford knew his business, was a master in the art of directing, and that the picture was going to be a success.

Clark's contract was coming up for renewal in the near future and he was not sure that he wanted to sign again with MGM. He was still considering formation of his own company for independent production, and was so sold on Africa that he wanted to return there to make a picture of his own.

I made out a Christmas list, sending it to Clark with gift suggestions for those concerned, and he returned it to me with his OK. The company had expected to return to Nairobi for Christmas, but the shooting schedule kept them in camp.

MGM went all out on a Christmas dinner, which was served in a large tent, with the entire company seated at one long table decorated with holiday candles and flowers. Menus were printed in Nairobi, and special food was flown in for the meal.

Ava and Grace and the other women dressed up for the occasion, and the climax of the evening was a show staged by Frank Sinatra—who had taught some of the natives from the Belgian Congo to sing "Silent Night." Frank himself closed the show with a medley of Christmas songs. It was a festive evening, but the extreme heat made it seem anything but the yuletide.

Crocodiles were a constant menace to the film colony beside the Kagera River, and the natives, who prized their meat, found them difficult to kill. The crocodile's thick hide is impervious to arrows, and the head is the only vulnerable spot.

"The natives set up a great clamor one day when they spotted a crocodile on a tiny island in the middle of the river, some hundred and fifty yards away," Morgan Hudgins says. "None of the hunters was around, so Clark got his gun; and as the natives watched in deep silence, he sighted, then shot the crocodile right between the eyes with one shot. Clark gave them the kill and they skinned it in nothing flat, divided the meat, and later sold the skin. After that," he continues, "Clark was their hero, their *bwana*, and they looked on him with great respect."

Clark and some of the men occasionally went swimming in the river despite the presence of the crocodiles and the many hippos which came down at sunset; but Ava and Grace never ventured near the water. They used the outdoor shower which was featured in the picture.

The two women became devoted friends, and Ava was very interested in learning some of the native dances; but she preferred to sleep late and leave the early morning hunting safaris to Grace and Clark. This was Clark's third picture with Ava, who was one of his favorite people, for he felt she had great talent. He thought it wonderful to see young actresses like Ava and Grace making a success of their careers.

Soon after Christmas, the cast and crew returned to Nairobi for a few days while the company broke camp at Kagera and moved to a new location in Uganda. Clark had heard that Malindi on the Indian Ocean was a beautiful beach resort, so he suggested a weekend trip there.

"The only transportation available was a ramshackle old plane that looked held together by baling wire," Morgan says, "but Clark talked to the pilot, who convinced him it was airworthy. So we got in—Ava, Grace, Frank, Clark and I—and away we went. I got cold chills for fear the plane would fall apart with all that high-priced talent aboard."

They found Malindi to be a beautiful spot indeed, with surf bathing that Clark thought far surpassed that in Honolulu. It was a most romantic place; the hotel was good; and they stayed several days, which was a refreshing respite after the heat of Tanganyika.

Clark became very fond of Asa Etula, a four-year-old native girl who was used in some of the film sequences. While waiting in Nairobi, Asa's mother approached Clark and offered to sell her child to him for twenty English shillings.

"Clark was in a spot," Morgan says. "He knew that if he refused point-blank she would be deeply offended. He finally told her that he would like very much to have the child, but felt it would not be fair to buy her for he had no wife to take care of her. The mother understood this explanation and was satisfied."

Isiola in Uganda was desolate desert country, with a completely different climate and lots of camels, which the natives used for transportation. Subterranean springs fed several waterholes near the film camp, which provided delightful swimming for the cast at the end of the day.

The company was at this location ten days; then they moved farther up-country for a few days to photograph a particular tribe called the Samburu—a savage, warring group who live by herding cattle, their diet consisting solely of blood and milk. The blood is obtained from the cattle by shooting an arrow into the neck of the beast. Enough blood is drained off for immediate needs, but not enough to kill the animal; then the vein is tied off, the hole plugged with mud, and the natives move on to the next animal.

Clark thought the diet must have agreed with them, for he said they were a colorful people, nearly seven feet in height, wore their hair down

Grace Kelly on location in Africa for **Mogambo.** *(1953)* COURTESY OF MGM

Clark in his tent during filming of Mogambo. He wrote to me telling all about the gala Christmas celebration the cast and crew had. He was probably typing one of those letters when this photo was taken. (1953) COURTESY OF MGM

to their shoulders and covered themselves with paint and trinkets.

At home the studio was receiving glowing reports from John Ford about the cooperative spirit and teamwork of the *Mogambo* cast, and Ford's great admiration and respect for Clark, all of which I relayed to him.

Location shooting in Africa was finished by the end of January and the cast and crew left for London for four weeks of shooting on the sound stages. Clark flew to Rome with John Ford for a few days, then went on to London, after making arrangements to have his Jaguar shipped to him there. He called me early in February to tell me that he was at the Connaught Hotel, which he preferred to the Dorchester.

"It's damned grim and cold here after Africa," he said. "I don't think I'll ever get used to this climate."

English production moves at a slower pace than in Hollywood, and there were many delays while awaiting the arrival of the African sequences and background shots. When John Ford was able to start work, Clark said it kept him busy trying to learn his lines to keep pace with Ford, but he liked it that way because it made the time pass faster. He found London incredibly dull.

He had occasional dates with Grace Kelly and others, but was asked by Sam Zimbalist to help with the editing of the picture and was frequently tied up with him or with John Ford.

The MGM publicity mills were beginning to grind with exploitation for the film. Various interviews were set up for Clark. George Chasin of MCA flew over to discuss a film called *Holland Deep*, which MGM had under consideration for production in Holland. George also wanted to go into the matter of a proposed two-year extension of Clark's contract. Clark was still talking about forming his own company and going in for independent production, and refused to make any decisions until he had had a long-delayed vacation.

Al and Julie Menasco had planned a European trip with Clark, and their arrival in mid-March was supposed to coincide with the finish of the picture, but they found Clark still hard at work. Clark wanted them to go on to Paris, arrange for a car and await his arrival, but they elected to stay in London and go sight-seeing until he was ready to leave.

The picture was finished in mid-April. Clark saw Grace Kelly off to New York on the nineteenth, then left immediately with the Menascos for Paris, where they rented a car for their trip, since the Jaguar would not begin to hold all the luggage.

For the next month, Clark phoned me from various hotels en route, as he, Al and Julie toured Switzerland, France and Italy. Occasionally Suzanne Dadolle joined them for weekends, and they had a wonderful reunion with Wayne and Elinor Griffin in Florence, going on to Venice and then to Capri and Rome. They explored museums, went to concerts, and did all the tourist spots.

"It was interesting to note Clark's pleasure and enthusiasm for the cultural side," Wayne says. "He seemed eager to broaden his knowledge of people, places and things."

I was able to cable Clark at the end of May that his divorce decree had come through and that he was now a free man.

When the Menascos sailed for home, Clark continued his tour of Europe, stopping at all the little Italian

With Al Menasco in the steamy kitchen of the La Fenice Restaurante in Venice, Italy. The chef had prepared Western Cowboy beans—the kind Clark loved—and he wanted to compliment him on them (1953) COURTESY OF AL MENASCO

Al Menasco, Suzanne Dadolle (a Parisian model), and Clark aboard the Andrea Doria. Al and Julie Menasco were heading back to the United States. (1953) COURTESY OF AL MENASCO

and French coastal towns which are off all the tourist routes, and slowly working his way back to Paris.

He called me now and again, as I had no idea where to reach him. "I may as well make the most of this trip, Jeanie," he said. "I don't ever expect to see any of this again."

Mogambo was previewed in Hollywood in midsummer, and Clark received wires of congratulations from Nicholas Schenck, Eddie Mannix, Howard Strickling, Howard Dietz and Joe Vogel. The consensus was that they had a smash hit on their hands. Clark was quite modest about it. He called me very early one morning to discuss the picture. "I helped Sam cut it, so I know its shortcomings," he said. "I hope the public doesn't discover them as quickly as Sam and I did. It's good but could have been better."

By the end of July, Clark was established at the Hotel Raphael in Paris and was reading the script of *Holland Deep*, the story of an intelligence officer in occupied Holland. It had been revised and tightened considerably. Sam Zimbalist was to produce and Gottfried Reinhardt had been signed to direct. Lana Turner was set to co-star and Victor Mature was the "heavy" in the cast.

George Chasin and I read the script and liked it. We talked it over, then advised Clark that we had high hopes for Reinhardt's direction and, since his contract had some months to run, we thought Clark should give the script serious consideration.

Clark felt fit and rested and, since he was already in Europe, he decided that rather than go off salary he would make the film, but the many changes in management at MGM made him determined that it was to be his last under the Metro banner.

In mid-August Clark shipped his Jaguar home and flew to London for story conferences with Gottfried Reinhardt and wardrobe fittings for *Holland Deep*, which was now called *Betrayed*. A tentative schedule called for shooting to begin in Holland in late September.

Clark stayed at the Connaught again, for he liked its gentility, the ancient servants and the coal fire he had in his room. He found several of his MGM friends in town and went with them to dine at Ava Gardner's flat in Abbey Lodge. It was very sumptuous with crystal chandeliers, lots of red velvet furniture with gold fringe, and several fireplaces. The kitchen had two refrigerators but only a tiny stove where Ava cooked her "seven-hour-long spaghetti."

He called me early in September to tell me that he'd agreed to do a week's good-will tour through Holland before the picture started shooting, and that MGM had assigned publicists Paul Mills of their London office and Emily Torchia from the Culver City lot to travel with him. The three flew to Amsterdam via KLM on the morning of the twenty-third, and were met at the airport by huge crowds; then they went on to the Amstel Hotel where a press reception had been arranged.

From Amsterdam they drove to Delft, picking up a police escort equipped with sirens several miles outside of the town, and were taken to the Town Hall in the public square where immense crowds of fans waited and the Burgomaster and other officials had a reception for them.

Driving on to Rotterdam the next day, they found the usual throngs awaiting them at the Rotterdam zoo, where Clark was presented with two lion cubs, one named Mogambo and the other Gable.

Clark took a lion cub under either arm and posed for photographers. One cub promptly nipped him, the other made a nuisance of himself, and before Clark could remedy the situation, the lion trainer appeared with a snarling Bengal tiger on one leash and a ferocious Belgian police dog on another.

He was heading directly for Clark, and Paul and Emily thought it was time to rescue him. So they rushed Clark into a nearby pub to get cleaned up, only to discover the name of the place was *Lion d'Or* (Golden Lion).

"I've had enough lions for one day," Clark said, which broke them all up, and they almost "fell apart laughing," according to Emily.

Their next destination was Maastricht, far to the south, where they were met again by police escort, and taken to the town square. Eight thousand citizens and a display of tanks and guns were massed there to celebrate the anniversary of the glorious day when the Allies marched in to liberate Holland from the Nazi occupation.

The Burgomaster and reception committee were waiting at the Town Hall. Clark, Paul and Emily were served champagne in beautiful crystal goblets manufactured in Maastricht. After toasts were drunk, the goblets were presented to them as gifts.

The Burgomaster made a speech about the Hollanders' love for the Americans who liberated them from the Nazis, and Clark responded in like manner, claiming kinship with them through his Dutch mother, whose name was Hershelman. This made a tremendous hit with the crowds and a pretty girl was chosen to give Clark a kiss of thanks.

That night the party stayed in a castle set in a seventeen-hundred-acre park of beautiful trees. Built in 1350, the castle was the former home of an impoverished countess who had turned it into a hotel.

During the evening, Clark wanted his companions to sample some dark Holland beer, served from a pitcher, and Emily managed to spill some on her suit.

"That makes us even," Clark said. "Now you smell of beer and I smell of lion."

Utrecht, The Hague and other cities were on the good-will tour itinerary. Everywhere, in cities and in quiet villages, people did double takes when they saw Clark. In The Hague *Mutiny on the Bounty* and *San Francisco* were playing at the theaters in his honor.

"Everywhere Clark went he commanded respect," Emily says. He had such innate dignity and courtesy that he was never pushed and pulled about as so often happens with other stars. Actually they were a little in awe of him.

Back in Amsterdam, they were joined by the newly married Lana Turner and Lex Barker, Victor Mature and his wife Dorothy, and Mr. and Mrs. Reinhardt. Shooting began in Amsterdam and the company subsequently moved to various locations in Holland. In Arnhem, the company took over an entire country inn called *Koonings Jaght* (The King's Hunting Lodge) which everyone thought particularly appropriate because of Clark. An exciting motorcycle sequence was filmed in National Park, which Clark enjoyed very much. Everywhere enthusiastic crowds gathered to watch the shooting and the publicity was enormous.

When the Holland location shooting was finished at the end of October, the company moved to London for studio filming. Paul Mills and Clark elected to return by boat and Clark phoned me from London to tell me that he was at the Connaught, expected to finish sometime in December, and would be home for Christmas.

"Get Fanny back as soon as you can," he said. "I can't wait to eat her fried chicken and chocolate cake."

We were in a whirl of activity at the ranch, for, at Clark's request, extensive redecorating had been going on under the direction of Dorothy Paul, a clever decorator.

Sylvia's sitting room had been made into a library for Clark, and the desk given him by David Selznick had been moved down from his bedroom and additional antique furniture brought in.

Sylvia's room had been recarpeted and refinished in soft tones of green, for Clark had specifically asked that I get rid of "that damned pink."

The living room furniture had been reupholstered in its original colors and the kitchen completely remodeled with stainless steel sinks and new hardware.

The matter of Clark's contract now became urgent at MGM. Eddie Mannix flew to London to offer Clark a renewal which he refused to sign, for he was determined to end his association with the studio.

Betrayed finished shooting and Clark flew home via Pan American Airline in mid-December. The ranch never looked lovelier and he was even more excited this time than he was when he returned from the war.

Wayne and Elinor Griffin had invited Betty Chisholm and a few of his intimate friends to a small homecoming party for him, and he seemed glad to settle down for the first time in nearly twenty months.

Clark was delighted with the changes and doubled my bonus check at Christmas. When I protested his generosity, he said, "Money is so little—I can never repay you for the wonderful way you have handled my affairs." This unexpected praise was the finest Christmas present I could have received.

Clark and Betty Chisholm flew to Amarillo, Texas, to spend New Year's with Betty's friends, the Harringtons. Don and Sybil Harrington have homes in Phoenix and Amarillo, and the Big Bull Ranch northeast of Amarillo.

The turkey, duck and quail shooting at the ranch was superb and the foursome had a wonderful time. When Don said, "I must get back to Phoenix," Clark shook his head. "If I had a place like this I'd never leave," he said.

Early in January Clark had to go back to the studio for a few retakes on *Betrayed* and to make some publicity stills. That completed his contractual obligations and he was free to leave. The day before his departure Emily Torchia (who had been with him in Holland) came to him and asked if they might have a farewell party for him. "Absolutely not," Clark replied.

On his last day many of the men and women with whom he had been associated over the years came to say good-by and wish him well.

Larry Barbier dropped in just as Clark was leaving. Clark looked at him and said, "Well, Larry, this is it!" Then he got in his car and drove through the gates of the studio for the last time. It had been his working "home" for twenty-three years!

Clark's future plans were now paramount in his thinking. After he came home we sat down and had a long and serious discussion about his career. He was receiving advice from all sides as to his course of action. Many thought he should form his own company, others suggested that he direct, still others thought he should retire.

It was a time for stocktaking, and we discussed the situation from all angles. I reminded him that *Mogambo* was a smash hit, his popularity was never higher, and that he was (and had been) on the distributors "top ten" star list, despite the fact that he was fifty-three and graying at the temples.

"I don't understand it, Jeanie," Clark said humbly. "How did I arrive at all this? I'm really not a great actor and by rights I should be playing character parts at my age, or thinking of retirement."

With many studios in town bidding for his services, I told him it was foolish to think of retirement. My advice was to keep going, to put himself in his agents' hands and see what was offered . . . and that is the way we left it.

Having arrived at a decision, Clark took off for several weeks in Phoenix, to ride and to play golf with Betty Chisholm.

Later that spring, the Stricklings invited Clark and Betty to go fishing with them off Newport. Betty decided to pull a gag on Clark, and went shopping at one of those "trick" stores and bought a horrible-looking fish. It was a foot long and covered with white fur, and had staring eyes and buck teeth.

When they were out at sea, Betty waited until Clark and Howard were napping in the bow of the boat, then got Pepito, the skipper, to attach her trick fish to Clark's line. The fish floated, however, instead of sinking beneath the water. Pepito gunned his motor and got up sufficient speed to cause the fish to sink.

Clark roused with a start, felt the pull on his line, thought he had a strike and yelled to Pepito to cut the motor

Clark mopping Betty Chisholm's brow after a terrific struggle to land a huge marlin. (1954) COURTESY OF BETTY CHISHOLM

as he began to reel in and "play" his catch. Howard ran to get his camera in order to get a good shot of the action.

Clark kept roaring at Pepito to cut the motor until Pepito had to do so, whereupon the phony fish popped up in the air and Clark practically collapsed at the sight of it. Betty, fearing she had gone too far, panicked. "For an awful moment Clark's face was like a thundercloud," she says, "then he laughed and took it like a good sport."

Gracy Kelly was nominated for an Academy Award for her supporting role in *Mogambo* and Clark escorted her to the Awards in March. Grace didn't win, but her serenity was undisturbed.

She had a tiny burro shipped to Clark from Mexico. When it arrived it was very shaggy and unkempt and covered with Mexican burrs, but we were all crazy about the little beast, whom Grace had named "Ba," her African nickname for Clark. Sunny and Melody had been brought back from Wayne's ranch and Ba fell in love with them and could not be induced to leave their sides.

Al Menasco had a jeep with special racks fitted on the back and Clark decided he must buy one like it. He had the seats upholstered in a zebra skin he brought home from Africa and thereafter loved to go tearing around the hills in it.

One morning before I'd left for the ranch, my neighbor called to warn me there was a rattlesnake on our property. Russ had gone and I was afraid that either the cat or the dog would tangle with it, so I called Clark to see if he'd like to come over and bring his gun.

"I'll be right there," he said.

He arrived, dressed for the occasion in full safari regalia—shorts, wide-brimmed hat, cartridge belt, gun.

"Ham," I said, pointing to the coiled snake.

"I'll show you who's a ham," he replied, and killed it with one shot.

I did some stocktaking of my own that spring. It had been fifteen years since I'd taken over the management of Clark's affairs. While it had been an interesting, often exciting and certainly rewarding job, it had left me very little time for a private life of my own, especially when he was away.

Russ's realty business kept him busy on the weekends and I hardly ever saw him. We never had an opportunity to visit or go anywhere together except on our yearly vacations, and I felt that the time had come for me to retire and devote myself to my husband and my home. I suggested to Clark that we consider a replacement for me.

He refused to consider my resignation or even to discuss the matter. "If you need time off, take it," he said, "but I won't let you leave. You're my right arm and you know it. I don't care what arrangements you make to get the work done, work it out to suit yourself, but you've simply got to stay on here and help me."

At first I tried taking a day off in the middle of the week but that was unsatisfactory, so we finally settled it that I would be at the ranch from ten to four every day, which gave me a little more time for my husband and my own affairs.

All that summer Clark continued to loaf about, and saw a great many of his friends. He was sunning himself in Tucson when the Stricklings and Joan

Clark with his catch of Yellowtail at Newport. (1954) PRIVATE COLLECTION OF HOWARD STRICKLING

Fishing at La Paz, Mexico, in 1954. COURTESY OF BETTY CHISHOLM

This is the way I saw Clark so many times—relaxed and happy with his special friends, Bobby and Rover. (1954) COURTESY OF BETTY CHISHOLM

With Sonja Henie at a party she gave for Liberace. (1954)

Harrison arrived to take him on a fishing trip to Guaymas in Mexico.

En route they stopped for lunch at a little restaurant.

Clark said, "I'm not sure you're going to like the food down here, Joan."

Joan, who had never tasted any Mexican food but was determined to be a good sport and show she was ready for anything, replied very airily, "I love it."

Clark ordered for the group and when the meal arrived, Joan attacked her plate with gusto, while Clark covertly watched.

"The first bite was so hot with peppers that it set my mouth and throat on fire," Joan says, "but I would rather have died than admit it."

"Can you take it?" Clark asked anxiously.

"Of course," Joan replied blithely, "but it needs 'hotting' up a bit with some catsup, don't you think?"

Clark roared with laughter.

When they arrived at Guaymas and went aboard the fishing boat, Joan, who suffered from *mal de mer*, quietly took a double dose of seasickness pills in order to keep in character as an outdoor girl. She became so drowsy that when she did get a "strike" she fell asleep while reeling in the fish and Clark had to take over and land it for her!

MCA had been submitting scripts to Clark for weeks and various picture deals had been discussed, but nothing seemed just right for him until George Chasin came up with an offer from Twentieth Century-Fox calling for Clark to star in two films for them, with a possible third in the offing, at a salary of 10 per cent of the films' box-office gross.

This was an attractive proposition, and the initial script, *Soldier of Fortune*, with Clark's role that of a devil-may-care adventurer in the Far East, seemed tailormade for him.

The Fox contract was dated July 12, 1954, and the picture was scheduled to be filmed in Hong Kong in the fall. It was with high hopes that Clark looked forward to this venture into the free-lance field.

CHAPTER ELEVEN

KAY (KATHLEEN) WILLIAMS, whom Clark had seen a great deal right after his return from the service, now came into his life again. In that interim, the twice-divorced Kathleen had married and divorced Adolph Spreckels II, the sugar heir.

A former Powers model, Kathleen was fifteen years Clark's junior, a beautiful blonde with very blue eyes and a sparkling wit. She lived in Beverly Hills with her two children, Bunker (Adolph Spreckels III), who was six, and Joanie, four. They were both darlings and Clark became very fond of them. Clark began dating Kathleen frequently and when he left for Hong Kong, in early November, she was number one girl on his list.

Eddie Dmytryk, the director on *Soldier of Fortune,* made the trip with Clark. They stopped over in Tokyo for a press conference and some sightseeing and went to the Kokusai Theater for a performance of the traditional *Dance of Autumn.* When the girls on stage spotted Clark, they stopped the show! Afterwards, Clark and Eddie visited them backstage.

Susan Hayward, who was to co-star with Clark, was unable to go to the Orient, so only background shots and sequences in which she did not appear were to be filmed in Hong Kong. George Chasin and I went out to Twentieth Century-Fox to see the tests Clark had made with Susan and they were splendid. We were all keeping our fingers crossed that this would be a good picture!

When Clark arrived in Hong Kong, he cabled me for my measurements. I was terribly excited, and wondered what he was getting me—but lost no time in sending them. I also had to send him the sad news of Lionel Barrymore's death and knew he would be deeply grieved, for Clark felt that Lionel had been his guiding genius in the early days.

Although he was free-lancing, Clark always insisted that his "boys," Lew Smith, his stand-in, and Don Roberson, his make-up man, work with him on his pictures. The entire company stayed at the Peninsula Hotel in Kowloon. Don recalls that one evening they were all so hungry for American food they decided to buy some of the Chinese pork sausages and have a "wiener roast" in their sixth-floor rooms. They found a small stove, built a fire in it, and were in the midst of the roast when Clark appeared.

"He joined in with us and we all had a ball," Don says. "If the management had known about it, they would have thrown us out."

Some of the exterior shots were filmed aboard junks in the harbor. "Clark was fond of a cute kid—a little Chinese boy," Don continues. "He took him clothes and toys—a little gift of some kind every day. I think if it had been possible for Clark to bring the boy home with him, he would have."

Clark returned to California, just before Christmas and Kathleen met him at the airport. He brought her

With Jane Russell in The Tall Men.
(1955) COURTESY OF TWENTIETH CENTURY FOX

beautiful fabrics and other lovely presents from the Far East, a model of an old ship for Bunker, and a doll for Joanie; and my present turned out to be a gorgeous black silk Chinese housecoat, made to my measurements.

Clark's second picture for Twentieth Century-Fox, *The Tall Men,* was scheduled to begin location shooting in Durango, Mexico in the spring of 1955. The story was about a post-Civil War drive of Texas Longhorns from San Antonio to Montana, with the usual hazards of weather, Indians and cattle stampedes, plus the problems involved when Clark, Robert Ryan and Cameron Mitchell all vie for the favors of Jane Russell who just happened to be along on the trip.

The film did not have a Mexican background, but was being shot there because the Mexican Crillo cattle bear a close resemblance to Texas Longhorns, which are now relatively scarce.

Clark went to Palm Springs to prepare for his role by doing a lot of riding and roping. He and Jane and the company left for Mexico in mid-March. Clark phoned from Durango to report that they had rented a nice house for him with two servants and a housekeeper and that he was very comfortable.

"We've got three thousand head of cattle, three hundred horses and a company of seventy here," he said. "Fox is really going all out."

The first sequences were shot in Vicente Guerrero, a remote community about sixty miles south of Durango. The entire population turned out to watch the proceedings.

John Campbell, the Fox publicist assigned to the film, recalls that when Clark appeared in complete cowboy regalia and flashed his famous smile, there was no sign of recognition from the people, not one of whom had ever even seen a movie!

"Guess I won't have to sign any autographs today," Clark remarked with wry humor.

Jane was not involved in the first scenes but drove out anyway to wish the company good luck on the first day's shooting. She was wearing a blouse and pedal pushers and her arrival created a sensation among the Mexicans. Clark was puzzled until a local English-speaking schoolteacher explained that Jane had created a stir not because she was recognized as a screen star, but because "not many here have seen a lady in trousers."

The teacher also explained to Clark that his pupils knew nothing of the custom of asking for autographs, but if Clark wished he would instruct them to come forward. Clark was emphatic in his rejection of the idea!

Clark phoned frequently, for there was a good deal of his personal business pending. He felt that Raoul Walsh, the director, had been a wise selection. "He knows his job, gets it done in a hurry and *well*," he said.

Clark was also impressed with Jane's talent as an actress. There were the usual gags on the set and when the script called for Clark to pick Jane up and carry her out to a carriage, she hid thirty or forty pounds of weights in the voluminous period costume she was wearing.

Clark picked her up and carried her out, making no word of complaint. Finally Jane could stand it no longer and asked, "Was I very heavy?"

"Well, I know that I've got a real woman in my arms, but you're not heavy," Clark replied gallantly.

Jane laughed, removed the

weights and showed them to him. "I'll be light as a feather for the next take," she said.

"The only time I saw Clark angry was when I brought a woman columnist out for an interview," John Campbell says. "To my surprise, as well as his, she asked him to kiss her so that she could describe the sensation. He was furious and turned on his heel and walked off. I was not surprised that he bowed out of this situation, but his vehemence was unusual. 'Sheer concupiscence!' he exclaimed later.

"I felt he had taken bigger problems pretty much in his stride," John continues, "but this seemed to irritate him for he felt it was an invasion of his person and his privacy. Otherwise in my experience with him he was pretty casual and hard to ruffle."

Lew Smith and Don Roberson also worked this picture with Clark. There was little in the way of diversion in Durango on the weekends, so Clark spent his free time at the hotel with them, the electricians, the sound men, and the rest of the crew.

"Clark was never one to pull star rank," Don says. "We'd sit around, talk, have a few drinks, tell jokes or discuss sports with 'Shotgun' Britton, Jane's make-up man and bodyguard, who was a former football star."

Soldier of Fortune and *The Tall Men* were good, run-of-the-mill films, nothing exceptional. They made money at the box office because Clark's fans were legion. But they never *did* anything for him!

Once more, Clark found himself at the crossroads, career-wise. Everyone now "got into the act," tried to tell him what to do, shoved stories at him, suggested pictures he should make, advised him to produce, to direct, to retire. It was characteristic of Clark to listen to everyone, then brood over the situation.

I felt the pressure, too. People came to me constantly saying: "Why doesn't the guy just give up and retire? Doesn't he know he's *had* it?" Or: "Gable's too old to play leads now. He's got to settle for character parts."

Again Clark and I had one of our serious, searching discussions about his future. He thought the idea of his directing was fantastic.

"Direct!" he exclaimed. "Why, I haven't learned how to act yet! . . .

"I've got a stubborn Dutch streak, Jean," he went on. "It's been the cause of most of my mistakes. I've tried to lick it, for I can't afford any more of those now. Am I finished? Should I really retire?"

"Nonsense!" I replied. "You'll never be finished. Your fans won't *let* you retire!"

For months, plans for the formation of an independent company in cooperation with Jane Russell and her husband, football star and coach Bob Waterfield, had been under consideration.

Clark now decided to go ahead with this independent venture. Although the corporation was not activated until the fall, the papers were signed that spring and *Gabco-Russfield* came into being. Clark was president, his attorney Bill Gilbert was vice president and I was secretary-treasurer.

Gone With the Wind had been reissued the year before. One of the big women's magazines now conducted a poll to determine the most popular actor of the year, and Clark won the award hands down! Even his detractors had to admit that he was still number one at the box office.

Suddenly every studio wanted him!

Kathleen had been a frequent visitor on the studio sets of *Tall Men*, and she and Clark were seen together everywhere, so it was no surprise this time when Clark came into my office one day and said, "Jean, I'm going to marry Kathleen. I think we can be happy together."

"Wonderful!" I said. "Now you'll have a family."

"Yes," he replied. "I really love those kids of hers. It'll be great having them around."

He made me promise I would stay on, particularly since I was now involved in the independent production setup, and I agreed.

We discussed the office situation, since the guest house would be taken over entirely by the children and their nurse, Dody. A bed-sitting-room, bath and kitchen were to be added, so that each might have his own bedroom and bath.

Clark offered to build another office at my home but the size of our hillside lot precluded any further additions, so he suggested that I move to an office of my own choosing in a regular office building. I began looking for a place at once, located a building in Encino, near the ranch, and had a lot of fun redecorating and furnishing my new office. With green walls, green matchstick draperies and the yellow leather furniture and accessories, it was most attractive.

Clark and Kathleen were married on July 11, 1955. As usual, Clark wanted no publicity and, since he was no longer with MGM, he asked his old friend Al Menasco to make the arrangements.

Al and his wife Julie scouted several locations and decided on

Minden, Nevada, a tiny town just across the California line. They drove there the week before to clock the time and mileage so they could brief Clark and set up an exact schedule for meeting him and Kathleen.

On the appointed day, Al and Julie chartered a plane and were flown to Minden from their ranch near St. Helena. Arriving early in the afternoon, they rented an old car and drove to a clump of cottonwood trees just south of Minden where they were scheduled to meet Clark, Kathleen and Kathleen's sister Elizabeth (Liz) Nesser at exactly five o'clock.

"We were there on time and waited and waited, watching the road to the south for Clark's car," Al says. "Knowing Clark's predilection for being on time, we couldn't understand why they didn't show up. When they did, they came in from the north."

It seems that Clark and his party had arrived early and gone to a motel in Minden to freshen up. To prevent their being recognized by the motel owners, who might tip off the newspapers, Liz acted as "advance woman" and engaged two rooms for her "mother and father," and the motel management didn't know the identity of their famous guests until later.

Al and Julie drove the wedding party to the home of the Court Clerk, the papers were filled out, and the clerk called Justice of the Peace G. Walter Fisher at his home. He was in the middle of dinner, but stopped when they arrived, and married them in a fifteen-minute ceremony.

After the wedding, Al and Julie drove Clark and Kathleen to an airstrip five miles north of the town, where the plane and pilot were waiting to fly the newlyweds to the Menasco ranch at St. Helena. Al, Julie and Liz then drove to Carson City to call Howard Strickling, who "broke" the story to the press. Needless to say, Mr. Fisher's phone rang all night long!

Julie Menasco had arranged to have a lovely wedding supper of roast chicken, salad, a wedding cake and champagne ready when Clark and Kathleen arrived. After supper they called Bunker and Joan, who were delighted to hear about "Pa." Then they called me to say their marriage was a *fait accompli*. They both sounded so very happy!

The Gables returned to the ranch in the late afternoon on the nineteenth. I had the house full of fresh flowers and dinner waiting. On arrival, Kathleen came to me and put her arms around me, and I told her how happy I was for her and Clark. We were on a "Jean" and "Kathleen" basis from the start.

Next morning there was the usual madhouse in connection with the press conference at the ranch, arranged this time by John Campbell of Twentieth Century-Fox. Kathleen looked very lovely in a smart black linen dress, its square neckline trimmed in white.

"Clark was charming and witty," John recalls, "but he didn't want to be photographed by the newsreels (which were supplying TV footage). They had set up their equipment, however, so he said, 'Oh what the heck, let 'em in.' "

Justice of the Peace Walter Fisher, who had performed the ceremony, appeared on "What's My Line?" the Sunday night following the wedding, and the panel (Bennett Cerf, Dorothy Kilgallen, Arlene Francis and Robert Q. Lewis) had no difficulty guessing his "line."

Work on the guest house went forward after the wedding, and Bunker, Joan and Dody moved in as soon as it was completed. They were delightful, well-mannered children and both Kathleen and Dody insisted on firm but warm and loving discipline.

Kathleen was eager to have me feel like one of the family; Bunker and Joan called me "Aunt Jean," and always remembered me on Valentine's Day, my birthday and at Christmas with cards and gifts. The children called Clark "Pa," as did Kathleen. Clark called her "Ma" and sometimes "Kathleen."

Soon we all settled down to the new routine. Clark came over to the office in Encino every day or, on certain days, I went out to the ranch, for I gradually took over Kathleen's business affairs and those of the children. I was happy with the new office arrangements and glad to be relieved of the household management and responsibility.

The servant staff, Fanny, Martin and Juanita, remained the same. Kathleen brought her own maid, Louisa, with her, on a part-time basis.

Kathleen loved to cook Clark's favorite vegetable soup on Fanny's day off and always made a tremendous pot of it in order to share it with us. It was exceptionally good.

The ranch was an ideal place for the children. Clark got another burro to match Grace Kelly's Ba, so each of the children could ride. Joanie had a fall from her burro, however, and soon after that, Clark thought it wiser to dispose of them.

One day Clark found Bunker in the gun room inspecting his guns and decided that he'd remove the temptation. The gun cases were torn out, bookshelves installed, and the room was converted into a den.

Every evening at five-thirty Bunker and Joan had their dinner on trays in the den with Kathleen and Clark. After dinner, there was a "parent-children's hour," with games or perhaps TV; then the children retired to their cottage with Dody, and Kathleen and Clark sat down to the evening meal.

The Gables gave no big parties, just small, quiet dinners with intimate friends. Kathleen's brother Vincent (Bud) Williams, a radio announcer, and her sister Liz were frequent guests, together with their families.

Russ and I were vacationing in the East in October when I got a wire from Kathleen and Clark, telling me that I was going to be a "grandmother." I was delighted, for I knew how much Clark loved children and how the prospect of having one of his own must please him. We read the newspaper stories about his announcement of his impending fatherhood at a party given by director Mervyn LeRoy.

We were on our way home in early November when we heard distressing news of the Gables over the radio. Kathleen had lost the baby.

On November tenth, Russ and I celebrated our twenty-fifth wedding anniversary. Kathleen and Clark sent us a beautiful silver vase filled with huge white chrysanthemums, together with a loving note, signed by both.

That fall, the deer wandered down from the hillsides and devoured everything in sight; they practically laid waste the flower gardens. Clark was very upset, called the city authorities. Their solution for the problem was to issue him a special permit to shoot the deer, which Clark could not bring himself to do. After that, when they came down, he peppered them with shot from his shotgun. Bunker and Joan loved watching the deer leap paddock fences in their retreat toward the hills!

I took this picture of Kathleen and Clark on the deck of a friend's yacht. They were just about to sail off on a cruise of the Panama Canal and the Caribbean. (1956)

Kathleen asked me to come up at Christmastime to help with the wrapping, and the ranch was a gay and lively place that year because of the children. Richard Lang was disguised as Santa Claus to surprise them.

Clark and Kathleen gave Joan a darling black female poodle called "Missy." It was in a huge basket, all done up with red ribbons, and Joan was beside herself with pleasure, for she and Bunker had no pets other than some lovebirds. (Later Clark gave Bunker a dog of his own.)

Bunker got the usual boy stuff, a football and some games. I gave both the children books, for they loved to read.

Clark regaled the children with stories of his boyhood Christmases in Hopedale when Jennie, his beloved stepmother, sent him out to chop down the Christmas tree, which he had to lug home.

"I nailed it to a base but we never brought it into the house until Christmas Eve," he said. "We put a white sheet around the base to simulate snow, and decorated it with strings of popcorn and real candles which were not lighted until Christmas morning. None of that phony tinsel stuff for us! I always had an orange in the toe of my sock, and a handful of hard candies."

"Pa, what was your best present?" Bunker asked.

"A pair of skates and a Horatio Alger story," Clark replied.

At the end of January, Clark and Kathleen were invited to join Kathleen's close friends, Frances and Ray Hommes, on a month's cruise with D. K. Ludwig, the shipping magnate, and his wife Ginger, aboard the Ludwigs' magnificent yacht.

Martin and Juanita took the Gable luggage to the yacht the day before and the Stricklings, Dody, the children and I drove down to Wilmington Harbor with Clark and Kathleen to see them off.

The yacht was a miniature floating palace, with four luxurious master suites and a huge covered afterdeck. Their itinerary called for a leisurely trip down the West Coast, and a call at Acapulco; then a flight to Mexico City, while the yacht negotiated the Panama Canal, followed by a cruise in Caribbean waters.

Kathleen and Clark wrote letters to the children and me from various ports. Kathleen had appointed Bunker "gentleman of the house" and Joan its "gracious lady" in their absence, and I must say both lived up to their responsibilities. Dody brought them to my office frequently so we could get off letters to the travelers, and of course I "kept an eye" on things at the ranch.

The yacht trip down was marred somewhat because of bad weather, and the children were concerned to hear that the Ludwigs' pet monkey and poodle were very seasick. Kathleen said they did nothing but sleep and eat. Clark had arrived at the stage where it was necessary for him to watch his weight and his waistline, which he found difficult to do because of the ship's splendid cuisine. They tried to call me one evening, but the connection was so poor the operator advised us to give up.

After calls at Caracas and other ports on the islands of Trinidad and Jamaica, the yacht proceeded to Florida, where the Gables were the house guests of the Carl Leighs for several days before flying back to California, where the "family" waited to give them a royal welcome.

The search for good stories for Clark was unending. George Chasin, Clark's agent, was untiring in his efforts to scout good properties for him. We all read constantly—books, plays, screenplays, stories of all kinds. Now that Clark was going into independent production, we began considering the relative merits of directors, writers, and other players.

Kathleen, Clark, George and his wife Eileen, Russ and I spent many hours in projection rooms at various studios, looking at completed films. Afterwards we sat around and discussed the performances, the direction, the production values. "We must have only the best," Clark said, and we all concurred.

In the spring of 1956, plans for Gabco-Russfield's first production got under way. Clark read a script called *Last Man on Wagon Mound,* which Bob Waterfield thought would be a natural for him to play. It had an intriguing premise. A handsome, devil-may-care adventurer learns of some hidden loot on a remote ranch and goes to locate it. On the ranch are a grim matriarch and her four daughters-in-law, all waiting for husbands who may never return. All four young women make a desperate play for the man, one wins out and they depart together with the loot.

Clark liked the story. Raoul Walsh (who had directed *The Tall Men)* was chosen to direct it and a United Artists release was arranged. Jo Van Fleet was cast as the matriarch and Barbara Nichols, Jean Willis, Sara Shane and Eleanor Parker were signed to play the four daughters-in-law. Everything seemed to point to a box-office success.

Clark and Kathleen left for St. George, Utah in mid-May for the location shooting. They lived in a small rented house in a residential section of St. George, and Louisa went along to help with the cooking.

St. George is in desert country and the weather was miserably hot. Kathleen got up early every morning to prepare Clark's breakfast, and had dinner ready for him every night. She never visited the location, as she felt it might interfere with Clark's work. Instead, she made herself an integral part of the town life, joined the local sewing club and did quilting and needlework with them, gardened and even mowed the lawn.

In the evenings, Clark studied his lines for the next day's shooting, and Kathleen either read or did needlework.

Everyone ribbed Clark because he waived his five o'clock quitting time while on location. "I'm willing to save money when it's my own picture," he said.

Until this time Clark had steadfastly refused all television offers. He felt that TV was making inroads on the motion picture business and that he would be disloyal to the industry where he'd made his success, if he were to do TV. "I'm still a motion picture man and I'm going to stay one as long as I live," he always said.

He had hired Chip Cleary as his public relations man on the production, and when United Artists wanted Clark to do some television, he refused. Chip suggested that it would be good promotion for the film if Clark were to let Ed Sullivan shoot some sequences on tape while they were on location, and Clark agreed if United Artists would pick up the tab, which they did.

United Artists put a writer on the script and Sullivan's schedule was arranged to bring him to the St. George location to shoot on Memorial Day, Wednesday, May 30, in order not to interfere with the regular production schedule.

Chip received the script on Sunday night and thought it was dreadful. He'd made arrangements, however, to rush it up to Clark via TWA flight to Las Vegas, then by local plane to St. George, so he sent it on as planned.

Monday morning I had calls from practically everyone on location saying that Clark wanted to talk to Chip. When Chip was located, Clark said, "Chip, this is a bad script. I won't do it. What do we do now?"

"We'll work it out," Chip replied. "I'll come up and write it myself."

He flew to St. George and found that Bob Waterfield and Jane Russell had also gone up. Everyone was tense and jittery.

"They all stood around looking at me as if I had committed murder," Chip says. "I had no idea what to write,

but I got up early the next morning and pounded it out, then took it to Clark.

"I'll scream when it hurts," Clark said and began to read.

Chip held his breath as Clark read the whole thing through.

"I like it," Clark said.

"That made me the fair-haired boy," Chip says.

He went into town to meet Ed Sullivan and his entourage and handed the script to Ed. Ed read it as quietly as Clark had, then said, "Good script, Chip. A little long, isn't it?"

"Gable likes it," Chip replied.

"O.K., then, that's fine," Ed said.

The show was shot on Memorial Day and everyone was happy. During the filming, Clark said to Walsh, "Raoul, it was Ed who named me 'King.' "

Ed showed the tape on his Sunday show just before the picture was released, and it came off very well.

Clark had long since abandoned all idea of making the ranch a paying proposition. After his marriage to Kathleen, the stables were closed and Sunny and Melody sent to pasture on the Strickling ranch. The cows were gone, no more chickens were being raised and no farming was done. As there was no longer any need for a resident caretaker and wife, the upkeep of the ranch was turned over to a couple of gardeners who came in by the day.

Kathleen decided to convert the empty caretaker's cottage into a guest house. While the Gables were in Utah on location, I followed her instructions and supervised a thorough redecoration and paint job, installing new carpeting and furnishings, which resulted in a most attractive cottage.

When Kathleen and Clark returned

in June, Kathleen was not at all well. Russ and I left for a vacation in the Pacific Northwest, and on our return I found she was in the hospital and that Clark had moved into an adjoining room to be with her.

Kathleen suffered from a heart condition. She was in the hospital for three weeks, then was brought home under strict doctor's orders to remain in bed for some time. As she was unable to climb stairs, the library was made into a downstairs bedroom for her, and Clark became her most solicitous attendant.

Kathleen continued to have discomfort and was still in bed on their first wedding anniversary, July 11. Since it was the "paper" anniversary, we brought in all sorts of colorful paper decorations, flowers and paper gifts, and tried to make things as gay and cheerful as possible for her.

Before long, she was able to be up and about, but her activities were curtailed. For her August 7 birthday, she was well enough to enjoy a quiet dinner party with her family in the dining room.

In the fall, she was so much improved that she insisted that Clark go on one or two hunting trips with his friends, but he was concerned about her all the time he was away and usually phoned several times a day to check on her well-being.

Kathleen's first public appearance after her illness was at a premiere of *Giant* in late October. It was her first drive in Clark's new Mercedes-Benz 300 SC two-door coupé. The car had light tan leather upholstery with fitted luggage of matching shade, made to Clark's order. Later he ordered similar luggage for Kathleen. Clark was inordinately proud of the Mercedes, and never permitted anyone to drive it but himself.

Last Man on Wagon Mound acquired a new and provocative title, *The King and Four Queens,* before its release in December 1956. The consensus of the reviews was that it was a mediocre film that had failed to live up to its initial promise. It was far from the smash hit we'd all hoped for, and everyone agreed that, while it did Clark no harm at the box office, neither did it add to his stature as a star.

When MCA came to him with an offer from Warner Brothers to star in a picture called *Band of Angels,* at a salary of 10 per cent of the gross, Clark decided not to attempt further independent production for the time being. Gabco became inactive, and he signed for the Warner film, which was to co-star Yvonne de Carlo, with Raoul Walsh as director.

Clark celebrated his twenty-fifth anniversary as a screen star in January 1957. The representative from Ohio paid tribute to him on the floor of the House of Representatives, calling him "a home-town boy who made good in Hollywood." The tribute was read into the *Congressional Record* and said, in part that "Mr. Gable still reigns unchallenged as one of the world's most popular and best-known movie personalities. Time cannot wither nor custom stale his infinite appeal."

Noting that Clark was born in humble circumstances in Cadiz, Ohio, the Congressman said that he was an example of "how a young American lad can advance himself and become famous."

Kathleen and Clark left for Baton Rouge, Louisiana in mid-January, for the location shooting on *Band of Angels.* Adapted from Robert Penn Warren's best seller, it was a pre-Civil War story of a Southern plantation belle who discovers that she is really a slave and is sold on the block to a wealthy New Orleans gentleman, a former slave runner, who makes her mistress of his home. The Civil War complicates things and the man, now in love with her, escapes with the girl to the North.

The Gables stopped in New Orleans en route and were assigned the "international suite" at the Roosevelt Hotel. Kathleen said the drawing room looked like Yankee Stadium. Clark paced it off, and found it was sixty feet long and thirty-five feet wide! They toured the *Vieux Carré*, dined at Antoine's, and left the next day for Baton Rouge, where the studio had booked a suite for them at the new two-and-a-half-million-dollar Bellemont Motor Hotel.

Mr. and Mrs. Lewis, the Bellemont owners, put their Cadillac at Kathleen's disposal and she promptly went shopping with Louisa, who had accompanied them south. She bought a hot plate and other equipment, and set up a little kitchen in the dressing room so she and Clark might have respite from the wonderful but very rich French and Italian cuisine they found everywhere. (Clark was still watching his waistline!)

Kathleen and Clark were lionized socially. Invitations to six or eight shooting clubs, dinner parties and affairs of all kinds poured in, along with bids for TV and radio appearances. While Clark was busy on location, Kathleen had lunch at the Governor's mansion with Mrs. Earl Long. (Armed guards had surrounded their car en route, which traveled with sirens screaming!)

At home, we were coping with an unusual freak snowstorm which damaged many of the trees and vines. Howard sent photographers out to take some pictures of the ranch, which looked lovely covered with snow. We sent them down to Louisiana to show the Gables what was happening in "sunny California." The children had great fun making a snow man.

Much of the film's shooting was done at The Cottage, a plantation mansion built in the 1800s, and also aboard the *Gordon C. Greene,* the last of the famous river packet boats. "Pa looked so handsome in his white linen suit and broad-brimmed Panama!" Kathleen said.

She staged a birthday party for Clark and the cast on February 1, at the Baton Rouge Country Club, and sent me the menu, which featured dishes bearing the names of the production, the director, the stars and the crew. "Swampwater" sherry and "Mississippi River" *vin blanc* were served. Later they heard the film's Negro chorus of one hundred voices sing spirituals.

Cloudy weather held up shooting several times, and Clark went quail hunting on horseback with a local judge while Kathleen made a trip to Natchez, Mississippi, where the Mayor presented her with the keys to the city and she toured all the antebellum homes, raving about the antique furniture. (Mrs. Lewis also took her antique shopping in New Orleans one day.)

The location sets were mobbed by local fans. Harry Friedman, the Warner Brothers publicity man at the location, said, "I've worked in many places with many stars, but I've never seen anything like the adoration they had for Gable." Kathleen said the fan mail almost snowed them under.

We were in constant touch with them by telephone. (Clark broke up a conference with Raoul Walsh one day when Joan asked to speak to him.) When they were ready to leave, Kathleen asked me to have Fanny broil chicken and make a chocolate cake (still Clark's favorites) for dinner on the night of their return. We had all been saving our birthday gifts so we could have a party for him then.

Soon after Clark finished *Band of Angels* for Warner Brothers, he was offered a picture by William Perlberg and George Seaton at Paramount. The title was *Teacher's Pet,* a comedy about a cynical, self-made newspaperman who hates journalism school graduates. He turns down an invitation to lecture before a journalism class, then is ordered to do so by his publisher. He goes to the school, is mistaken by the teacher for an older student, and goes along with the idea. He lives to change his opinions about journalism students and marries the teacher.

Perlberg and Seaton had a long string of successful films to their credit. Clark was impressed with them and eager for the chance to do comedy again. He signed for the picture at the usual 10 per cent of the gross.

Shooting started in April with Doris Day as the journalism teacher, and Gig Young, Mamie Van Doren and Nick Adams in the cast. Messrs. Perlberg and Seaton proved themselves to be master showmen by inviting sixty-odd newspapermen and women from all over the United States to come to Hollywood at their expense and appear in the film's newspaper city room scenes, playing themselves as reporters and columnists.

As a result the picture got fantastic publicity while in production, for each newspaper representative wrote daily dispatches on the stars, the producer and director, and on all aspects of film making. Almost all of them interviewed Clark, and the consensus was that at fifty-six he was still the King of the Movies, a real "pro," a "champ," who was always on time, up on his lines, unruffled, and able to conjure up the right mood as the scene demanded.

One of the highlights of the newspaper people's visit was a barbecue party given by Doris Day and her husband Marty Melcher on the grounds of their newly purchased home in Beverly Hills. Kathleen and Clark and other stars and film personalities were among the guests.

Tables and gay striped umbrellas were scattered about the lawn, and Doris had gone to a great deal of trouble to make this a very festive affair. But the weather man double-crossed her and it began to rain! The guests all scrambled indoors, where they sat on the floor in the empty house, which was in the process of being redecorated before the Melchers moved in.

While *Teacher's Pet* was in production, Kathleen asked Bruce Alan Clark, the decorator who was doing Doris Day's house, to help her with some redecorating at the ranch. Clark, who loved to be consulted, helped decide on colors and fabrics for new draperies, lampshades and bedspreads, as well as the additional antique furniture selected. When the work was finished, the whole house looked fresh and lovely.

At the finish of the picture, Clark and Kathleen went up to Del Monte Lodge at Pebble Beach near Carmel, California, for the Fourth of July, and stayed on for a few days' rest and change. Frances and Ray Hommes went with them and Julie and Al Menasco joined the party for several days.

Before leaving, they saw Bunker off to his first summer camp. He was so excited over the prospect! Clark had had a great deal of fun supervising swimming lessons for both Bunker and Joan, and while Kathleen was at Pebble Beach she had scouted summer camps for girls, having promised Joan (whose nose was slightly out of joint over Bunker's departure) that *she* might start summer camp the next year.

The Gables spent their second wedding anniversary at Pebble Beach and gave a dinner party for their friends at a small French restaurant in Carmel to celebrate the occasion.

They returned to the ranch at the end of July and left almost immediately by plane for Honolulu, thence to the Island of Maui, where the Butterfields, managers of the Hana-Maui Hotel, made them welcome. (Russ and I had found it a delightful place and recommended it to the Gables.)

The children were now under the care of a splendid, elderly French governess whom we all called "Mademoiselle." When Bunker returned from camp in mid-August, we got both children and Mademoiselle ready and put them on a plane for Honolulu, where Kathleen and Clark were to meet them.

Russ and I drove them out to the airport. Bunker and Joan were so thrilled at the thought of joining "Pa" and "Ma" they could hardly speak. En route to the airport, we passed several billboards advertising *Band of Angels*. Bunker pointed them out to me and said, "That's my stepfather," with such pride in his small voice!

The children had a wonderful vacation with Kathleen and Clark. Joan went everywhere in a muu-muu and learned to do the hula. The family picnicked, swam, sunned, played golf. Both Kathleen and Bunker won the daily golf tournament.

They all came home early in September and Martin and I met them at the airport. They were loaded with leis and other Hawaiian souvenirs, and were tanned and happy-looking. Joan brought home some Hawaiian records so she could continue with her hula!

On September 16, Clark started a new picture for Hecht-Lancaster called *Run Silent, Run Deep*. As a free-lance star he was to receive the standard 10 per cent salary deal.

(Clark's 10 per cent on his film's grosses had proved to be a most profitable arrangement for him. Although the films he made were not outstanding and sometimes did little more than recoup their production costs, *he* still made money because his percentage came "off the top.")

Run Silent, Run Deep was a "he-man" picture after Clark's heart. He played the role of a submarine skipper prowling Japanese waters in World War II. Burt Lancaster co-starred in the role of the sub's lieutenant. The skipper loses and then regains the respect of his crew before his death.

Location shooting was done in San Diego, and the Gables took an apartment at La Jolla during that time.

Chip Cleary handled Clark's publicity and set up a trip out to a submarine tender in San Diego Harbor, where Clark and Burt were made honorary members of the submarine squadron. They had the opportunity to go aboard a submarine and were briefed on equipment and actual procedures while the sub is in action.

Afterwards they were invited ashore to the Naval Training Center at Point Loma, which was under the command of a famous submarine captain whom everyone called "Captain Red." Clark and Burt stood in the chow line with the Boots (trainees), had lunch with them in the mess hall, and signed autographs. Later they went on to Advanced Training School and reviewed a Boots dress parade.

Next morning, Clark and Burt went out to the submarine again aboard Harold Hecht's *Pursuit,* a ninety-foot M-boat. They transferred to the submarine and spent the entire day on board, while her skipper made practice dives.

"It was Clark's idea to go on the sub," Chip says. "He was a careful workman. He wanted the action in his role to be authentic, so they let him take the sub down a few times and cruise around."

This attention to detail paid off, for *Run Silent, Run Deep* turned out to be one of the best submarine stories ever made and it did exceptionally well at the box office.

In the fall, Kathleen was feeling fit again and began going on hunting trips with Clark. Jane and Ray Barnard, Frances and Ray Hommes, Martha and Martin Smith and Barron Hilton were among the Gables' friends who belonged to the Club Patos al Vientos (Ducks on the Wing) at Point Mugu. This was a jointly owned cooperative venture, and Clark bought into it at an original investment of two thousand, five hundred dollars.

The club had a Ladies' Day "for shooting only" twice a year, and Kathleen always went up with Clark and loved it. They frequently stayed with the Barnards at their Rancho de Las Flores near Ventura or at Martin Smith's Colonial House in Oxnard. On the latter occasions they left very early in the morning, taking Larry, one of Smith's employees with them, and Larry cooked breakfast at the Club.

A new location for my office became necessary in November due to conditions in the building over which I had no control. I was scouting for new quarters when Clark said, "For Pete's sake, why pay rent when we have that guest cottage on the ranch? Kathleen and I want you to move back there."

So, after two years, I returned to the ranch. On the morning of my arrival, I was greeted by Kathleen, who said, "It's about time you came home. Happy to have you aboard."

She and Clark had arranged a huge bowl of red garnet roses on my desk and it was a happy home-coming.

Bunker and Joan, who were now attending the Buckley School, liked to visit me in the office after school. Both loved to play "secretary," using my adding machine and typewriter.

Kathleen's dressmaker moved into the cottage's sitting room for a week or so to work on Kathleen's wardrobe, for she and Clark were leaving in early December for a trip to New York to shop, see the new shows and to have a "fun time" when Clark had finished *Run Silent, Run Deep.*

Kathleen bought some beautiful clothes in New York, but wore a Kelly-green satin California gown to the Bachelors' Ball. All the ladies were required to wear tiaras. Kathleen's was loaned by one of the smart jewelry firms, and she had to have a police escort to guard her "crown."

Kathleen had taken Louisa along, and when they were ready to go home the Gables gave her their Christmas present: a ticket south, so she could visit her family before returning to California.

Clark, as usual, was delighted to get home. The ranch was his touchstone and he was never entirely happy when he was away from it.

CHAPTER TWELVE

WHILE at MGM Clark had always refused to make personal appearances in connection with his films. In fact, he almost never went to their premieres, nor even to the sneak previews at outlying theaters. Up until the time of his marriage to Kathleen, Russ and I always attended those showings and no matter how late it was at night, Clark expected and always waited for me to call and give him a report. He wanted an honest opinion, and I never pulled my punches, but told him exactly what I thought, assessing the audience's reaction and what I believed the picture's box-office potential to be.

After his marriage, however, Kathleen usually prevailed on him to go to the previews, and so they were on hand for the Hollywood premiere of *Teacher's Pet* in March 1958. Kathleen wore a black satin Mainbocher gown with matching stole, and she and Clark made a handsome pair.

A week later, the 1957 Academy Awards presentation ceremonies were held at the RKO-Pantages Theater and George Seaton asked Clark to accept the Academy's invitation to present some of the Oscars. Clark hated public appearances of this nature, but he admired and respected both George Seaton and Bill Perlberg.

"I'll do it for them," he said.

All of us were there to see Clark and Doris Day introduced by Bob Hope, the master of ceremonies, as "two of the most popular stars in Hollywood." They presented the writers' awards for the year, which went to Pierre Boulle (*Bridge on the River Kwai*) and George Wells (*Designing Woman*).

When a film goes into release, public appearances by its stars always generate a lot of publicity and good will which is reflected at the box office. Now that he was free-lancing and on a percentage basis, it was obvious to Clark that it was to his advantage to go on tour when *Teacher's Pet* was released in the spring of 1958. Doris Day also agreed to personal appearances, but their schedules did not coincide.

Chicago, Washington and Cleveland were on Clark's itinerary and Kathleen went with him. It was to be a "crash" program with a two-day stop in each city, where a round of press conferences, cocktail and dinner parties, and private showings of the film were to be held for the press and invited guests.

Ted Taylor, executive assistant to the Messrs. Perlberg and Seaton, was assigned to accompany Clark's party. Ted told me that never in his experience had he seen anything like the public's reaction to Clark.

"His walk, his carriage, his dignity commanded respect everywhere," he says. "As we walked down the street together it was interesting to watch people turn to look after Clark, or simply stand in awe as he went by. Huge crowds would gather, but he was never mobbed; they just wanted to look at him."

All the newspaper reporters who

had appeared in the film with Clark gave him a big welcome and the news coverage he received reflected their enthusiasm.

Washington was the second stop on the tour. Senator Kuchel of California took the Gables to the State Department and, according to Kathleen, Clark's appearance threw all the secretaries there into a dither. They had lunch with the Senator in the Senate Dining Room and sampled the famous bean soup for which the chef is famous. (Kathleen managed to wangle the recipe!)

While they were on a regular "tourist" trip through the White House, President Eisenhower heard they were there and invited them into his office, where they chatted with him for over an hour. When Clark and Kathleen asked if he were going to the special preview of the film that night, "Ike" laughed, saying Mamie was away and that he'd have to babysit so his son and daughter-in-law, Major and Mrs. John Eisenhower, could attend.

A reception followed the screening and Ted says it was amusing to see society leaders, Congressmen, Pentagon brass and the press vying for the opportunity to talk with the Gables.

They took off for Cleveland immediately after the reception and the same pattern of activity was repeated. In commenting on the fans who crowded the airports and streets to see Clark, Ted Taylor said that the number of teen-age girls was astonishing. Clark's old films were showing on television, and a new generation was discovering his ageless appeal.

The publicity, and the evidence of his continuing popularity, were of course gratifying; but the write-up that impressed Clark most was Bosley Crowther's article in the *New York Times*. Crowther saluted him as one of "Hollywood's genuine, changeless 'pros.'" He thought Clark's talents had matured and said he deserved new respect for having reigned so long as a top film star.

"It's the best vote of confidence I've ever had," Clark said.

Exhausted by the strenuous tour, the Gables accepted Marion Davies' invitation to make use of her Palm Springs home for several weeks' rest. Bunker and Joan, still in school, joined them on weekends.

Clark played golf and had a wonderful time trying out his new Mercedes-Benz 300 SL sports car. It had those batwing doors which required some dexterity when entering or leaving the car.

"Keeps me young, climbing in and out," Clark said.

At the ranch I was busy getting things in order so Russ and I could leave on a European tour. Kathleen offered the services of her dressmaker to help with my wardrobe and had her work in the guest house, so it would be convenient for my fittings.

We left on April 30 via SAS flight for Copenhagen. Kathleen and Clark sent me a lovely corsage, which I pinned to the curtain of my berth so I could enjoy the fragrance of the flowers all night.

After a seventeen-hour flight, we arrived in Copenhagen at three o'clock in the morning and were met by a reporter. Somehow her paper had learned that I was associated with Clark Gable, and she wanted an interview. While Russ was clearing us through customs, the newswoman began questioning me about Clark and his latest film. I was half-asleep and could hardly remember my own name, much less the name of his picture, so I sug-

Clark, Kay, and President Eisenhower, September, 1958. The picture is autographed to me: To Jean, with our love, Kathleen and Clark.

gested that we continue the interview at our hotel sometime later, as I was too weary even to think at the moment.

We changed our hotel accommodations, however, and I didn't see her again. But when we left Copenhagen, other reporters turned up, and this time I made more sense. I learned that few Hollywood films reached Copenhagen until they were quite dated. None of the reporters had seen any of Clark's latest films, and they said they'd have to go over to Sweden to do so.

When we returned to California in July, I had a long session with Clark, for I was eager to be brought up to date on his future plans. He had verbally agreed to star in another Perlberg-Seaton film, *But Not For Me*, which would go into production some time in

1959. Meanwhile, he was still reading many stories—particularly comedies, which were high in favor at the box office. *Teacher's Pet* was such a success everyone seemed to feel that comedy was really Clark's métier.

Although he was now fifty-seven and gray at the temples, and had to watch his waistline, he still had the charm and magnetism that had kept him at the top of the distributors' lists for years. Nevertheless, I could sense that Clark was a little concerned about his career. "I'd like to find a good story right away," he said.

"What's the rush?" I inquired. "Why don't you just take it easy until the Perlberg-Seaton script is ready? You really don't *have* to work until then, Mr. G."

"Perhaps not," Clark said, with

the old worried look. "But I've got a family now, and a big responsibility."

(My two months' absence had given me a new perspective. I could see that maturity and a happy marriage had mellowed Clark but there were still the old basic fears and insecurities.)

"But, Mr. G———," I started to protest, when he interrupted.

"Perhaps I'll just give up and start directing," he said.

It was characteristic of Clark to make such statements in order to get a reaction. I knew he had no intention of retiring or of directing. What he really wanted me to do was to reassure him, argue against such a course of action.

"Why quit when you're ahead?" I said. "You can pick and choose your own stories now and can afford to wait for the good ones."

He switched his strategy then, and came up with what Kathleen called his "annual plan" to sell the ranch.

"This place is too much of an expense," he said. "I may just sell it and we'll buy a house in Beverly Hills."

I began to laugh. "You're not going to sell it and you know it," I said.

He grinned like a small boy who has been caught out. "You're right," he replied. "I love it. My roots are here. Besides, it's such a good place to raise children."

In September Kathleen and Clark went out to look over the exclusive Hidden Valley Gun Club near Riverside. The club owned two thousand acres of land; the duck, dove and pheasant shooting there rated among the best in California. (Clark never liked deer hunting.)

The Gables were particularly interested in joining this club because women were permitted to shoot at all times, and Clark wanted Kathleen with him when he hunted. She had been doing a good deal of skeet shooting at the local Aqua Sierra Club and had become a good shot.

Ed Nichols, one of the co-owners, showed them through the magnificent clubhouse and Clark asked to inspect the kennels, where he met Ivan Brower, the trainer and club manager. The first dog Clark saw was a red cocker spaniel, registered as Caminos Red Rocket, but called Red. After an hour spent looking over the other dogs, Clark returned to Red.

"What will you take for this dog?" he asked Ivan.

"I wouldn't sell him for a thousand dollars, but I'll give him to you if you'll let me take him back to New York for the National Field Trials," Ivan replied.

"It's a deal," Clark said, "and I'll pay your expenses."

The Gables joined the club, made reservations for Tuesday of each week, and usually spent the entire day there.

"Kathleen roughed it with the best of them, was a good sport and a good shot," Ed Nichols says.

Occasionally they took the children with them and Bunker and Joan rode horseback while Kathleen and Clark hunted.

Clark was excited over the prospect of owning Red. He'd long wanted a good hunting dog. Bobby, his German short-haired pointer, had died some time before, full of years and ice cream. As he'd grown older he'd developed a fondness for the sweet, and Clark fed him some every night. If none was served at dinner, he went to the refrigerator for it.

"As long as Bobby is with us," Clark said at the time, "he's going to have his ice cream."

He'd had another hunting dog after Bobby, a *Deutsch Drahthaar* (now known as the German wire-haired pointer) called Rusty. Dogs of this breed are supposed to be good hunters, but Rusty never measured up to expectations, so Clark gave him to Bunker. Now he could hardly wait to hear the results of Red's performance in the field trials.

Winter conditions in the East that year were severe. The ground was frozen and Red worked against dogs accustomed to cold weather, but he won the National Championship. I don't know when I'd seen Clark as thrilled as he was when Ivan wired him of Red's victory and said he was shipping the dog to him by plane.

Clark went to the airport to meet him and immediately called his friend Ray Barnard in Ventura to ask if he could come up and work him. They went up the next day, for Clark was eager to show off the new champion.

"The dog had had a long plane flight, spent the night in a new home and came right up here," Ray says. "He was so confused that when we worked him, he brought in a decoy instead of a duck. Clark was certainly crestfallen."

After he'd had some rest and was oriented to his new surroundings, however, Red lived up to his championship status and was a wonderful hunting dog. Bob Pelgram, one of the club members, made a sixteen-millimeter film of Red in action, which showed him retrieving, and bringing in, not one but two ducks at the same time. Clark saw the film and was so crazy about it that Kathleen called Ed Nichols and asked if he could get a print for Clark. Ed did so, and gave it to Clark as a Christmas present.

Clark was so proud of Red that he insisted on having him sleep up in his bedroom for a while. Owning "the Champ" was one of his great satisfactions.

Just before Christmas, Clark told me he wanted to get some sweaters for Kathleen, so I called Doris Fields at Saks Fifth Avenue. Doris and Kathleen were friends and had been Powers models together in New York. When I told her Clark wanted to do some shopping, she said to have him at the store early some morning and, if he came in through the men's department, he'd have reasonable privacy.

On the appointed morning, Clark set out with my written directions and Bunker in hand. Doris met them and Clark introduced Bunker by saying, "This is my son, Bunker."

"Bunker looked as though Clark were his whole world," Doris says.

She had some special sweaters shown to Clark, and he and Bunker were very choosy. "Pa, do you think Ma will like this one?" Bunker asked before they made any selections.

"Remember, now, this is a secret from Ma," Clark warned. "And I don't want you to say anything to her about it."

"It was wonderful to see the mutual admiration those two had for each other," Doris says.

When Clark had selected several sweaters, Doris asked if he'd like to shop in other departments; but by this time the news that he was in the store had gotten out and people were beginning to gather around.

Clark shook his head. "I've had it," he said, then turned to Bunker, "I'm ready, Bunker."

"I'm ready too, Pa," Bunker replied.

When Bunker got home he came over to my office to tell me that he and

Pa had a secret, and he seemed very proud that Clark had entrusted him with it.

But Not For Me was a remake of *Accent on Youth* and co-starred Carroll Baker with Lili Palmer, Lee J. Cobb and Barry Coe in the supporting cast.

"Carroll was very excited over playing with Gable, and very much in awe of him," Ted Taylor says.

When Clark arrived at his dressing room on the first day of shooting, he found that Kathleen had decorated it with garnet-red roses, huge buckets of popcorn, and the special hard candies that he liked.

Walter Lang, Fieldsie's husband, directed. After the long years of friendship, this was the first time Clark and Walter had worked together, and they had a wonderful time.

"Walter is all business on the set, and I like that," Clark said.

Lew Smith and Don Roberson were working with Clark. Don recalls that Clark was in a devilish mood one day and decided to do a take-off on all of them.

"You old guys—I'll show you what you're like," Clark said, and then he did a devastating imitation of Don, Lew and "Swede," the wardrobe man, while the rest of the crew roared with laughter. "It was a panic," Don continues, "the more so because he was so good!"

When the picture was finished, the Gables left for Palm Springs. Things were very quiet at the ranch, and once again I took stock of my personal situation. I had the strong conviction that the time had come for me to retire and devote myself to my husband and my home. This was indeed a hard decision to make, for the job was an integral part of my life, and I'd had so many wonderful years of association with Clark.

I had no qualms about his affairs. His family, and George Chasin, his agent, and his attorney, Bill Gilbert, and Russell Bock, his tax consultant, were all looking after him.

After talking it over with Clark, I agreed to remain at my post until my successor had been selected, so I could instruct and initiate her into all the minutiae of the complex Gable affairs.

MCA interviewed a number of applicants and Margareta Gronkwist, an attractive Swedish woman, was engaged by Clark and Kathleen. Actually, it was two months before everything was straightened out, and the transfer of business affairs into her efficient hands was effected.

The breaking of ties, the severing of long associations, are not accomplished overnight. There were many telephone calls from the ranch in the months that followed and I never quite lost touch.

Still exploiting Clark's flair for comedy, Paramount signed him for *It Started in Naples*, which was to be directed by Melville Shavelson on location in Italy.

The Gables sailed from New York in late June of 1959, together with Bunker, Joan, and a new nurse named Jo, who had replaced Mademoiselle when she retired. Jo was Dutch and when the family disembarked in Holland, the children remained there with her for a visit, later rejoining Kathleen and Clark in Austria, where they all celebrated the Gables' fourth wedding anniversary in a lovely old villa overlooking the Wolfgangsee.

They moved on to Rome in early August, and settled down in a villa outside the city while Clark was working in the picture, which co-starred Sophia

Loren and Vittorio De Sica. (Clark's role was that of a Philadelphia lawyer who comes to Italy to settle the estate of his late brother and finds himself involved with Sophia and a child.)

Jo brought the children home in September in time for the opening of school, but the Gables did not return to the ranch until sometime in November.

While they were in Italy, Kathleen and Clark had looked over the plans of a house being built at Bermuda Dunes near Palm Springs, which Ernie Dunlevie, co-owner of the development company, hoped they might like well enough to purchase.

They inspected the completed house on their return. It adjoined the golf course, and both fell in love with the desert-type architecture of the low, rambling structure. Clark bought it for a "between pictures" winter vacation residence. Decorators Harry La Chance and his wife Edlene designed the décor and furnishings of the spacious beam-ceilinged interiors, using a color scheme of chalk white and cool greens and beiges, accented with lacquer red, the whole in keeping with the locale.

Clark and Kathleen now began to take their golf seriously. Clark bought and studied numerous books on the subject, and both spent a great deal of time on the game.

Early in 1960, Howard and Gail Strickling visited them in the new house and found Clark shooting in the high seventies. He was interested in losing weight, because he had just signed to star in John Huston's production of *The Misfits*, which would roll in midsummer.

"I've got to get in shape," Clark said. "If I'm to play a lean, tough horse wrangler I need to drop about thirty pounds."

"Why knock yourself out?" a friend asked. "This is going to be a rough picture."

"I know," Clark replied, "but I can't turn down that kind of money. I'm getting a guarantee of seven hundred and fifty thousand dollars against 10 per cent of the gross, and if the picture runs over schedule, I'll get overtime."

The Gables remained in Bermuda Dunes most of the spring, and Clark continued to golf and diet for his role in *The Misfits*. At Sonja Henie's black-tie party for forty friends, Clark and Kathleen lingered late with several of the guests and Clark sang cowboy songs with the guitar player from the orchestra.

Everyone was amazed at his good voice. "We didn't know you could sing like that," one friend said.

"I used to sing for my supper," Clark replied. "Now I'm doing it to get in the mood for my new picture."

Just prior to filming, Kathleen and Clark asked Al and Julie Menasco to meet them in Minden, Nevada, to help them celebrate their fifth wedding anniversary.

Al and Julie waited for them under the same cottonwood trees outside of town, and watched the road to the south as they'd done five years before; and, as in 1955, Clark and Kathleen arrived from the north. They'd rented an old Model T Ford and came chugging down the road in it, just for a gag.

They had a happy reunion, then all drove to the house the Gables were to occupy in Reno. It was a beautiful area, had a swimming pool, and was right on a golf course.

The Misfits with Marilyn Monroe was Clark's last film (1961) COURTESY
OF UNITED ARTISTS

"It was a real showplace," Al says. "We got there after dark and had a terrible time trying to locate the light switches."

Later, Jo, the children and Louisa joined Kathleen and Clark for the summer. Clark had lost thirty-five pounds by then and looked very fit.

The Misfits started shooting on July 18. Clark's role was that of Gay Langland, a rugged, free-roaming cowboy of the old school, "a misfit" in the changing times on the Nevada ranges. Marilyn Monroe, his co-star, played a bewildered divorcee who meets and is attracted to Clark but is also besieged by other "misfits" (Montgomery Clift and Eli Wallach).

The script was by Arthur Miller and Clark felt it was a strong one and had "something to say." Clark had long wanted to work with John Huston. In fact, they'd talked years before about doing a picture together in India, but somehow had never gotten around to it.

Harry Mines, the public relations man on *The Misfits*, said that Clark's impact on Reno was tremendous. "They gave him a standing ovation practically everywhere he went," Harry says. "All the local people wanted to have their pictures taken with him."

One day Harry found Clark in town, flat on his back under his Mercedes, which had stalled.

"All the fans had gathered around and were telling him what to do and how to do it," Harry says. "Clark was really swearing and sweating."

Harry set up many interviews for Clark but the writers and newsmen found that he would rarely talk about himself.

"We sure got a good story from Gable," they'd report to Harry. "All about the motors in foreign cars and what that Mercedes can do on a desert road."

"Clark was good about helping Marilyn on her interviews," Harry continues. "You know how persistent some newsmen can be and the leading questions they ask. Often Marilyn would be in a tight spot and Clark would come to her rescue, taking on the questioners."

There is a saying that "no man is a hero to his valet." It is also applicable to stars and publicity men. When Harry left the location he gave Clark a book, *Portrait of Max* by S. N. Behrman, and Clark was touched and pleased.

"It was the highest tribute I could pay him," Harry says, "for I don't often give a star a gift."

Wayne Griffin called Clark one day and said Wayne Junior would stop in and visit him on his way home from Stanford. Wayne asked how things were going and Clark said "very well." He thought the troupe was wonderful. "John Huston is one hell of a fine director in addition to being a very nice guy," he continued.

Wayne Junior arrived at the end of what had been a particularly grueling day for Clark, but he sat down and talked with him for two hours. Wayne Junior wanted advice about going into the Air Force, for he knew Clark had had great experience.

"If I were in your shoes and had all the fire power you have at your age, I would fly no matter what your old man says," Clark told him.

"It was wonderful to hear Clark talk to the boy," a friend says. "He always took time for the things he thought worthwhile and his advice was honest and sincere, right from his heart."

Later, when Wayne Senior came

over to the location, Clark told him what he'd advised his son to do. "I hope you don't mind," he said. "I had to say it, because that's what I really thought."

"Of course I don't mind, you old tiger," Wayne Senior replied.

In August, Clark announced to the company that he was going to be a father. "He was almost bursting his buttons with pride," a friend says.

"Imagine a wonderful thing like this happening to an old guy like me," Clark remarked. "It's an extra dividend from life and I want to make the most of it."

To him it was unthinkable that the baby would be anything but a boy. He constantly referred to the "little fellow" who was on his way. His concern over Kay was touching.

The first location site was about a ten-minute drive from the Gable residence. Later, the company moved to a dry lake near Dayton, Nevada, for the rodeo scenes and also did some shooting near Pyramid Lake. Clark had a chauffeur-driven car at his disposal, but drove himself to and from location a great deal of the time, which meant a fifty- or sixty-minute drive twice a day.

Doc Erickson, production manager on the film, said Clark enjoyed his role. "He felt he understood it better than most any other role he had ever played," Doc says.

Wrangling of wild mustangs on ranges was an integral part of the film's action, and the searing heat of the Nevada desert was rough on everyone. Marilyn collapsed from heat exhaustion. There were other delays. Dust storms and a forest fire held up the shooting for days.

Doc and Clark played golf a great deal during the delays, and Clark said

to him, "You know we are going to be here until it snows."

Doc laughed, but one morning in early October Clark called him at six-thirty. "Look out of your window," he said. "I told you it would snow."

"Sure enough it had," Doc continues. "It lasted only a day, but it *was* snow, and in October."

On October 18, the production moved back to the studio for interior scenes and process shots on the sound stages. The picture ran a week and a day over schedule, for which Clark collected an extra fifty-six thousand dollars, bringing his total "take" on the film up to eight hundred and six thousand.

On the last day of shooting, Friday, November 4, there was a studio party to celebrate the end of the picture. Clark looked in for a little while, then drove home. He had a date to look at a horse on Saturday with Howard Strickling, but called him in the morning to say that he didn't feel too well and would like to postpone their appointment until Sunday.

Early Sunday morning, Kathleen called the Stricklings, saying Clark was in Hollywood Presbyterian Hospital. He'd had a heart attack and she meant to stay right with him.

No visitors were allowed to see Clark; but calls, wires, letters and cards from friends and fans poured in, expressing their love and concern. President Eisenhower, himself a former heart patient, wired him "not to worry, not to get angry, and follow your doctor's advice."

Howard got daily bulletins on Clark's condition and I was in constant touch with him during the next week. He told me that Clark was much better and that if he continued to improve the doctor felt that by the twelfth day he would be out of danger.

We were greatly relieved at this news. The Menascos started driving down from St. Helena, and all of us were happy in the knowledge that the "King" was going to be all right.

Early Thursday morning, November 17, I had a phone call from Howard.

"Jeanie," he said, "we've lost Clark."

"Oh no!" I cried, shocked, incredulous.

"Yes," he said, "last night. About eleven o'clock."

The end had come quietly, unexpectedly.

Clark had had a visit from his doctor, who talked of permitting him to go home in a few weeks, provided he took care of himself.

"Don't worry," Clark said. "I don't intend to do a lick of work until after my son is born. I want to be right there when he arrives, to look after him and watch him grow. You couldn't tear me away."

About 11 P.M. Kathleen, who had been with Clark all evening, retired to an adjoining room. The nurse was settling her patient for the night. Clark leaned back against his pillows, sighed gently, and was gone.

Funeral services with full military honors by the United States Air Force were held for Clark at the Church of the Recessional at Forest Lawn Me-

morial Park in Glendale. They were conducted by Chaplain Johnson E. West, USAF, with the dignity, simplicity and privacy Clark himself would have liked and approved.

General Harvard W. Powell, USAF, and Lieut. Colonel James D. Hunter, USAF, together with a special color guard and ten airmen from March Air Force Base represented Secretary of Air, Dudley Sharp.

Prior to the service, Captain Richard Mealoy, USAF, and Chaplain Lieutenant Darrel Harper, USAF, marched down the aisle to lay beside the casket the folded flag that afterwards was given into Kathleen's keeping.

The pallbearers were Al Menasco, Howard Strickling, E. J. Mannix, Spencer Tracy, Ray Hommes, Robert Taylor, James Stewart, George Chasin and Ernie Dunlevie.

Russ took my hand as the sound of "Taps" floated out in the bright autumn morning. Memories of Clark's generosity, his kindness and his courage flooded my thoughts. Then the realization came to me that life is eternal and that all the qualities we admired and loved in Clark were indestructible and would live on. With this came a deep sense of peace.

John Clark Gable was born at 7:48 A.M. on the morning of March 20, 1961.